WALK
LIKE
A GIRL

WALK LIKE A GIRL

Prabal Gurung

HarperCollins *Publishers* India

First published by VIKING 2025
An imprint of Penguin Random House LLC
1745 Broadway, New York, NY 10019
www.penguinrandomhouse.com

This edition published in India by HarperCollins *Publishers* 2026
HarperCollins Publishers India, Cyber City,
Building 10-A, Gurugram, Haryana – 122002, India
www.harpercollins.co.in

2 4 6 8 10 9 7 5 3 1

P-ISBN: 978-93-6569-068-2
E-ISBN: 978-93-6569-288-4

Designed by Cassandra Garruzzo Mueller

Printed and bound at
Thomson Press India Private Limited

MIX
Paper | Supporting responsible forestry
FSC www.fsc.org FSC® C010615

This book is produced from independently certified FSC® paper
to ensure responsible forest management.

★

HarperCollins *Publishers*, Macken House, 39/40 Mayor Street Upper, Dublin 1,
D01 C9W8, Ireland

To be girlish is to be powerful,
because power is redefined.

ROBIN GIVHAN

In the realm of brave souls,
Where difference is dared,
In their stride, we find a world unfurled,
In the courage to simply walk like a girl.

PRABAL GURUNG

To my mother, Durga Rana, who always
made sure I had the perfect shade of lipstick.

To my sister, Kumudini, who never made me feel alone
with the stories she shared and the dresses she let me borrow.

To my brother, Pravesh, who always carried on
his shoulders the light that shone upon me.

To my nephew, Arhant, for reinforcing the power of femininity in me.
By being unapologetically you, you made me even less afraid to be me.

To my niece, Vaidehi, who is my dreams, promises, and hopes manifested.
In every shade of pink matched, in every tear and moment of joy shared,
I soar higher because of your unwavering and unconditional love.

To the Rosas, Shirleys, Glorias, Angelas, Mayas, Graces, Yuris, Oprahs, Marshas, Hillarys, Michelles, Malalas, Angelinas, Annas, Madonnas, Shabanas, Arundhatis, and Kamalas: Your names are not merely syllables; they are beacons of hope, courage, and resilience. Forever grateful, we watch your light inspire generations to come.

Author's Note

Walk like a girl.

The phrase constantly hurled at me in an attempt to diminish me eventually became my life mantra. It is no longer just a verb or an adjective but rather an emotion, an intention, and an act of resistance.

This is my story, told the way I remember it. I understand that each of us experience life in our own unique way, and for this reason, several people's names and identifying characteristics are changed in this book.

This book is the celebration of matriarchal beliefs. A celebration of feminine-leaning people, for in their authentic and unapologetic existence lies the inspiring world yet unseen. I believe existing in this manner is the only way we can save this world.

Contents

Foreword xvii

CHAPTER ONE 1

CHAPTER TWO 19

CHAPTER THREE 37

CHAPTER FOUR 51

CHAPTER FIVE 65

CHAPTER SIX 81

CHAPTER SEVEN 101

CHAPTER EIGHT 119

CHAPTER NINE 133

CHAPTER TEN 151

CHAPTER ELEVEN 175

CHAPTER TWELVE 191

CHAPTER THIRTEEN 211

CHAPTER FOURTEEN 229

CHAPTER FIFTEEN 247

CHAPTER SIXTEEN 259

CHAPTER SEVENTEEN 269

Afterword 283

Acknowledgments 287

Foreword

My name, Prabal, means "the strongest one." Powerful, mighty, and fierce, we're described as fearless and brave individuals willing to take risks. With every challenge that seems more daunting than the previous one, we emerge even more determined and resilient. For me, it is not just about strength but also about courage and perseverance. My name has always been a reminder of the strength I have within.

My sister's name, Kumudini, means "white lotus flower that blooms in darkness." It stands for "magical and creative." It is the flower on which the goddess of wisdom and knowledge, Saraswati, resides. It is no surprise to anyone in our family that my sister Kumudini is the most academic and loves art and literature. Creative, artistic, and imaginative, those named Kumudini are known to have a strong sense of intuition and empathy.

My brother's name, Pravesh, literally means "entrance" or "beginning," signifying the innate ability to find, with each new dawn, hope amidst uncertainty. Those named Pravesh are also considered creative, reflective, and on a constant quest for knowledge. Generous hearted, compassionate, and gracious—it is to my brother Pravesh whom we always turn to for insight and wisdom.

Both of my siblings live up to their names—they're universally liked.

I, on the other hand, am not for everyone.

People in India and Nepal have no problem with my name, but in America, people find it challenging.

"It's so difficult to pronounce!"

"Do you have a nickname? Can we call you P or PG?"

"No," I would reply. "My name is Prabal. Like 'trouble' with a P."

I would help them—but also a subtle forewarning: if I can try to learn your name, then you shall try to learn mine.

I've been called Pablo, Pebble, and Pray. Not pronouncing my name correctly is a power play for so many people. It doesn't say anything about me, but it says a lot about whoever mispronounces it.

Other Asian friends of mine have changed their names: Jin Yun became Jenny; Abu now goes by Abe. I came to America as an immigrant and a misfit. I wanted to be a designer, and to find a place for myself where I would feel like I belonged. I wanted to find my people.

Instead, I was asked to change my name.

WALK
LIKE
A GIRL

CHAPTER ONE

In one of my earliest memories, I was five years old and sitting on the ivory, raw silk, tufted stool in front of my mami's mahogany wood vanity. I was staring at her collection of lipsticks, a neat row of compact cylinders lined up between several bottles of face cream and perfume. There were photos of my siblings and me to my right, next to a fresh bouquet of jasmine plucked from my mother's garden, and a picture of my grandmother who died before I was born.

Hindi music was playing in the living room, where my older sister, Kumudini, was engrossed in a book and snacking on titaura, a special treat made of Nepali hog plums. My brother, Pravesh, the responsible middle child, had already finished his homework and was now helping with household chores. Everyone was quietly in their own corners, including our housekeeper, who was in the kitchen prepping ingredients for my mother, an excellent cook, who always made dinner when she arrived home from work. My favorite time of day was when I was sitting with her and my siblings around the dining table, sharing stories.

As I sat in front of the mirror, I ran my fingers over the top of all those glossy tubes, pausing at a shiny gold cylinder with YSL etched in brilliant black on one side. My heart quickened as I picked it up, pulled off its top, and twisted the bottom to reveal the most beautiful dark ruby-red tip.

A light summer breeze danced through the window, making the ivory silk curtains flutter. My heart was fluttering, too. I looked in the mirror, puckered my lips, and began to smear the red tip over them, nervous and excited.

I'd watched Mami sitting in front of this very vanity countless times, mesmerized by the transformative power of lipstick and eyeliner, which took her from daytime polish to evening chic in a matter of minutes. I'd also witnessed her work magic with concealer and powder to camouflage the bruises and scratches from fights with my father, never once wincing or flinching. Stoically gazing into the mirror, she would apply the foundation, then powder, then blush, methodically making herself even more beautiful than she already was. Witnessing this nightly ritual made me believe she was invincible.

This afternoon, I channeled Mami as I continued to paint my bottom lip with awkward jabs that seeped beyond my lip line. I was holding my breath: what I was doing felt illicit and thrilling. It felt wrong and even a bit dangerous, as my effeminate ways were often a reason for my parents' fights.

The door behind me suddenly creaked open, followed by the sound of glass bangles jangling. The scent of perfume came next, in a warm wave, a familiar floral concoction. I froze, lipstick clutched in my right hand.

"Prabal?" Mami's voice wafted across the room, more searching than stern.

My heart started to pound in my chest as my mother, dressed in her crisp, ivory and beige salwar kurta, walked toward me.

"What are you doing, kanchu?"

She seemed concerned.

My heart was now pounding in my ears.

As she sat down next to me on the stool, I braced myself.

"That's not how you apply lipstick," she said, and she gently held my chin in one hand.

She took the lipstick from my clenched fist and delicately, as if holding a paintbrush, swept it over my bottom lip, and then traced the tip along the contour of my upper lip before using a tiny brushstroke motion to fill the rest in.

She pulled her head back, my chin still in her hand, and smiled broadly.

"This is how you apply lipstick," she said, then swept her hand through my hair as she stood up to walk out toward the living room.

I looked in the mirror and gasped: I was beautiful.

"Hungry?" she asked, pausing at the door, smiling.

I nodded yes and pulled a tissue paper from the tufted dispenser to wipe the lipstick off.

"It's okay, leave it on. You look beautiful," she said. "But only if you want to."

I nodded and watched her head toward the kitchen. But when I looked back at myself in the mirror, I decided to wipe the lipstick off anyway.

At our house, we never knew who might show up for dinner. My aunt and uncle. Any of our relatives. Always annoying. Always disapproving. They wouldn't understand. This would be our secret.

THAT RED LIPSTICK WAS Mami's favorite, and mine, too. Almost every evening, I'd watch her change from her business clothes into a robe before sitting at that vanity to brush her long, straight, jet-black hair back into a low chignon, or sometimes leave it loose, cascading down her back. She'd then apply that same red lipstick as rouge, gently dabbing it on her finger and patting it up and down her cheekbones and then to each side of her nostrils. Next, she'd brush a bluish-gray-green eye shadow beneath her perfectly arched eyebrows, which she defined with her kajal, her eyeliner. She'd finish by painting her lips, just as she had done for me. Only then would she begin to get dressed in an elegant sari, her evening outfit.

My mother had many saris, in a variety of colors and fabric weights. I learned at a young age that how a woman wore her sari said something about her style. If Mami wore one during the day, it was cotton. For evening, she'd change to something with a little sheen, a mint-green French chiffon for the summer months, a chocolate-brown Tanchoi silk during winter, or a fiery, vibrant red silk sari for ceremonial or religious occasions. Sari fabric is seven yards long, and my mother would drape and pleat it around her petite frame, ending with a length that went over her shoulders. Most women cover only one arm and keep the end piece short, but my mom preferred to cover both arms and keep that last piece of fabric long, hanging down her back.

As a final touch, she'd spritz herself with either a blue bottle of Yves Saint Laurent Rive Gauche or the diamond-cut Chanel No. 5. The finishing touch, transformation complete.

As a child, I would watch, mystified. To me, my mother was beauty and strength personified, just like her name. According to the Hindu legend, the female goddess Durga was born to defeat Mahishasura, a demon who took the form of a buffalo and was so strong that the gods Brahma, Vishnu, and Mahesh could not destroy him collectively. Durga is the epitome of female strength and power. She's often depicted riding a lion, which I also found thrilling as my mother was born in August, a Leo. The goddess has ten arms, each holding a different weapon given to her by the various male gods specifically for her battle with the buffalo demon. She alone was able to defeat Mahishasura, and by doing so saved the gods—and mankind—against evil.

My mother has done the same for me.

I WAS BORN IN SINGAPORE, but my family moved to Nepal when I was four. My mom, Durga Rana, was born into Nepal's royal family. Jung Bahadur Rana, my mother's great-great-grandfather, was arguably one of the most important yet polarizing figures in the history of Nepal. Queen Victoria appointed him prime minister after he led the Kot massacre in 1846, which resulted in the slaughter of forty members of the royal palace, including the then prime minister. That started the Rana autocracy, setting up an oppressive dictatorship in Nepal that lasted 105 years, until 1951. This is considered a dark period in Nepali history.

Jung Bahadur Rana had two sons—and the eldest had two wives. My mother's family descended from the first wife of the eldest son. The second wife had more children, and because of their strength and numbers, my mother's family was exiled to Palpa, a rural city west of Kathmandu, when she was ten years old. The eldest of four brothers and three sisters, Mami regaled me with stories of her privileged childhood: the jewelry and fine clothing her grandmother, mother, and aunts wore; the vast lands her family owned; and the stables of horses she loved to ride as a child. She also shared stories of her dismay at how the women would get dressed for events and parties, only to be forced to stay behind curtains.

"We were not allowed to share the same space with men," she'd say with a stern look on her face. Even as a child she couldn't fathom why men and women sat separately or why women ate only after men had finished eating.

She also told the scary but exhilarating tale of the night her family was exiled, how the newly appointed Rana rulers were hunting her male siblings to assassinate them, and how my grandmother and aunts hid the babies in their big, elaborately embroidered hoopskirts. Once in Palpa, my mother was lucky enough to go to a good boarding school, where she was the principal's favorite, a trait that she passed on to my siblings, as well as a love for reading, writing, and poetry. She had dreams of going to London and studying politics, but fate had a different path for her.

My father, Baba Krishna Gurung, comes from a different caste: they're warriors and soldiers with strong roots in Nepal and ancient lineages tracing back to various parts of East Asia. Often lively and boisterous compared with the more stoic and uptight Ranas, the Gurungs also had a good standing and positioning in Nepali society, but their clan usually married among themselves. They were men of honor and valor. For them, the Ranas were debauched people with no integrity, who for the sake of power would betray their own children or families. A Gurung marrying a Rana was the coming together of two opposite worlds, like a WASP marrying a Jew.

My mother did it anyway. Just after she turned eighteen, she married my father and moved to Singapore.

As a young woman in Nepal, my mother was used to not having agency or power. But in Singapore, she knew no one, and did not even know the language. Whenever she tried to speak English, my father would make fun of her accent. And then, one day, she asked him for money to buy something, and he said, "Why would I do that?"

"That was when I knew I had made a huge mistake," she said.

And yet my mother had no other options. She did not have a family in Nepal to return to, as her mother died when she was young and her father had remarried. Her aunt made all the decisions in her family, and getting married was what most Nepali women did at her age. My father had promised her that she could get an education—her dream, and the reason she accepted his proposal. Plus, starting a new life in Singapore sounded exciting. She quickly learned that neither was the case. When I was growing up, my mother was always evasive about why her relationship with her family was strained—from what I could piece together, it seemed that they had opposed her marriage to my father, and once she had gone ahead and married him, divorce was unthinkable.

In Sanskrit, there is a phrase: *pati parmeshwor.*

Pati means "husband" and *parmeshwor* means "god."

Even though she had desires of being independent, there were no role models—in Nepal or in Singapore. She was totally on her own. Back then, the men worked, and the women stayed home to take care of the family. My father worked in the Singapore police, where many officers' wives knitted and crocheted as a hobby. My mother didn't have the patience for either, but she did see a potential lifeline for herself. She took whatever items these women made—coasters, crocheted cushion covers, tablecloths, ponchos, and more—and sold them to the boutiques on High Street. Suddenly, these stay-at-home wives had an income—as did she.

Like my mother, my father had a difficult upbringing. His mother died when he was young, and his father, who was second-in-command in the Nepali police force, remarried a woman who had two sons. She was the archetype of the evil stepmother. Even today my siblings and I laugh about how our father could eat an entire chicken by himself. But we also know that his stepmother would give her sons the best part of the chicken, giving my father the scraps. He never told us these stories directly, but my mom shared them with us. She was trying to humanize him. She wanted us to understand that people are not bad, circumstances make them that way. This was something she often said.

Also like my mother, my father was known for his style—always polished in a well-tailored suit. He was a football player and a musician, and one of my fondest childhood memories was listening to him sit in our living room, strumming his guitar, singing a beautiful but haunting song about a lonely, blind, orphaned boy who is "nobody's child," the name of the song.

My memories of Singapore are faded. But I remember going to see films at an outdoor theater with my parents. As soon as each movie was over, the street vendors would arrive, selling food and trinkets, including two-dimensional paper dolls. They were wide-eyed with dark hair and tiny lips. Black-and-white line drawings that you could color in—each wearing a simple A-line dress. I always begged my parents to buy me one, and they often did. Those dolls are the basis for every sketch I have ever made of my clothing designs.

My mother knew that I liked to play with dolls, draw pictures of beautiful gowns, and dress like a girl. She even encouraged me when I wanted to wear dresses—I have photos to prove it. I particularly loved one pink dress that belonged to my sister, Kumudini. I could not understand why my clothes—stiff shorts and a pressed button-down shirt—were so restrictive, compared with my sister's. I wanted something that fluttered and flowed with my every sashay.

Wearing a dress made me feel more myself. Sometimes, I'd pair that pink dress with my mother's white high heels and feel gorgeous. My mother never once questioned my penchant for so-called women's clothes. Nor did my sister or my brother. My father, however, struggled with it. I remember one day he returned home from work to find me prancing around in my mother's sari and stilettos. I watched his body stiffen and his face grow taut, all hard lines. He turned to my mother, who was reading quietly on the couch.

"Prabal cannot dress like that!" he shouted at her, as if it were somehow her fault. "He's going to be called a sissy!"

"Leave him alone," my mother replied coolly. "Who cares what anyone calls him? This makes him happy."

My father left me alone, but not my mother. These interchanges would escalate quickly. Often, it was about my effeminate ways, but the most violent fights were when my mother questioned my father's extramarital affairs. There were nights when he wouldn't come home from work. When he finally returned, sometimes days later, my mother would inevitably ask, "Where have you been and who have you been with?"

"How dare you question me?" he'd scream.

My father was a terrible husband, but he always supported my siblings and me. I never questioned his love for us. I don't know why he was so threatened by my mother. I do know that it did not deter her. In Singapore, her crochet and knitting business eventually started doing so well that she was making more money than my father.

"You keep doing what you're doing," she told my dad. "All you need to do is make sure our visas are good—I'll make money to put our kids in the best schools possible."

She had just made a deal with a Chinese manufacturer to grow her business and had all her workers lined up when, a week later, my dad said, "We're going back to Nepal."

MY MOM WAS HAPPY to be back home in Nepal even though it meant starting her company from scratch. My father had left the police force and was really struggling with his health. The panicky soundtrack from this period of my life is of my father wheezing, followed by the rat-a-tat-tat of his nebulizer, always in his pocket. He had terrible asthma, and anything could trigger the attacks—dust, food, allergies, stress. When we first came back to Nepal, they were so bad that we'd hear him gasping for air and watch his face grow beet red as his eyes went wide and wild. He'd suck on his inhaler, and when that stopped working, my mother would have to rush him to the emergency room. The doctors said he needed an operation. It was dire—but incredibly expensive. My parents didn't have nearly enough money to cover the cost, so my mother convinced my father that they should go ask his father.

At the time, my grandfather was stationed as a police officer in Dhangadhi, in the western part of Nepal on the Indian border. It was an all-day journey for us—a car to a bus and then sixteen hours later, we climbed onto an oxcart called a ladiya, which took us the rest of the way, down dirt roads through rice paddy fields. My grandfather sent guards to escort us for this portion of the journey. As we passed through the villages, people emerged from their thatched-roof houses and began calling to one another and running after our cart. These were Tharu, indigenous people of Nepal. The women stared at us, and I could not help but look back, mesmerized by their intricately embroidered, once colorful, now faded choli—a cropped and fitted blouse. They wore weather-beaten cotton saris draped over their heads and silver jewelry and tattoos adorned their bodies. The men had on lungi—a draped skirt, which they wore with a shirt and a scarf—all sun beaten and worn thin. They were huddled in conversation with one another, seemingly annoyed by our presence. The children, however, ran alongside our ladiya, barefoot, in T-shirts and tattered cotton sarongs, smiling as they pointed and shouted at me and my family.

Though I was only six, I was struck by the vast—and seemingly arbitrary—difference in our circumstances. But what stands out the most was the children's laughter. It was so hopeful and joyous.

My grandfather's home was a stately brick structure surrounded by a gate, a stark contrast to the mud and thatched-roof homes that surrounded it. My mother went inside to chat with her father-in-law, leaving me outside in the cart to wait with my brother and father. When she returned, she seemed subdued. Disappointed. She climbed back into the cart and shook her head without saying a word.

"I told you we should not have come," my father said angrily.

My mother remained quiet until my dad made a grunting sigh, which prompted her to say, "We must try. We must make an effort."

I knew then that my grandfather had said no to paying for my father's operation. It shocked me that he did not have the heart to take care of his own son.

BACK IN KATHMANDU, my mother went to see her cousin Prem. She was working on starting a garment company and had asked him to review her contract with the manufacturer. That was when she learned that he had taken over the licensing deal himself. Rather than waste time on feeling angry, my mother simply started another business. She considered Prem almost like a brother, and the relationship was worth more to her than the company. To this day, he oversees a multimillion-dollar company that my mother started. So instead, she pivoted. She bought saris in India and sold them in Nepal. Eventually she opened her own boutique, as well as a tailoring company. Her lesson in all of this was "make sure to have wood in different fires."

In Kathmandu, my father started working as a freelance journalist for a local newspaper, which meant that he was often gone, traveling for work. He never got the surgery—we simply could not afford it. Instead, my mother made sure to monitor his diet and was constantly worried about dust and other allergens, which meant our house was spotless. He continued to use his nebulizer, and even had an oxygen tank for the bad days. In addition to journalism, he also started an employment agency where he would recruit people from villages to work abroad as migrant workers, Nepal's biggest export. Both jobs meant he was often gone, which I preferred. Our home was peaceful when he was not there.

One afternoon, I was playing in the garden courtyard on the green lawn when a woman approached our wrought iron gate.

"Does Baba Krishna live here?" she called out to me.

I was struck by how confident she seemed as she called out my father's name.

"Yes," I said. "Who are you?"

"I'm his wife."

Shocked, I ran inside to tell my mother, who was sitting there with her sister, my aunt Manju, who was living with us at the time.

"Mami, there's a woman at the gate looking for Daddy," I explained, and the words felt hot in my mouth. "She said she's his wife!"

I was waiting for a reaction that would match the thumping of my heart, but my mom did not flinch. "Don't say a word, Prabal," she said. "Let her in."

I went back and opened the gate, and my mother greeted her at our front door and introduced herself as my father's sister. She then invited this stranger into our home and offered her tea. They sat in our living room, and I hid just outside the door, straining to hear the muffled conversation. What I was able to make out was that she was from Dharan, a ten-hour drive from Kathmandu, and again claimed that she was married to my father.

When my father came home that evening, my mother said coolly, "A woman came looking for you today. She claims she's your wife."

"I have no idea what you are talking about," he said.

I felt the tension course through the house and quickly hid in the same spot behind the living room door where neither of them could see me.

"She's lying!" he said, throwing his arms in the air.

My mother remained calm but firm, listing the details she had gathered that day.

I watched my father shift from defensive to defiant.

"Yes! So what? I can marry whomever I want!" He was now shouting and gesticulating. My mother didn't flinch—nor did she back down.

She always won with words, leaving him all he had left: his fists.

FIGHTING SEEMED TO FOLLOW me wherever I went, whether it was at home or at school. I was always getting in trouble at school—for my grades, for my attitude, and for the fact that I fought back whenever anyone bullied me, which was often. It was so bad that I would end up in the principal's office for defending myself and would still be punished.

I was the opposite of my two siblings. My brother, Pravesh, is two years older than me and was a star student, the president of the student council, and the lead actor *and* director of school plays who won countless awards. He was also the most popular kid in the school and had been voted "Best Boy" by his classmates. He was a kind, thoughtful, and very responsible child who was not only well liked in school but universally loved by our relatives and neighbors. He did everything by the book and in my eyes could do no wrong.

My sister, Kumudini, the eldest of us, was a mix of both Pravesh and me: a genius, an A-plus student, and a total badass. One afternoon, when I was ten years old, I was walking with her through the streets of Kathmandu when two teenage boys shouted, "What a chakka!" as we passed by.

That translates to "sissy" or "pansy" in English.

I had begun to understand all the ways in which words could be used as weapons against my very existence, and I ignored the jeers. But Kumudini did not. I watched her face shift from soft to rigid in a flash.

She turned around and marched right up to those two boys.

"What did you say?" she yelled, pointing a finger toward them, her nostrils flaring.

Her rage startled them into silence. As she inched closer, the boys let out high-pitched laughs before speeding off on their bikes. Like my mother, Kumudini always had my back.

But whether with those boys in the streets, or with the kids in my classes at school, the abuse I experienced had a similar thread: I'd get pushed around in the hallway, called names, or tripped on the street. The taunt I heard the most was "You walk like a girl!"

They meant it as a criticism, which did not make sense: The women in my life were strong, brilliant, and opinionated and always spoke their minds. How was being girlie a bad thing?

Besides, I could not help it. It was simply who I was, then and now. I knew that boys were supposed to love *Superman* and *The Incredible Hulk*, but *Wonder Woman* was my favorite TV show at the time. I would run around our house wearing just underwear, with one of my mother's silk scarves tied around my neck as my cape. I spent hours meticulously fashioning cuffs from gold chocolate foil and would box the air with them on, jump off the couch, high kick, and loudly sing the theme song: "Wonder Woman!"

I also practiced Diana Prince's amazing twirl in the mirror, which reminded me of my mother's nightly transformation. From her daytime business outfit into her gold cuffs, her red, white, and blue bodysuit, and her knee-high boots, Diana Prince reminded me so much of the strong, justice-seeking women in my family.

No outfit could protect my mother, however. I recall one night when shouting woke me up. I was still in bed when I heard a crash, followed by a gasp, and then silence. Terrified, I ran to investigate and saw my mother slumped on the floor in our living room, surrounded by broken glass. My father had thrown her so hard against the coffee table that it had shattered. He was standing above her, his fist in the air, frozen. I ran into the room and screamed, "Stop it! This is madness! You could kill her!"

That snapped my father out of his fervor. I saw him shake his head as he registered what had just happened. He then lowered his arm and backed out of the room.

I learned at that moment how to use my voice to protect my mom.

Domestic violence was so common in Nepal—if anything, my mother was blamed for my father's anger. I witnessed similar incidents throughout my extended family where the attitude was "the woman must have done something to deserve it."

The beatings were bad—and usually occurred at home but would sometimes spill into the public realm, too. When he spotted my mother speaking to another man at my cousin's wedding, he struck her in front of everyone—aunts, uncles, and cousins. No one did anything to defend her.

My mother remained close with her cousin, my uncle Prem, despite his betrayal. We visited him and his wife Manorama often. They had just returned from a trip to Hong Kong, and I recall sitting in my cousin Karuna's room, watching her unpack. She was a few years older than me. I remember the moment she pulled out a butter-yellow ballerina dress from her suitcase that she had bought abroad. It was the most beautiful thing I'd ever seen, the poufy epitome of a Disney Princess dress. I felt a jealous pang, which must have flickered on my face.

"Oh, look, Karuna, Prabal likes your dress," my aunt Manorama said with a smirk.

I stifled my smile, but still watched, mesmerized, as Karuna carried the dress by its two delicate straps to her closet, where she placed it on a hanger. The ruffles on the edge of the skirt did a magical sweep, as if the dress were animated, waving goodbye before it disappeared.

A few weeks later, we returned to the house for a party, as my aunt and uncle often entertained. My siblings were closer in age to my cousins, so they were excited to go. I, however, had no one to play with. I just sat on the couch watching the adults chat, cocktails in hand, as my cousins and siblings laughed together in a corner. I felt a loneliness that was becoming familiar. Then I remembered that yellow dress.

It was an almost magnetic pull. I snuck upstairs and into my cousin's room, locked the door behind me, and walked straight to her closet. There, I opened the doors and stared at the burst of tulle sunshine among the more muted cotton sundresses. My heart started to pound in my chest as I slipped it off its hanger. I could feel the music from the party below emanating through the floorboards, coursing throughout my body, and merging with my heartbeat, to the point where I could not distinguish the two.

I quickly took off my shorts and shirt and stepped into the dress, which felt like wrapping myself in a cumulus cloud. I grew up watching Bollywood musicals and Hollywood epics like *Sabrina* and *My Fair Lady*, where the heroine's gowns were characters unto themselves. Suddenly, I was zipping myself into one.

I could still hear the chatter downstairs as I twirled and watched with delight as the layers of tulle swirled with me into the most dramatic shapes.

I felt like I was floating on a lemon meringue sky. It was less my wanting to wear this particular dress and more of what that dress allowed me to do: I was transported to a place where my very being made sense. I twirled a few more times and then sat down on my cousin's bed, crossed my legs, and watched as the fabric fluttered and settled around me. Peaceful.

I WAS PROBABLY TEN when we went to yet another gathering at my aunt Manorama and uncle Prem's house. This time, it was a housewarming party for them. That garment business that my mother had started and Prem had taken over had grown into one of the most successful companies in Nepal. It was doing well enough for my uncle and aunt to afford a four-story mansion, which was surrounded by a big gate with a security guard. We drove up the long driveway to a white stucco house that looked like a big square wedding cake. Everyone seemed excited about it. I, however, found it bland.

My brother and sister ran into the house to join the festivities, but I was dreading the gathering. The last time we had visited, Aunt Manorama had singled me out in front of everyone for being a sissy. I can't precisely remember what I had done, only that my very existence bothered her. That night, the house was packed, mostly with relatives, but also friends and neighbors. People were dressed up for a fancy party, everyone dancing and celebrating—and I was restless. I went back outside to wander around and escape the inevitable taunts.

Along the house was a generator, and next to it, I spotted a gallon of black paint and a paintbrush and was immediately drawn to them. The next thing I knew, I was dipping the brush in the pot of paint and drawing big, bold, black lines on this new white house. I loved the way the black popped on the white, making what I thought was quite a dull exterior visually compelling. I felt a surge of adrenaline flood my body, which compelled me to add another stroke here, and there. In hindsight, I can now see how I was grappling with internal turmoil and resentment toward my aunt. However, in the midst of that creative act, I felt free.

And then I heard a scream. I looked up and saw one of my aunt's maids running back into the house, still shrieking. That snapped me out of my reverie: I knew that I was in trouble. I stood still as my aunt came storming outside, yelling, "Prabal, what are you doing!"

She had tucked her sari into her belt and was stomping toward me, her arms raised, hands balled into fists, yelling so loudly that a stream of people followed her out of the house to see what the commotion was. My mother ran ahead of the pack and took her place by my side.

"Of course, Durga Maharani! This is all your fault!" my aunt was now screaming at my mother. "You can't handle your husband! You can't handle your children!"

Maharani means "princess." Manorama was seething.

My mom shielded me as my aunt started to circle me, slinging insults like rocks.

"What's wrong with you, Prabal?" she hissed. "Do you wish you were a girl? Are you a sissy?"

I stood statue still as she continued her barrage, my mother's hand on my back unwavering. I, however, could feel the tears boiling up inside me.

"Oh, so now you're crying?" my aunt continued. "Of course! He's a girl after all!"

My mother very calmly took my hand and said, "Come, Prabal, we're going home."

In the car, she remained quiet and looked straight ahead, her fingers still interlaced with mine. Her stoic expression was a shield against the waves of emotions crashing inside of me. I had put her in a terrible position with my aunt and was searching her face for any sign of disappointment or shame. Instead, she turned to me with compassion in her eyes and flashed a faint, tired smile. That was when I was finally able to release all the feelings welling up inside of me. I nestled closer to her and began to sob, still holding her hand, seeking refuge in her embrace.

We both knew I had done something wrong. Of course, you don't paint someone's new house at their housewarming party! But my mother also knew that there was something inside of me that I needed to express.

The following morning, I woke up to find a drawing pad, paintbrushes, watercolors, and pencils on my study table.

CHAPTER TWO

I was in sixth grade when my mother realized that my ability to grasp and retain information was a lot different from my siblings'. Both were stellar students with excellent grades—I was barely passing. When I think back to that time, it's so clear I was struggling with what seems like dyslexia, even though that was not a term anyone used or understood in Nepal. I also see how the traditional school structure did not agree with my restless and wandering mind. Instead of being inspired or encouraged, I was constantly punished. Everywhere I went, I was in a perpetual state of fight or flight, bearing witness to my father's abuse at home and being bullied by my peers at school.

At the time, I was attending St. Xavier's School Jawalakhel, a very strict Catholic all-boys day school in Kathmandu where I was teased daily. I was not a good student or athlete, but I was often cast as the lead in school plays as I had dramatic flair and a beautiful singing voice. This, of course, led to more ostracism. While I was not the only effeminate boy in my school, I was the only one who fought back whenever anyone bothered me, which generally landed me in more trouble.

My father was now hardly ever home, leaving my mother on her own to raise three kids. My siblings were perfect in every way—excellent students, role models, and citizens. I was decidedly the black sheep. Still, I was a bit shocked when Mami told me that she was sending me to Saint Xavier's boarding school, which was in Godavari, on the outskirts of Kathmandu. That was the first of the Jesuit-run schools in Nepal, founded so that the ruling Rana family's children could be educated in their country, versus being sent to India or Europe.

My mother said that she had no choice. My brother and sister were A-plus students—meanwhile, I was borderline failing and constantly getting into trouble. After I got over my shock, I found myself intrigued. It meant a fresh start. I was so sick of the kids who tormented me daily in my school. Plus, my only friend, Deep Rana, was already at Godavari.

Deep and I had met on the very first day of third grade at St. Xavier's. I remember other students looking at me like I was a weirdo, and then Deep approached me and asked, "What's your name?"

He was way taller than me, lanky with buckteeth, which earned him the nickname Camel. There was something so kind in the way he talked to me.

"Come sit with me," he said.

In a classroom where I felt immediately judged, he made me feel welcome.

He was my one friend throughout fourth grade, so I was sad to learn his parents were sending him to St. Xavier's School, Godavari, the original boarding school in the same Catholic network of schools in Nepal.

Now I'd be joining him. It only went through sixth grade, so I only had to survive one year. At least I had a good friend to help me navigate being away from home for the first time in my life.

MY MOTHER HIRED A CAR to take us to my new school. I watched with wonder as the chaotic city streets morphed into a lone highway, with rice fields on either side, a vibrant green dotted with optimistic mustard-yellow blossoms. I was equal parts excited and unsure. Deep said it was a great school.

More than anything, I hoped I would make new friends. I was praying for a change, the promise of a new beginning.

At some point along the journey, "I Have Confidence," my favorite song from *The Sound of Music*, began playing on the car radio. I loved the movie and knew the entire soundtrack by heart. I started to sing along, channeling Maria.

As our car started to slow down, I saw a large iron gate ahead flanked with security guards. Students were running around the large lawn that sprawled behind it, boys playing football in one field, volleyball in the other. Those not playing were all dressed alike: white shirts and navy trousers or shorts. Black shoes. The school uniform.

As we approached the security booth, a massively tall white man, dressed in a black-and-white priest outfit, came running toward us.

"You must be Prawwabal Gooroong?" he said, nodding his head. He was flushed pink and wore thick glasses that slipped down his sweaty nose. His smile was big, warm, and kind.

My hand disappeared in his gigantic, outstretched hand. I nodded and he smiled. Then he turned to my mother and said, "Mrs. Gurung?"

My mom smiled politely and said, "I prefer to be called Durga."

"Well then, Durga, I'm Father Pascale, the principal," he responded. "Welcome to St. Xavier's Godavari."

The way he said Godavari—overemphasizing the *da*—in his American accent made me chuckle. He took us on a tour of the school, speaking in both English and Nepali. I was amused by how effortlessly he was able to navigate those two languages. The semester had already started—I'd been on a waiting list, so the minute a spot became available, we rushed to fill it. I appreciated how thoughtful and attentive Father Pascale was to me and my mom. Something about him made me feel safe.

As we neared the dormitory, Father Pascale said, "Well, now I leave you with the dorm supervisor, Jhamke Dai. He'll take care of you from here."

Jhamke Dai was a short, pleasant-looking man wearing a white shirt, khaki trousers, sneakers, and a Nepali topi. He greeted my mother and me with a namaste and a big smile.

"Welcome, welcome," he said, and then he turned to me. "I'm your dai. Your big brother. So if you need anything, let me know."

He showed me where I would sleep—a top bunk in a gigantic room filled with two-tiered beds. My mother helped me unpack and then quickly taught me how to tuck in my sheets and fold the sirak, a handmade comforter with cotton covers. Anyone who has lived in Nepal knows how soft, warm, and comforting these sirak are.

Then she placed my clothes in my assigned dresser and arranged all the snacks and candies she had brought on my bedside shelf: dark and milk chocolates, bourbon biscuits, dried noodles, and some titaura and other dried fruits, which she covered with a mulmul khasto, a thin, organic-cotton voile shawl.

"Leave it here so you have it to wear when it gets cold," she said.

After I settled in, she found Jhamke Dai and gave him some money.

"Keep an eye on my son," she said.

He promised he would.

Right before she said goodbye, my mother explained that this new school was a good thing for me.

"A fresh start," she said, though her eyes were brimming with tears.

It was a new beginning—and the first time in my life that I was leaving my mother. One of my favorite rituals was going to her bedroom as soon as I woke up. I'd crawl beneath her blanket, and we'd have tea in bed and talk. Those morning conversations made me the person I am today. And yet I knew that she was struggling at home. My father had been in and out of our lives my entire childhood, and this was a period where he was gone. I was used to his not being there, and to be honest, it was a relief. When he was not around, I didn't worry about my mother's physical well-being. But I also knew that money was tight. My mother was raising three kids on her own; we had moved from a house we owned to a rental. I needed to be one less thing for her to worry about.

It was late afternoon when she said goodbye, and I'll never forget the panicky feeling in my stomach as I watched the car drive down the driveway and out the gates. As it disappeared in the distance, tears started to roll down my cheeks.

Right then, Jhamke Dai came and patted me on the shoulder. He said, "Don't worry, you'll be okay. Plus, in a few months, you'll get to go home for your holidays."

Deep walked up at that moment, smiling, and I immediately felt at ease. I thought, "Well, I have my best friend with me now. What could be so bad?"

I gave him a big hug.

As we were walking down the hallway, I noticed all these boys stopping and staring at me. I was the new kid. Deep looked a little nervous and kept on walking, looking straight ahead.

"Don't stop till we get to the dining room," he whispered under his breath.

That was foreboding. At dinner, a boy my age introduced himself. He seemed kind.

"What kind of movies do you like?" he asked.

"Musicals," I said, and then rattled off my favorites. "*Sound of Music, My Fair Lady, Singin' in the Rain.* And some Bollywood, too."

We talked about our favorite actors, as well.

"If you could be one character in a movie, who would that be?" he asked.

"Wonder Woman," I said without hesitation. "Or Rekha."

Rekha was my favorite Bollywood actress and one of *the* most stylish Hindi movie stars ever. I also wanted to say Maria from *Sound of Music* but decided against it.

Later that night, as I was brushing my teeth, another student bumped into me.

I was startled, but assumed it was an accident and anticipated an apology.

Instead, he pushed me again—more forcibly this time. My body slammed against the ceramic sink.

"So, you want to be a wonder *woman*?" he hissed in my ear. "Or was it Rekha?"

As if on cue, several boys surrounded me. Their ringleader pushed me again, this time into another boy, who pushed me back into the center.

"So, you're a girl then? That means you must want to get fucked!" one of the boys shouted as the others laughed, egging each other on.

"That can be arranged," another shouted.

I curled my fist around the toothbrush and placed both hands protectively around my head, my mouth still frothy with minty toothpaste suds as the circle closed in on me. Just then, Jhamke Dai arrived. He yelled at the boys, and the crowd dispersed before any more harm was done. I washed my face and saw Jhamke Dai looking at me in the mirror. He smiled as if to say sorry, but his eyes looked worried. He slumped slightly and walked away.

That night, I cried myself to sleep.

The next day, I found my friend Deep in the dining hall and felt a wave of relief. I ran up to him, my smile matching his. But then another guy approached and said, "Who is this chakka?" I watched Deep's face deflate as he realized that being my friend was a dangerous liability.

THE BULLYING AT ST. XAVIER'S was the most intense I'd ever experienced. I was targeted for all the things I loved to do—singing, dancing, sketching girls in dresses in my notebook. Deep suggested that I keep my head down and ignore the jeers. Instead, I always fought back with the goal of landing at least one punch. The abuse was so consistent that, to this day, I still have a shoulder injury from those early scuffles.

I put on a strong face during the day. I had to. But at night, I would sit in my bunk bed and look at the window at the main gate and fantasize about my mom coming to take me home.

THE ONLY TIME I felt safe was onstage. Playing a role. Singing a song. I was a terrible student, but I had a beautiful soprano voice.

All the boys were assigned to dining tables. Mine had six or seven boys. Every week, there was a school talent show where each table had to perform a skit or song.

At our first performance, the boys at my table panicked: "What should we do?"

One kid said, "Prabal, you can sing. What if you do a song, and we will stand behind you?"

I was thrilled to be the recipient of positive attention for once and chose a difficult Hindi song to perform. It was well received. The kids in the audience stayed quiet, and the boys at my table were relieved. I liked being the hero—but it was short-lived.

That night, in the bathroom, another boy from my dorm room sneered, "Sissy."

Another said, "You sing like a girl," as if that were an insult.

I ignored them, brushed my teeth, and got ready for bed.

Every evening, a teacher made the rounds to make sure all the students were settled in. On that night, our teacher, Edon Richards, was on duty.

Each bed was domed in mosquito netting and, for the most part, Edon would quickly walk by each bunk, doing a head count. Every so often, he'd stick his head into the net to say something to a boy. It struck me as odd. I didn't know why, but I did not want him to do that to me. I was already being called names. I didn't want his attention.

That night, after the talent show, he approached my bed.

I lay very still, eyes shut tight, pretending to already be asleep. "Please keep walking," I thought to myself.

Instead, he pulled my net up and put his face close to my ear. "Prabal, you sang so beautifully," he whispered. I could feel his breath against my cheek.

My body tensed up and I said a very quiet, curt "Thank you." I was relieved when he replaced the netting and continued his rounds.

The next time I saw him was in the swimming pool. It was our physical education class, and I was just learning to swim. I wasn't good at it at all. Part of the strategy of the PE teacher was to throw kids into the deep end of the pool. Of course, there were lifeguards, teachers, and other students who were skilled swimmers there to save people from drowning, but I found that "sink or swim" approach terrifying.

That afternoon, I was thrown in the pool and was flailing around underneath the water, panicked, when I suddenly felt strong hands beneath my stomach.

As my head broke above the water, I looked up and saw that it was Edon Richards who had saved me.

He was tall and muscular, with light blond, wavy hair and dark brown eyes. Even though I was only eleven, I thought that he was terribly handsome. I threw my arms around his neck, grateful. But I had also heard the rumors.

"Don't ever get stuck alone with Edon Richards," the boys in my dorm would say. They never explained why. I found it confusing, as he was one of the very few teachers who was nice to me.

A MONTH OR SO into the school year, I auditioned for the lead role in a play called *The Never Never Nest.* There was another student who wanted the same part, and everyone assumed he'd get it because his brother had played that role the year before. I knew I was the better choice and fought hard for the role—so I was especially proud when I got it.

Everyone's families were invited to the opening night. Finally, after all those nights pining for my mother to come save me from the testosterone-driven nightmare that was sixth grade, she was coming to see me. That visit would be the inoculation I needed to make it through to the holidays.

On the day of the performance, I woke up with butterflies in my stomach and hurried through breakfast, thinking if I moved quickly, so would time. Deep and I went outside together to wait for our parents. I heard fellow students shouting as their family members arrived; I felt their thrill with each reunion. The running, the open-armed hugs. Some families brought picnics; others were carrying gifts. The anticipation kept mounting. I strained my neck and even stood on my tiptoes looking for my mother, her signature sari, both shoulders covered. Her perfect red lipstick.

I saw Deep light up and watched his parents emerge from behind the front gate. Pravesh was right behind them, and my heart began to dance in my chest—I didn't expect him to come. I ran toward him, and we met in a big bear hug. As I squeezed my big brother, I scanned the small groups of parents still arriving in his wake.

"Where's Mami?" I asked.

"She couldn't make it," he said quietly, pulling back and looking at his feet.

He didn't explain why, and the feeling of sadness I had was overwhelming. I had been holding in so much frustration and confusion—at not fitting in, anywhere. I was counting the seconds until I saw Mami, knowing that she'd help me make sense of it. She was my ballast, my haven.

"She wishes she could be here," Pravesh said, pulling me back into his chest.

I had also been excited for her to see me in this play. It was the first time I'd done something that I was proud of, and I was devastated that she wouldn't see me in it. But I didn't let that get in the way of giving my all to the performance. Inhabiting a character onstage meant that I didn't have to be myself. Acting didn't just bring me joy—it was also a place where I felt safe. Up onstage, I knew that no one was going to attack or tease me.

I CAN'T TELL YOU how many times I cried myself to sleep that year. Deep was my only friend. There was another student who I thought could be a friend. He was kind to me, to the point where I began to trust him. One evening, I confided in him how much I liked dressing up in my sister's clothes. I didn't have a desire to be a girl—that never crossed my mind. But I loved dancing and much preferred how dresses moved when I danced in them versus how men's clothes moved. I also told him how much I loved *Wonder Woman* and *Charlie's Angels.* Why wouldn't I? They all reminded me of my mother!

The next morning, I walked into class and felt all these eyes staring at me. One boy started laughing, then another, and another.

Our teacher said, "What's so funny?"

Someone blurted out, "Prabal wants to be a girl."

I saw my "friend" snickering, one hand over his mouth, the other pointing at me.

AT LEAST WINTER BREAK was on the horizon. I was counting the days until I could leave. When the morning finally arrived, I hopped out of bed, elated. My mother was coming. I was finally going home.

It was a rainy, dreary day. I put my yellow raincoat over my jeans and sweater and then headed down to the dining hall for breakfast. Afterward, as I made my way back to my dorm, I heard music wafting out of the open windows of the staff quarters, catty-corner from my dorm. It was Sister Vivencia and Sister Josephine, two nuns at our school, singing "Edelweiss" from *The Sound of Music*, accompanied by piano. Hearing their angelic voices lifted my spirits even higher. I started to sing along, lost in my thoughts as the soft sprinkle of rain speckled my face and body.

Just then, I felt a tap on my shoulder.

"Prabal, what are you still doing here?"

It was Edon Richards.

"Just waiting for my mother to pick me up," I replied. "She's running late."

He was holding up an umbrella and wearing a cream-colored button-down shirt with chocolate-brown polyester pants. My heart raced a bit. I was just discovering my own intense feelings for boys and had many crushes at that time in my life.

"Why don't you join me for a stroll?" he said as a warm smile spread across his face.

He motioned for me to join him beneath his umbrella, and as I did, he gently took my hand. Most kids had been picked up by then, so the campus was empty. We began to walk and talk, and while holding hands is common in Nepali culture between men, it felt somehow wrong. We then passed another teacher, who laughed and said, "Edon, is that your new girlfriend?"

Edon shook his head, laughing as well.

The rain picked up. Even beneath the umbrella, we were both getting wet, so he suggested we wait for my mother in his apartment, which was adjacent to my dormitory, in between the fifth- and sixth-grade dorm rooms.

"Let's go dry off," he said as he opened the door for me and motioned for me to enter.

I did, and then heard the door lock behind us. He then escorted me into the second room, which was his bedroom and study.

"Take off your raincoat," he said. "Make yourself at home."

I was both excited and a bit nervous. He was paying attention to me. I felt special. But this also felt dangerous. I figured I could handle it either way, so, after I removed my coat, I sat down on his bed, my hands folded in my lap.

"Prabal," he asked as he sat next to me. "Why are you always so curt and rude with me?"

My mind started racing. I wasn't sure how to respond.

"Every time I see or talk to you, I feel like you don't like me."

All the rumors I had heard swarmed in my head. I blurted out, "I heard that you kissed boys."

"Oh!" he said, laughing. "Is that it?"

I was trembling as I nodded my head yes.

"Prabal, there's nothing wrong with kissing boys," he said as he moved closer to me on the bed. I kept looking straight ahead, my hands now balled into fists in my lap.

I saw him smile through the corner of my eye, and then felt him lean toward me and kiss my cheek.

His soft lips against my skin gave me the shivers. I was a mix of emotions: unsure, aroused. Then he unbuttoned his shirt, took my hand, and placed it on his chest.

This was my teacher. He was so good-looking, kind, attentive, and caring. Everyone told me I was a bad student, a bad kid—except him. I was beginning to feel wildly uncomfortable and pulled my hand away. At that moment, he scooped me up in his arms and held me tight.

The next thing I knew, he had slipped off his pants and was sitting back down next to me, completely naked. He asked me to touch his penis. "Just rub up and down," he said in a whisper.

He then guided my hand down to his penis.

I was eleven years old and had never seen or felt a hard-on before.

I was paralyzed: I did not know what he meant, or what to do. It was so overwhelming. Then he asked me to kiss it. Again, I was a mix of scared and curious. It was all happening so fast. I just started following his orders, like a puppet.

He asked me to take off my clothes, and I did. He next pulled me into bed with him, and that was when I began to panic. His hands were all over me. I was relieved for a moment when he told me to sit on him. I could finally get out from underneath him. But then, I experienced a pain so searing, I began to tear up. I wanted him to stop but worried if I opened my mouth to say so, I would cry.

When he did, the relief I felt was staggering.

We chatted a bit—I can't remember what he said—and then he began kissing me again. I did not mind—I was just so glad for that pain to be over. This was so tender in comparison.

A knock on the door shocked both of us, and I saw his face go from serene to panicked. "Put on your clothes!" he hissed and then jumped up and into his clothes.

"Edon, are you in there?"

I immediately recognized Father Pascale's deep voice penetrating the locked door. Edon quickly opened a window that looked out onto the corridor where Father Pascale was waiting.

"Is Prabal here? His mother is looking for him."

My heart leapt to my throat as I hopped off the chair and ran to the door.

As I was leaving, Edon whispered in my ear, "This is our secret."

I looked at him blankly.

"Is that okay?" he asked, running his fingers through my hair.

I was a young, scared boy, on the brink of puberty, so not yet fully aware of my sexual orientation. I didn't know how to answer that question. For the first time in my life, I felt at a loss for something to say.

Once outside, and walking to see my mother, Father Pascale said, in an almost stern way, "Prabal, never be alone with Edon Richards."

Again, I remained silent.

Father Pascale stopped midstride and looked at me, alarmed. "Did he do anything to you?"

I could hear Edon Richard's whisper still lingering in my ear.

"No," I said.

I could sense that he knew I was lying, but he seemed more relieved to hear that than the truth.

It breaks my heart to think back to this moment. I was a kid who never had any validation. I was not a good student. I was not a good athlete. I had very few friends. So, to have gotten this attention from my teacher, who was handsome as well, had been both confusing and thrilling. I felt special. But the way Father Pascale asked that question made me certain what had just happened was terribly wrong. Thinking back on this now, it makes me so angry—he obviously knew how dangerous Edon was. And yet he did nothing, choosing to protect Edon over me and perhaps countless other children.

My mother was in the school lobby and seemed a bit frantic.

"Kanchu!" she said as I ran to her for a hug.

I was so happy to see her that I didn't want to let go. I felt safe in her arms, like I'd be okay. I squeezed her so hard she started to laugh.

"I have missed you, too!" she said. "Let's go home. You brother and sister are waiting for you."

When we were back in the car, she looked at me quizzically.

"Are you okay?" she asked.

This was much more direct than her usual, "How are you?"

It was as if she sensed something was wrong.

"Is something bothering you?" she asked as she reached her hand over to grab mine. That was when I saw the spots. Pale pink and white splotches formed an abstract web on her hands and arms. I looked up, alarmed, and saw a similar pattern on her neck and shoulders. I had seen these spots before, but never so many. Even as a kid, I somehow understood they were caused by too much stress. The last thing I wanted to do was add my troubles to her list. I knew things were hard at home and did not want to add to her burden. "I'm fine," I said, and forced a smile.

She looked at me suspiciously, but then I saw a smile emerge across her face.

"Good," she said. "This is all that matters."

I WAS SO RELIEVED to be back home, eating my mother's food, laughing with my siblings. For two weeks I left the pain of my boarding school life behind, and I just fell right back into my family life. This was the one place where I felt like I could be myself. Safe.

That time passed quickly. When I returned to school, I told myself that I'd keep my experience with Edon Richards locked away. I began to compartmentalize. If I told myself enough times that it didn't happen, I could pretend that was so.

Still, I dreaded going to his class, to the point that my whole body would stiffen. I refused to make eye contact and did everything I could to avoid interacting with him.

THAT SPRING, I WAS forced to play volleyball in gym class. I absolutely hated it. I was a scrawny little kid and the youngest in my sixth-grade class. As the ball was bouncing from one kid to the next, it suddenly came flying toward me. I tried to hit it with one hand and felt an immediate crack in my thumb. The pain was red hot and shot up my arm. I curled my throbbing hand toward my chest and started crying.

"Stop being a sissy!" one classmate yelled.

"Toughen up!" another added.

"What a crybaby!"

I was numb to the jeers, but not the pain pulsating from my thumb. Later that afternoon, at the nurse's office, I learned it was broken. Not that it mattered. The diagnosis would not get me sympathy—if anything, just more ridicule.

I knew then that I was these pubescent boys' greatest effeminate, limp-wristed fear, the very person they were taught *not* to be. I was the sissy, the eunuch, the half man/half woman. I also knew that the only way to survive was to fight back.

I decided to write my mother a letter detailing the abuse I had suffered thus far in sixth grade. While I didn't mention Edon Richards, I did document all the other bullying I had experienced. I knew that once she received it, she'd come rescue me. I could once and for all go home.

I was working on the letter in class, during recess, when my Nepali teacher, Ramesh Sir, approached my desk and said, "Oh, Prabal, your handwriting has vastly improved. Let me have a look."

It was more a demand than a request. As he read, his eyes grew wide. He then confiscated my letter and told me I couldn't send it.

The next night, Edon was doing the night rounds and made a straight line for my bed. I pretended to be asleep, willing him to keep walking past me. My body was so tense I thought I might implode when I felt him lift the mosquito netting. I sensed his breath on my neck and bit my lip to stop myself from screaming.

"How's your thumb?" he whispered. "Do you want me to kiss it and make it better?"

I stayed silent, kept my eyes shut, and held my breath until he lowered the netting and left the room.

Of course, the next morning, all the kids who saw him stop by my bunk asked me what happened.

"Nothing," I said.

After my letter was confiscated, I had to navigate the school carefully. But I also knew that bolstering myself internally was essential to my survival.

I started coming up with my own affirmations. I'd hum "I Have Confidence" to myself whenever I needed some self encouragement. I also liked to recite lines from Rudyard Kipling's poem "If—":

If you can dream—and not make dreams your master;
If you can think—and not make thoughts your aim;
If you can meet with Triumph and Disaster
And treat those two impostors just the same.

It was during this period that I turned to things I could do, on my own, that brought me peace and happiness—whether singing or sketching figures of girls in different types of dresses in my schoolbooks and notepads.

LATER THAT SPRING, I was in swimming class and once again, Edon Richards was there. In front of everyone, he pressed his body against mine while we were both in the pool. I felt humiliated and enraged as I knew his attention would lead to more taunting from the boys. I swam away quickly, and from that moment on, I aggressively ignored him, to the point of being rude.

I first started hearing cusswords at St. Xavier's, so I tapped into that energy and doubled down on my defiance. In my head, I thought, "Fuck him." If I passed him in the hallway and he said, "Good morning," I said nothing in return.

I was counting the days until graduation—I knew if I could make it to June, I'd never have to return to this place again, as St. Xavier's Godavari ended in sixth grade.

But then, roughly a month before graduation, Edon Richards made an announcement in class.

"The following students are in danger of failing my class," he said.

I was in my seat, in the first row. The best students were placed in the last row, the mediocre ones were in the middle, and the worst in the front of the class. Still, when I heard him call my name, my heart sank in my chest, leaden. This news was not surprising—I was actively not doing my work in his class—but devastating, nonetheless.

Then he said, "The students I just named will have to repeat next year."

A full-blown panic unleashed within me. I didn't want to repeat the class—and certainly not with him. I also did not want to disappoint my mother again.

That evening, I broke my rule and went to his room. I was crying, begging him to pass me.

"My parents will be so upset," I said, tears streaming down my face. "I have to pass. What can I do?"

"Change your attitude," he said coolly.

I knew this was not about my inability to grasp the material in class. It was bigger than that. This was not about my grade, or my papers: he wanted to break me.

I don't know what happened in that moment, but something inside me unlocked.

"If you don't pass me," I said, looking directly into his eyes. "I will tell everyone about what you did to me."

He sat up straight, surprised.

"You would never do such a thing," he said. "It's our secret."

"Not if you don't pass me," I said.

He looked at me with such anger that I thought he'd either hit or kill me. I did not look away. I needed him to know that this was not a veiled threat.

I knew one thing: I would be graduating from St. Xavier's that spring.

CHAPTER THREE

I felt remarkably calm as I entered seventh grade back in Kathmandu. After what I'd been through the previous year, I figured I could handle anything. Mostly, I was excited about my new uniform: instead of the white shirt with a navy-blue tie, trousers, and blazer (or sweater), I now got to wear a cerulean-blue shirt and white pants. The new uniform felt like a metaphor. It reminded me of a crisp summer sky dotted with clouds, one that I could stare into for hours and dream of a bright, happy future.

I was also excited about being at the same school as my brother, who was in tenth grade. I was in awe of him—and wanted to be like him. He was in the top five in his class academically, and he was president of the student council. He was popular with his peers and his teachers, which makes sense, as he's one the kindest, most thoughtful, and most generous people I know. Our relatives loved him as well, and many of my friends liked him more than they liked me.

Kumudini went to a neighboring school called Adarsh Vidya Mandir (AVM). A voracious reader and an exquisite writer who was also very popular, revered and respected by her peers, she was an even *more* brilliant student than Pravesh. She was—and still is—confident, feisty, and no-nonsense, always telling the truth, never mincing her words, very much like our mother. Perhaps because she was the first child, or because of the way my mother raised her, Kumudini exuded a confidence that was astonishing for a woman in Nepal, where daughters were generally not treated equally to sons. Some people called her snooty, and some, including our cousins, feared her. But she was my role model. She never ever made me feel bad about who I was. On the contrary—she was my best friend, protector, and advocate.

As much as I loved them, it was hard living up to them. Being in the same school as my brother proved especially difficult because of the inevitable comparisons. During my first parent-teacher conference in seventh grade, my academic adviser said, "Prabal is good, but not as good as Pravesh."

I had been working hard, and my grades were improving—but it still wasn't enough.

I felt tears welling up when my mother grabbed my hand. Her body stiffened as she smiled and said, in her calm, graceful, but searing way, "I have two sons. Both are special and each has different talents. I don't compare them. So why do you?"

On the car ride back home, she said, "Kanchu, there's no substitute for hard work—but don't ever let anyone make you feel less than who you are or make you doubt your own worth. Take the good in that critique, learn from it, and move on. Your time will come. I have full faith in you."

I felt her love—but as strong as it was, I still struggled. Whenever I stepped outside of my house, I was on high alert. I always felt like I needed to be prepared for the next attack, but I never knew where it was going to come from. This made me an emotionally conflicted, angry kid with a very short temper—so different from my siblings. I was also completely confused about my own sexuality.

Back then, in Nepal, there was no concept of gay. I never heard anyone even mention homosexuality, but I was often called a hijra. They're formally considered a third sex in both Nepal and India and viewed as aggressive social deviants by society at large who often had to resort to stealing or prostitution to survive. To be called a hijra was considered an insult.

THE FIRST TIME I ever saw hijras was when I was in New Delhi visiting a relative. My cousin and I were in a car, sitting in traffic. There were several hijras going up to car windows asking for money. They weren't like other beggars—they had a certain dignity to them. They demanded attention and were unabashed about begging. It was more like they felt they deserved to be given money. I was awestruck. The group I saw wore open blouses with very low necklines, their saris wrapped loosely, revealing more skin than I'd ever seen in public. The color combinations were garish, as was their makeup, heavily painted on to camouflage their weathered, sun-darkened skin. The result had a heavily powdered ghostlike effect.

As they came near our car, I could see the beads of sweat on one's brow, like small pearls in a glistening crown. They each had a big red bindi in the middle of their forehead, eyes heavily lined with kohl. Some wore fake gold costume jewelry around their necks and dangling from their ears; another had a flower tucked in their long, braided hair. Their lips were a dark cranberry red, which bled onto their teeth stained by the paan they'd been chewing. Their voices were loud but cracking, masculine in sound but feminine in their delivery. They walked with exaggerated hip movements, clapped their hands, and shouted loudly at the cars. The only words that I could understand were "haye haye," a dramatic version of "oh my god."

I was fascinated by their fearlessness, mesmerized by their boldness. They didn't fit in, but rather than hiding, they were holding up traffic, creating a ruckus, demanding to be acknowledged. They were misfits and they owned it. Compared with how they were portrayed in the media, they seemed almost endearing. I never understood why people feared them so much. It was often said that the blessing of a hijra comes true—and so does their curse. People revered and feared them, and mostly cursed and rejected them. I was completely lost in their world when I heard one of my older cousins, who was in the car with me, laughing loudly and saying, "Fucking chakka hijras."

Those same words, hurled at me constantly—in school, on the streets, in my own home—crashed me back to reality. This moment shifted the way I thought of hijras, from fear to awe.

Back in Kathmandu, I was navigating the tricky terrain of seventh grade when a kid from my class said, "Hey, Prabal, a few friends are coming over after school. Do you want to come hang out, too?"

This was toward the end of the year, and I was pleasantly surprised—but also suspicious. This guy had never paid me any attention before. That said, he had never been mean to me either. Intrigued, I decided to go.

That afternoon, I went home and changed from my uniform into a pale pink loose tank top beneath a colorful knee-length black, white, and red graffitied long-sleeved shirt, which I wore unbuttoned over baggy acid-washed jeans. I stacked lots of colorful plastic bracelets on either arm, very eighties eclectic. A mix of Madonna, Boy George, and David Bowie—my style icons.

I rode my bike to the boy's house to find several of my classmates already there. It was a pubescent cauldron of hormones. Some kids were smoking cigarettes, which shocked me. Others were playing guitars and singing and asked me to join, which I did. For the first time that year, I felt welcome, like I was part of a group. Lost in music, singing, laughing, and silliness, I realized I was actually having fun. I was happy.

At one point, I left to go to the bathroom. When I finished and opened the door, I saw a boy who often ridiculed me at school waiting outside. He immediately pushed me back into the small, tiled room and slammed me against the wall. I braced myself, waiting to be punched, but instead, he held my face and started to kiss me. I was so shocked that I froze. This was the same boy who often called me names. I thought he hated me—but it now seemed like he was possessed by an almost ravenous attraction to me. For a brief moment, my teenage hormones and desires gave in to his strength, and the warmth of his body pressing against mine. I had my own feelings and desires—we kissed for some time, and then he put my hands down his pants.

Just then, someone yelled for him in the other room. That broke his fevered spell—he looked at me, spat on the floor with disgust, and then laughed as he left. I stood where I was, against the wall, alone, and engulfed with a deep sadness. I felt so foolish for trusting these guys, and angry at myself for thinking it would be different this time around.

The next morning in class, I heard the boys whispering and snickering to one another:

"Prabal is the person to go to if we can't have girls."

"Yes, he's our whore."

IT WAS A CONSTANT betrayal—desired, not desired. I cannot tell you how many boys I kissed throughout seventh and eighth grade, including football captains with girlfriends. I was the keeper of secrets for boys who were sexually attracted to me but would never admit this to anyone but me. Some even sent me love letters. I never told anyone whom I kissed, ever. Not even my sister. It was my secret. I knew no one would believe me, and I had terrible anxiety about the physical repercussions if it ever got out. I also knew that if and when the time came, I could use those letters to save myself, like I had done with Edon Richards.

In private, boys would be very intimate and kiss and caress me. In public, they'd call me a hijra or bully me. I got used to the tension between how these boys behaved when we were alone and how they protected themselves—by humiliating me—in front of others. I could even empathize with them. But as much as I understood and learned how to navigate these toxic relationships, I also knew that I deserved better. This belief in my worth was a fire inside of me. Sometimes roaring, sometimes a small flame, but always alive.

MY ROLE MODELS HELPED feed the flame. There was no room for misfits in Nepali society, so I found inspiration elsewhere. Bowie. Hendrix. Prince. I was so inspired by how they expressed their defiance through their music and art. At St. Xavier's Godavari, I often found refuge in the library, which had subscriptions to *Rolling Stone* and *Life*. I pored through these magazines and read about my role models and subconsciously started to emulate them—not just how they looked, but how boldly they were challenging the status quo. Unapologetic and unafraid.

I continued to give myself pep talks: "If they say I'm different, then I'll do things differently. Present myself differently. Act differently."

In ninth grade, that translated into tweaking the dress code: instead of the obligatory sky-blue cotton polo shirt, I wore a silk shirt that was a few shades lighter than the mandatory hue. The cut was roomy—it hung beautifully on my slight frame, and the color was perfect for my skin tone. Most people want to blend in, especially when they're being bullied. I decided to stand out. That palest blue almost steel-gray silk shirt was my first act of public defiance. Every single time I wore it, I was called into the vice principal's office. But the power and confidence I felt when wearing that shirt was well worth it.

I also found refuge in my notebooks: I continued to fill them with sketches. As my interest in wearing my sister's clothes had worn off, I'd become more interested in clothes themselves. I started to see that fashion was about transformation. I'd witnessed it with my mother and experienced it directly with that pale blue shirt. I created entire universes, my version of beautiful people—dressed in exquisite gowns and fantastic outfits. Those sketches allowed me to dream and escape. They saved me.

So did Madonna. It was around this time that I began listening to her, and I loved what a badass she was. My friend Deep was still in my life—though he was sent to another boarding school after we finished sixth grade. I'd see him during his school breaks, and somehow he got a bootleg copy of *Madonna Live: The Virgin Tour* and invited me to watch it at his house during one of his breaks. It was filmed in black and white and opens with Madonna looking straight into the camera: "I wanted to be famous, I wanted everybody to love me. I wanted to be a star. I worked really hard, and my dreams came true," she says in her iconic New York accent. Then it cuts to her song "Dress You Up."

I was blown away. I'd never seen anyone so unapologetic about their ambition. I was completely hooked by the way she used fashion, music, and creativity to challenge the system and society. Yes, my other role models were equally revolutionary, but there was something about Madonna's provocative and defiant glamour that really spoke to me—including that she and my mother were both Leos! While their approaches couldn't be more different, both were fighting against male-dominated societies that told women how to behave. I was obsessed with Madonna's music, style, and—above all—her courage to not give a fuck.

THE BEST-LOOKING STUDENT IN our school was Abhiyaan. He was a year older than me—in tenth grade—and was captain of both the basketball and football teams. All the girls at our sister school, St. Mary's, had a crush on him, as did I. But I wouldn't even dare look at him or his friends. They were the most popular kids in school—everyone admired them.

I took the bus to school. Every time we'd cross the Bagmati bridge from Kathmandu to Jawalakhel, I'd see Abhiyaan and his crew on their bikes riding to school. I'd watch him from afar, his wavy dark hair blowing wildly in the wind, the leather jacket he wore over his school uniform. His friends would inevitably give a middle finger to the school bus as they rode past it, but he never even bothered to glance at the bus or the kids on it. He was that cool.

At that time, TCs, short for Teenage Confessions, were very popular. A TC was a sort of personal yearbook. You'd take a journal or notebook, decorate, and personalize it, write down your likes and dislikes, and then pass it on to other students to fill in their own confessions. My TC was a Madonna shrine—cluttered with photos of her from magazines and newspapers. I kept it with my textbooks, which we stored inside our school desks. One day, I opened my desk and saw that someone had left several items inside. A ziplock bag with a Madonna cassette inside. A *Rolling Stone* magazine with her on the cover, a rare find in Nepal. Several buttons and pictures of Madonna. I was thrilled—but also cautious. I started asking everyone in class, "Who gave this to me?"

No one knew.

Whoever it was, I was so touched. It was the sweetest gift ever.

Later that day, I was waiting for the bus when I saw Abhiyaan with his posse. I immediately started to walk the other way. I was not looking for trouble. My whole body tensed as I became aware of someone following me. Then I saw a bike tire next to me.

I stopped and I looked up to see Abhiyaan. My heart was beating so fast that I was sure he could hear it. I was excited that he seemed like he wanted to talk to me, and also wary, wondering why.

He got off the bike and started to walk alongside me.

"Did you get it?" he said.

"Get what?" I asked.

"The package? I left in your desk?"

"What package?" I asked him nervously, certain that I was being pranked.

He stopped walking and looked at me.

"Madonna," he said with a warm smile.

My smile was the answer. As he rode off on his bike, my heart went with him. My crush grew into love in an instant. I was the happiest I'd ever been.

THE NEXT DAY IN SCHOOL, when he saw me in the hallway, he smiled and said hello. Afterward, astonished classmates kept asking me how I knew him.

I didn't tell anyone. I did not want Abhiyaan to get teased for being nice to me. Deep was back at boarding school, so there was no one else I could trust with the truth. I kept it to myself.

Abhiyaan was always kind to me. We didn't hang out much in school—as we were in different grades, plus he was a classic high school jock, whereas I was a theater kid. That said, I'd often stay after school to be part of these school productions, and Abhiyaan would sometimes come watch. He had other friends in the troupe, so it was not just to see me. But having him in the same vicinity gave me the jitters. He was so hot. Plus, no one would hang with me at the risk of being called a sissy himself—except Abhiyaan. He'd come sit next to me, and we'd laugh together. He was my first crush.

He was a boy of few words, but would throw back his head and laugh every time I'd say something that he found funny or ridiculous. I soon started hanging out with him at his parents' house, listening to a mix of his favorites: Bon Jovi, Guns N' Roses, and Alice Cooper. Every so often, he'd indulge me with Madonna, Whitney Houston, and even a little Prince and Michael Jackson.

One weekend, he played me a song by a band I hadn't heard of.

"They're called the Bangles," he said. "I think you'll like them."

"Walk like an Egyptian" blared from his speaker, and I got up and started to dance while he stayed on his bed, watching me, amused. He put on another song and said, "I thought of you, Gurung."

Calling me by my last name reminded me of my father, who was still absent at this period of my life. I was used to it by then. The song was "Eternal Flame," a slower Bangles ballad. I looked at Abhiyaan as he got up from the bed and came closer to me. He then took my hand in his and put his other hand on my waist and started to slow dance with me. He was muscular, strong, and way taller than me, and all I remember thinking was, "Is this really happening?" I had dreamed of this moment: slow dancing with my high school crush, the coolest kid in our school.

Right at that moment, he held my face in his hands and kissed me. It was magical. His lips felt surprisingly soft. I'd never experienced such a tender kiss. It had always been without my consent or forced.

We kissed for what simultaneously felt like hours and also just seconds. The song ended, and he stepped back and stared at me. I must have looked confused or even scared. I was waiting for his reaction. Would he be angry? Ashamed?

Instead, he looked at me, ruffled my hair, and laughed. Then he hugged me and said, "Oh, Gurung, you're special. Very special. Remember that."

I held back my tears. For the first time, I knew what it felt like to be truly seen.

THAT YEAR, I HAD an English teacher named Michelle Monnin. She was from Ohio and extremely thoughtful and kind. She reminded me of Meryl Streep from *Out of Africa*—beautiful with long, curly, reddish-brown hair, pink-peach skin, and the most pleasant demeanor. On special occasions, she'd wear a gorgeous yellow cotton dress with black pumps—and I was mesmerized. She saw how badly I struggled in school with my peers and always assured me, "It's going to get better."

She was also unafraid.

"Knock it off, all of you," she'd yell whenever anyone said something mean to me in her presence.

During class breaks or at lunch, she'd invite me to go for walks with her. I opened up to her about the bullying I was experiencing daily and even shared hints as to how troubled my parents' marriage was. I never revealed too much about the abuse I had witnessed because I didn't want to get my father in trouble. She seemed to understand. She was my secret keeper.

One day, I was walking up the school driveway, through the main gate, when I saw Sanak, the biggest bully in school, chatting with Michelle Monnin and a bunch of other boys from my class. As I grew near, Sanak said, "Oh, so it's like him."

Everyone started laughing—except Michelle, who started turning pink.

"Gurung," Sanak said. "We're talking about gay, homos."

That was the first time I'd ever heard those words, but I could tell by the way Sanak spat them from his mouth that this was not something anyone wanted to be.

"Michelle was explaining it to us," Sanak continued. "It sounds just like you."

The laughter got louder, and while I had no idea what they were talking about, I knew from their jeers that it was something to be ashamed of. Michelle's face was now crimson. I quickly walked away, queasy. She'd been my confidant—why was she talking to these bullies about me? I was also completely confused, as I had no idea what *gay* even meant, and I had no one to ask, not my brother or my mother. There was no internet back then. No Google search, nothing.

A couple of weeks later, I spotted "The Gay Disease" on the cover of *Parade*, a magazine published in India. I picked it up from the newsstand and flipped to the story, which was about AIDS in America. I had never heard of this disease. I immediately bought the magazine and read the article. My first thought was that the men pictured in it, dancing at a nightclub in New York, were incredibly attractive. And then I continued to read and learned about this terrifying disease that was targeting—and decimating—the gay community. It mentioned that Rock Hudson had died from HIV/AIDS. My first idea associated with "gay" was death.

While there was no manual to being gay, I realized then I might be that. The images of those shirtless, handsome men were scintillating but the stories about this incurable and fatal disease were also terrifying. I was so confused how being oneself could lead to death. If that were the case, then boys liking boys must indeed be wrong. And yet, deep in my heart, it felt right.

Meanwhile, every day, someone called me a chakka or eunuch or hijra to the point where I'd simply disassociate from it. My survival was based on that. Even more confusing was how many boys continued to be attracted to me, and wanted to kiss me in secret, but would never publicly admit it. They were also ashamed, which further confused me.

Abhiyaan was different. He was incredibly private and aloof. So no one knew how much we enjoyed hanging out together—except us. Our attraction to one another was so pure.

"You are who you are, Prabal," he said to me one day. "The world sees that. And I'm envious of that."

Looking back now, I wonder if he saw in me certain parts of himself that he was not brave enough to acknowledge. Men are so trapped in their fear of being emotional. Abhiyaan was in my brother's class, which meant when I went to see Pravesh at his senior prom, I also saw Abhiyaan on the dance floor with a girl in a green dress. That was the last time I laid eyes on him.

By tenth grade, I could navigate the bullying. I knew all the perpetrators, and they knew that they couldn't beat whatever it was that they hated out of me. They had tried and lost. Plus, the girls at St. Mary's loved me. I'd get invited to all their parties because I liked dancing, singing, and having fun, and was not at all creepy. It was wild to see how some of the worst bullies stopped treating me badly simply because they wanted access to the girls. I played that card well.

By the end of tenth grade, I was preparing for the school leaving certificate. In Nepal, eleventh and twelfth grades are our college. I needed a 65 percent or above to be placed in the first division, which I wanted to do for my mother. Just for pride. Second division would be shameful. I took the test and, to most people's surprise, including mine, I got first division. I was pleased, but my mom was ecstatic. I will never forget how relieved she looked when I received the results.

She looked at me, smiling, and said, "I knew you could do it."

Then she asked, "Where do you want to go next?"

"St. Xavier's College, like Pravesh," I replied.

St. Xavier's was the best school system in all of Nepal—so it also had a college in Kathmandu. Its name was equated to safety, trust, and quality—everything that was promised, but not delivered, to me. My mom looked surprised by my choice. St. Xavier's was very hard to get into. Pravesh was thriving there, and amazingly, I got accepted. Then I had to choose what to study, which was difficult as there were no obvious pathways for me. The best students became doctors or engineers. Some students chose commerce or finance. I chose science—it had been my favorite course in high school, and it was also what Pravesh had chosen to study.

Right off the bat, I struggled. And then one day, less than a month into the college semester, I was in a mandatory lecture by the dean about attendance. I was sitting in the back row, eating as he spoke. In Nepal it's considered disrespectful to eat in class, but I didn't care. I was hungry. Afterward, the dean asked me to come to his office.

I sat down across from him, bracing myself. This was all too familiar.

"What was your score on the SLC?" he asked, more accusatory than curious.

I told him my score, which was fine, but not stellar.

"You would have never gotten into this college with that mark," he said, sneering. "You know why you are here?"

I shrugged.

"The only reason you are here is because of your brother."

When I got home that same evening, I made an announcement: I wanted to go to school in India. It was time to pursue my own path.

CHAPTER FOUR

India felt familiar. It was close to home and yet far enough away from the comparisons to Pravesh and everyone else's low expectations of me. I needed to forge my own future. I decided to study the arts and humanities, a choice that people outside of my family considered a sign of failure, but my mom and even my dad knew that it was the right choice for their creative dreamer son. Meanwhile, I didn't care what anyone thought: I just needed to get out of Kathmandu. A fresh start.

I was at the New Delhi airport going through customs when a tall, pot-bellied, fair-skinned officer with the most exaggerated mustache shouted, "Oye, chinky, idhar aa ve!" (Oh, chinky, scurry over here!)

A wave of shame washed over me, quickly followed by a seething anger, but I knew better than to mess around with the border patrol. It was nothing more than a routine questioning. Still, I walked away heavyhearted. Being called "chinky" upon my arrival in India felt like an ominous foreshadowing.

To understand my experience in Delhi is to understand the relationship between India and Nepal. Culturally, everything is very similar, but the class dynamics in India are even more intense. India was under British rule from 1858 to 1947, whereas Nepal, a landlocked nation sandwiched between China and India, was never colonized. We lacked the infrastructure to be economically independent or well off. Resources were rare, as were opportunities, especially for those who lacked access to education. Because we share similar cultures and religion, Nepalis often come to India for work—mostly as domestic help and sex workers. In Kamathipura, Mumbai's red-light district, many of the women were trafficked from Nepal as young girls. They're also called "chinkies" and have been commodified as sexual objects. It's heartbreaking.

Because college in Nepal started earlier than in India, I was able to begin the eleventh-grade school year at the prestigious Delhi Public School with the rest of my coed classmates. This was my first experience with boys and girls in the same classrooms. Even though the students were from all over India, the majority were from the north, which meant they had fair skin and more Aryan features than the southerners, who had darker skin, or the northeastern students, who had Mongolian features. While there were several Nepali students who tried to bring me into their fold, I wanted to get to know different kinds of people. As I said to my mother, "If I wanted to hang out with Nepali people, I would have stayed in Nepal!"

ONE WEEK INTO ELEVENTH GRADE, I was awoken in the middle of the night by someone shouting, "Wake up, wake up, wake up!"

The seniors had snuck into our eleventh-grade dorm and were ordering all of us to get out of bed and march to the courtyard. Twenty-plus boys—all new eleventh graders—were commanded to stand on the cold, tiled floor. The usually gleaming white floor had also, strangely, been covered in dirt. A senior named Himanshu shouted, "Strip!"

I watched, amazed, as all the boys around me started taking off their pajamas until they were only in their underwear. I did not budge.

Himanshu saw me and screamed, "*You! Strip!*"

I refused to move, stunned that everyone else was following such ridiculous orders.

Then several seniors poured buckets of water on the dirt and screamed, "*Swim!*"

All the near-naked guys got on their stomachs on the floor and started pretending to swim in the mud. I was shaking my head in disbelief. I may have even laughed, which triggered several seniors to circle and push me into a corner. They started punching the wall around my face, trying to intimidate me.

I didn't even flinch. My protective habits kicked in, and I found myself disassociating from my body, like I'd done so many times back in Nepal. My fear here, however, was heightened now that I was in a foreign land.

Someone screamed, "Teacher!" Overhead lights suddenly flooded the area, revealing a string of pathetic, half-naked boys, sprawled on the floor, soaking wet. Some scurried for cover; others tried to run away.

More teachers arrived, shouting, "Everyone line up!"

The interrogation began. Many of the boys had been in this school for years, so the head teacher focused on the new students. "What's this ruckus? Are you being hazed?"

Nobody said a word.

I was hiding in the corner, witnessing it all unfold, shocked. Hazing didn't happen in Nepal. Looking back, I understand now that it was a practice the British colonists had left behind. Eventually someone said, "We just wanted to hang out with the seniors."

Himanshu laughed and said, "Yeah, we were just hanging out."

At first, I wasn't going to say anything because I thought Himanshu was attractive. Yes, I was that shallow. But for a sixteen-year-old scrawny gay boy, a strapping, muscled, loudmouthed handsome senior who was also a star athlete did cloud my judgment—for a moment. Earlier that week, at orientation, he approached me: "Oh, you're a Gurung? Do you know Anand?"

When I shook my head no, he said, "Well, I'm sure you're an amazing football player like him. He was a star athlete who graduated four years ago. Gurung, you'll be on my team."

I just nodded yes, knowing that he was in for a major disappointment. Even so, I was determined to be in his good books—until this moment. Watching him outright lying, and seeing everyone go along with him, made me snap. I stepped out from my hiding spot and said, "Actually, that's not true. We *were* being hazed."

I proceeded to explain precisely what had happened, starting with being startled awake and ordered out of bed. As I spoke, I saw all my classmates, lined up, in their underwear, staring at me, eyes wide, as if to say, "What are you doing?"

Meanwhile, the seniors were glaring at me. They wanted me dead. Himanshu most of all. But their anger couldn't stop me. I had enough. All my life, I'd been bullied. I thought that coming to India meant getting to start over. Instead, it was the same old thing. So this time, I was going to speak up. I knew it would get me in even more trouble with my peers and likely set the tone for the rest of my time in that school, but I also knew that this was the right thing to do.

The night ended with the seniors being told that they had to report to the principal the next morning and my classmates and I scurrying back to our rooms. On our way, the juniors kept reliving the evening, talking about these seniors as big brothers. Several looked at me with disgust. One classmate, a tall, creepy-looking fellow named Rakesh, started laughing as he looked at me and said, "Teri to gayee. Ab gaand phatne wali hai teri."

He was predicting that I was going to get my ass whipped.

I was beginning to think I had made a huge mistake in coming to India. Just as panic began to rise in my chest, someone tapped me on the shoulder.

"Don't worry. You'll be fine," a kind voice said. "Himanshu is like my big brother. I'll speak to him."

I looked up and saw an incredibly handsome boy whose face matched his kindness. He had longish, wavy hair, slightly dopey brown eyes, a strong jawline, and a sharp but slightly broken nose. When he smiled, I saw he also had a crooked molar.

I don't know what came over me, but I hugged him tight—and he squeezed me tighter. I let him go, looked at him, and knew that he was going to be a big part of my life.

"I am Sid," he said. "I think your room is right next to mine."

KUMUDINI WAS LIVING IN Old Delhi at the time. My sister had gone to eleventh and twelfth grades in Mumbai, which was known as Bombay until 1995 when the government decided to revert to the city's original name. So when I was going to Delhi Public School, Kumudini was getting her bachelor's degree. She went to Sophia, one of the best girls' colleges in India. She was so brilliant. My parents did not have a lot of money, but education was the number-one priority. Nepali kids who could afford to study abroad often went to Indian schools because they were considered prestigious.

Kumudini was in her second year of college by the time I arrived and was dating a man named Rajesh. My mother liked Rajesh—we all did—but she did not want Kumudini to limit herself in any way. She used to say, "Just because you are dating him doesn't mean you have to marry him! If you get pregnant, I will help you get an abortion. I just want you to be free!"

Rajesh lived in his own apartment with his cousin, and Kumudini lived in one she shared with her college girlfriends. They were my weekend refuge! I could not wait for Friday classes to end so I could go spend my weekends with Kumudini and Rajesh and escape dorm life. I usually went by auto-rickshaw or tuk-tuk, and it would take at least forty-five minutes to go the fifteen kilometers between Old Delhi and New Delhi.

As always, my sister was my confidant and adviser, helping me get out of countless messes. We also shared a love for movies, music, food, and fashion. I lived for those weekends when she and Rajesh would indulge me. Rajesh always made a genuine effort to make me feel welcome: He also shared my love for singing and laughed at all my jokes. He accepted me for who I was and made me feel seen.

I also loved visiting my sister because her roommates were so much fun. They were in an all-girl band that did Whitney Houston, Madonna, and Janis Joplin covers. Their walls were covered with pages ripped out of fashion magazines like *Vogue*, *Elle*, and *Harper's Bazaar.* Their apartment was where I was first exposed to the world of supermodels: Christy Turlington, Naomi Campbell, Linda Evangelista, Cindy Crawford, Yasmeen Ghauri. I was mesmerized by their beauty and by the stunning clothes they wore, which were nothing like the styles I had grown up with in Nepal and India. My sister's world felt way cooler than mine.

After my first weekend away, I returned to my dorm and noticed that my bed was wet. It struck me as odd, but I didn't think too much about it and simply changed the sheets. The next time I left for the weekend, the same thing happened. The third time I came back to a wet bed, I mentioned it at dinner to classmates who lived in the same dorm. A few of them glanced at each other and quickly changed the topic. Something was up. I looked at Sid, who had become one of my best friends. He whispered, "I'll tell you later."

After dinner, Sid pulled me aside and said, "I didn't know how to tell you this, but when you're away on the weekend, some guys go to your room and pee on your bed."

I was horrified.

"Anytime I have seen them trying to go to your room, I have stopped them, but I'm not always there."

I discovered that the culprits were several seniors as well as some of my classmates who wanted to be in their good books. The ringleader was a senior named Jateen Masthogi, a gruff, testosterone-filled simpleton with a pea-sized brain. He was trying to impress Himanshu and Tenzin, two popular seniors who hated me after that first night of hazing. I also knew that Tenzin had a crush on Sarika, a tall girl with big, beautiful brown eyes whom I'd become friends with. Her hair was cut in a blunt bob, which she wore parted to the side so that it fell messily across her face. At first you'd think she was pretty, with her sharp lips and cheekbones, but the more you talked with her, you realized just how beautiful she was.

Himanshu was out for blood because I spoke out against him in front of the teachers. And Tenzin did not like that Sarika preferred hanging out with me over him. I learned from Sid that Tenzin was the quiet devil who convinced Jateen to vandalize my room. Jateen was so crass and clueless that he did their bidding, thinking he was impressing the seniors, who were simply manipulating him. I had seen this countless times: this idea of "brotherhood" is so problematic. Even today, if anyone calls me brother, I say, "Please don't, I have a brother." I don't mind when a bunch of gay guys call me sister, as that is playing on gender. But any mention of "bros" or "brotherhood" is triggering—and this experience is why.

When I learned that Tenzin was jealous of my relationship with Sarika, I made it a point to hang out with her even more. When she invited me to her birthday, the next morning, all of the seniors kept asking, "How was the party?"

Sarika came from a well-to-do family and loved fashion and models and Bollywood as much as I did. We started to go see films together, and then she invited me to her house for meals with her family. When she invited me to another party, I asked, "Does this mean we're dating?"

"I'd like that," she said.

We started dating and had so much fun together, dancing and gossiping about Bollywood stars. Even though I knew I was attracted to boys, I still fell in love with her. She was the closest I ever came to wanting to marry a girl.

One weekend, I took her to Old Delhi to meet my sister and Rajesh for lunch. She went to the ladies' room, and as soon as she was out of earshot, Kumudini said, "Don't mess with her heart, Prabal."

I know now that if I had never explored my gay side, I would have married Sarika.

Word got around that Sarika and I had started dating. The next weekend, when I got back from my sister's place, I saw that the door to my room had been broken and my bed was flipped over. My Tom Cruise *Cocktail* poster had been ripped down; my diaries were torn open. I ran into the common area and screamed, "What the fuck happened?"

"This is what happens when you go against the seniors!" said Jateen, who then slapped me so hard I fell on the ground.

"Well, I'm sorry if Sarika likes me and not Tenzin," I said, still on the floor.

That was when all the boys surrounded me, kicking me, punching me, and shouting, "Chakka soch le mar gaya." (Consider yourself dead.)

I was a scrawny little kid with acne. Tenzin was a stud with a motorcycle. And yet Sarika had chosen me. Tenzin's feelings were clearly hurt—though he did not hit me, his friends did. They couldn't tolerate that this gorgeous girl wanted me, a sissy.

Sid heard the ruckus and intervened. He was a star student and athlete, beloved by all, and he was able to get everyone to leave me alone. After he dispersed the crowd and helped me clean up my room, he said, "Okay, let's go get tandoori."

It was nighttime by then—we weren't allowed to leave the campus without permission. I said no. He looked at me and said, "Prabal, I'm taking you to my favorite dhaba for tandoori chicken, roomali roti, and lassi."

Dhabas are small hole-in-the-wall joints with arguably the best food in north India.

I was reluctant to break the rules, but Sid kept on insisting.

"Come on, you need this," he said. "And besides, I'm super hungry and I really want this tandoori."

I shook my head—I did not want any more trouble.

"Pleeaaase," he said, and smiled.

That crooked tooth always got me. I gave in and followed his lead. We snuck out of our dorm, ran across the football field, and were about to climb a giant wall, when the guard saw us. I froze. We were caught. I was sure we'd be expelled. But Sid ran up to him, put one hand on his shoulder, and said something that made the guard laugh. He then nodded and walked away.

We climbed up the wall and jumped off the other side onto the normally busy Mathura Road, which was relatively quiet.

"What did you tell him?" I asked.

"I said that we were in love and planning to elope," he said with a wink.

I looked at him, speechless. He laughed, "Oh, relax, Prabs! I told him that I was going to get him tandoori chicken as well. He loves it, everyone does. And plus, I've known him for eleven years, since I was in first grade! Everything is cool!"

That was the thing about Sid. He was not only charming, handsome, and an all-around stellar student, but also a good person. The only other friend whom I had a similar rapport with was Deep. I had a crush on Abhiyaan—not a deep friendship. With Sid, it was both.

It was a hot, balmy New Delhi night. The moon was bright enough to light the roadway and bounced its silvery beams off the rattling buses and whirring cars. Every so often the loud roar of a Mahindra motorcycle would startle me. I was still traumatized about being attacked by so many classmates, and by the state of my bedroom—breaking the school rules made me extra jittery. This was something my mom wouldn't approve of. But I was also thrilled by what might unfold that night.

As we walked, Sid told me his story—he was a Rajput, from Rajasthan. He grew up with horses and loved the outdoors. I felt like I could listen to his voice forever—raspy, excited, punctuated with laughs. We finally reached Nizam's dhaba, a tiny restaurant whose walls were corrugated metal sheets. Three tables surrounded by mismatched folding chairs sat on an uneven dirt-packed floor. As we entered, Sid yelled out, "Paa ji, paao lagoo," to an older gentleman with a long beard and sooty yellow turban and touched his feet.

The gentleman hugged Sid and said, "The usual?"

Sid nodded and the man placed two skewers of turmeric-soaked chicken onto the hot grills in the wood clay oven behind him. The charred curry scent followed by the sizzling made my mouth water.

"This place is like my second home," Sid said as we sat down. "Whenever I miss my mother's food, I come here."

The food arrived. I haven't tasted tandoori chicken, roomali roti, or lassi that delicious ever since. After we finished eating, Sid said, "Let's go for a ride."

We left the restaurant, and he hailed an incoming neon-colored autorickshaw. I felt giddy and hopeful, a first since I'd arrived at that school.

That night, our long, winding ride was made more magical by our driver singing an old Hindi Raj Kapoor song. We got off at Chandni Chowk, also known as Moonlight Square, one of the oldest and busiest markets. I'd been maybe twice before but only during the day, and both times I found the hustle and bustle overwhelming—a sensory cacophony made up of honking traffic, the throngs of people, riots of colors, and fragrances from the spice sellers. But on this night, there were enough people milling about to give the market a steady heartbeat, while everything else was quieted, from the turmeric, cinnamon, and cumin scents that now gently fragranced the air to the vibrant colors now muted by the moonlight. Old Hindi music was playing from one small radio, its strands mingling melodically with Qawwali music, a form of Sufi Islamic devotional songs, coming from another.

We walked around for an hour or so, stopping for kulfi—a sweet Indian ice cream—before heading back. It was past midnight, and what had happened earlier in my room seemed like a distant faded memory. It had been a while since I had felt this serene.

In the auto-rickshaw, I wanted to ask Sid why he was being so nice to me. How come he was not like the rest of the boys? What did he see in me? My friendship was so easy with Sid. He was playful. Less brooding than Abhiyaan. Both cared about what people said, but not when it came to me.

If anyone asked Sid, "Why are you friends with Prabal?" he'd answer, "Because he is a cool guy."

I will note that, at the time, Sid was dating a popular girl named Ronita. Looking back, I think that though we both cared deeply for the girls we were dating, we were also in love with each other. In another universe, Sid might have been my boyfriend, out in the open. But we both knew, without ever saying it out loud, that it was just not possible in India in the 1990s.

Still, that night I wanted to say thank you and let him know how much this escape meant to me. I wanted to hug him. I wanted to say so many things. We were sitting side by side in the rickshaw heading back to the school when I tapped him on his knee. When he turned to look at me, all I could say was, "I owe you."

"Don't worry about it," he said, laughing.

I insisted that I would pay him back, as he had paid for everything that night.

"Sure, sure," he said.

We got back to the school wall, and he climbed up first just to make sure the coast was clear. He came back down to help me get over it. As he held my waist and pushed me up, he said, "Prabs, I had fun tonight."

"So did I," I said. "Thank you."

"You may not know it yet, but you are special," he added. "And I know you're going to be someone big."

He kept saying, "Kuch to karega kuch to banega," which means "you will do something, you will be something."

I will never forget the way he said it and the way he looked at me. He meant every word. I could feel it.

I was suddenly overcome with emotions and blurted out, "I love you, Sid. I love you so much. I have loved you since the first day I saw you."

My heart was pounding. My hands were sweaty.

He looked at me shocked—eyes big and cheeks blushing. Then he held my shoulders tightly with his strong hands and said, "I love you too, silly."

When he saw the disbelief in my face, he laughed and said, "Why do you think I hang out with you whenever I can?"

Then he smiled that crooked smile and held my face in his hands and kissed me. It was electrifying. I could taste the tandoori chicken, onions, spices, and the burnt roti and the sweet kulfi we had eaten in Old Delhi. I wanted more.

Then he pulled back and said, "And don't forget, when you do become famous, you must take me out on a night like this. A magical night out and about in whatever city you are living in. That's how you pay me back."

I nodded yes. I couldn't wait for that moment to come.

MEANWHILE, BACK HOME IN NEPAL, I heard news that my father was having yet another affair. Kumudini was worried that my parents were on the brink of divorce, which stupidly was more scandalous than the affairs. The woman was always blamed. I did not want to add to the stress at home and knew I had to do well my third term or else I would be kicked out of school. So I decided to cheat on my mathematics exam—and was caught. That was a very low point in my life.

My parents were so concerned that they both decided to fly to India to meet with my teacher. And I was so panicked that I went to speak with my teacher, hoping she'd have some compassion. I explained that I was having a difficult time in the dorms, and she said, "Well, if you behave like a girl, you will be treated like a girl."

I was shocked.

"I'm also having a hard time at home," I said. "I just learned that my parents are getting a divorce."

That grabbed her attention. Divorce was unheard of back then—both in India and Nepal. That was my cry for help. My parents arrived a few days later. After meeting with my teacher, my father was apoplectic.

"What rubbish are you telling people?" he said. "That I beat your mom and that we're getting divorced?"

My mother shook her head and said, "It's okay, Prabal. You will stay here this summer with Rajesh. You will study and you will do better next time."

That summer is a bit blurry. I was relieved that I could stay in Delhi with Rajesh, and yet despondent that I had disappointed my mother. I felt that I had become an embarrassment to my family. If I had returned to Nepal, I'm sure everyone—except for my mother and siblings—would have said, "We knew he would fail."

I retook the exam and passed. The only other thing I remember from that summer was watching *The Phil Donahue Show* and discovering a series called *Style with Elsa Klensch* on CNN. This stood out because I had never seen anything like it. Klensch was a fashion journalist who spent an hour each week doing a deep dive on a famous fashion designer. I was utterly fascinated, as that was my first glimpse into the world of fashion. She focused mainly on European and some American designers, and included interviews with them, and then footage of their runway shows. I was mesmerized. That was where I learned about Yves Saint Laurent, Christian Dior, Coco Chanel, Christian Lacroix, Claude Montana, Bill Blass, Oscar de la Renta, and Azzedine Alaïa. I was transfixed by the magic they made out of fabric. And yet, their world was still a reverie—there was nothing quite like that in India that I knew of.

My senior year went by quickly. By now I finally had my own group of friends, mainly girls and a few quiet, thoughtful boys. I was no longer dating Sarika, but we had remained friends. Sid was still dating Ronita and having a secret affair with me. We loved each other. I still have the letters he wrote to me. Nobody else knew but the two of us. It was our secret.

The night before graduation, I was in Sid's room. We were slow dancing, listening to Eric Clapton's "Tears in Heaven." After that song ended, we both sat on the floor and cried. I knew it was the last time I'd ever see him.

"I don't think it will happen in this lifetime," he said. "But maybe in the next one."

Whenever I hear that song, I still think of him.

CHAPTER FIVE

Some classmates went on to study medicine, others to become engineers. Sid went to college in Delhi to study commerce and economics. Sarika became a model. A few girls from Punjabi families got married. Other students went to study in Canada. I graduated with a degree in humanities and had absolutely no idea what to do with it. One thing I was certain of: I did not want to go back to Nepal. But I also needed a break from the very toxic masculine energy I'd experienced in Delhi.

I chose to move to Mumbai simply because Bollywood was there. Those films had been a comforting escape from the bullying I experienced throughout my teen years. As a queer, effeminate boy growing up in Nepal and India, I sought joy wherever I could find it—books, music, sketching, and dreaming, as well as in films. Old Hollywood movies and musicals enthralled me, but my primary escape was Hindi films—big-budget commercial Bollywood films and smaller, independent art-house movies, which my mother preferred because they were thought provoking and often challenged the status quo.

While the independent films were poetry, the Bollywood musicals were over-the-top melodrama punctuated by colorful, larger-than-life song and dance sequences, with incredibly glamorous dolled-up leading ladies dancing (even in the snow) in thin chiffon saris. Movies like *Mr. India*, *Sholay*, *Hero*, *Himmatwala*, *Silsila*, *Umrao Jaan*, *Devdas*, *Hum Aapke Hain Koun..!*, *Dilwale Dulhania Le Jayenge*, and *Kuch Kuch Hota Hai* all brought me so much joy. For those three hours, I was transported to a place where anything and everything was possible, as long as you did it with conviction. Those movies gave me the hope and courage to dream impossible dreams—though they did ruin my idea of love! I'm still waiting for the five hundred singers and dancers to appear at the moment of my first true love kiss.

The leading ladies like Mumtaz, Rekha, Sridevi, Zeenat Aman, Parveen Babi, Madhuri Dixit, Tina Munim, Aishwarya Rai, and many more were always so glamorous. Even if the styling sometimes veered toward bad taste, their unapologetic commitment to looking fabulous made them unique divas.

That energy brought me to Mumbai, which felt more cosmopolitan, cultured, nuanced, and complex than New Delhi. It was a thriving hub of different cultures, religions, colors, and castes. It was electric and vibrant. It was also the first city where I saw vast wealth living side by side with abject poverty, fancy high-rise buildings adjacent to slums. I'd never seen that dichotomy up close anywhere in my entire life: in Mumbai it was right there in front of you.

Mumbai is called the city of dreams, or Maya Nagari. Still, I had no idea what my dream career was. Out of ambiguous desperation, I chose hotel school for a year. I thought a degree in hospitality would, at the very least, place me on a career path. I quickly learned it was the wrong one. Yes, I learned how to make a perfect bed, set a table, and even cook a few dishes—but I was not passionate about any of it. Then one evening, while working as a waiter at a wedding function, I noticed a little boy crying. He reminded me of myself at that age, and my heart ached for him. And then his mother said tersely, with a scowl, "Don't cry or else you will end up like him."

She pointed her finger at my friend, also a waiter. My whole body stiffened. I had moved to Mumbai to escape the toxic masculinity I'd encountered in Kathmandu and Delhi, only to find that it was everywhere. There was a guy in my class named Aditya. One night he came to my dorm room, drunk, got in my bed, and started kissing me. It could have just been a one-night stand, but afterward he stopped talking to me. I was used to this kind of confusing behavior, so I did not think much about it. I knew he had a girlfriend, as had so many other boys in the past who were attracted to me.

But then I noticed that he started becoming quite aggressive toward me. He and a few other guys teased me incessantly, calling me sissy and chakka. It was like boarding school all over again, though by then I knew that his homophobic name-calling was a loud and desperate attempt to shield his own struggle with his sexuality.

One night, while I was in the dorm bathroom getting ready for bed, he and three friends entered and locked the door behind them. As they all surrounded me, I had flashbacks to St. Xavier's Godavari, but these were grown men, not pubescent boys. One guy grabbed me and another tried to kiss me, while a third wrestled me to the floor. I was petrified. It was becoming clear that they were trying to rape me. I had to think quickly, and said, "Okay, let's do it, but let's go to my bed."

That caught them off guard—giving me a window. I jumped up, ran out of the bathroom and into my dorm room, and locked my door.

I told two friends. They both made excuses for the three men. "He was probably drunk," one said.

It was never "Prabal almost got raped."

It was "boys being boys."

That experience was devastating. I kept my head down and went to my classes, holding my books against my chest, counting the days until that year was over.

I GRADUATED WITH MY degree but knew a life as a concierge was not the right path for me. I felt more lost than ever. One weekend, while visiting my sister and Rajesh back in New Delhi, I was sketching and listening to music when Rajesh said, "Maybe you should give fashion a shot."

My sister's face lit up. "What a great idea!"

By then, thanks to my weekly Sunday night ritual of watching CNN's *Style with Elsa Klensch*, I'd fallen in love with fashion. When I first saw Yves Saint Laurent on that show, I remembered my mom's lipsticks, in their sleek gold tubes with the YSL logo etching. I was amazed at how a few strokes of lipstick could transform my mother, and in awe of the magic that Yves Saint Laurent, the man, could make with clothes. I got emotional watching models walk down the runway in his creations. Women in tuxedos, shift minidresses in Mondrian prints, and Van Gogh–inspired sweaters—he played with gender and literally put art on fabric to make his own. Through him, I understood fashion as poetry, a lyrical and universal language that needed no translation. I was hooked. Every Sunday evening, I'd be transported to a world of fashion that I'd never even dreamed of entering, as I had no road map. Nothing like that existed in Nepal—there were no famous designers. But Rajesh had planted a seed that my sister's enthusiasm watered. I didn't even know it could be a career until I began to entertain the possibility upon their insistence.

The timing was perfect, as the National Institute of Fashion Technology (NIFT) had recently opened in Delhi. India was such a huge country that the design historically catered to an Indian aesthetic—saris for women and Nehru jackets and kurta pajamas for men—so this was an attempt to bridge the enormous gap between the two countries. While India has an incredibly rich history of textiles and craftsmanship, it was not until the 1980s that younger Indian designers started to make their mark beyond the country's borders. The school had already caused quite a stir as several graduates had turned into star designers on the Indian fashion scene. Still, the fashion designers who most excited me were far away in Europe and America—not in Nepal or India.

I applied to NIFT and moved back to Delhi when I was accepted. I was the only Nepali there. On my very first day, a young woman with kohl-rimmed eyes and short hair tinted auburn motioned to me. She was sitting on the stairs leading up to the school, smoking a cigarette and wearing a tight cropped burgundy T-shirt and low-cut jeans. She had piercings in her nose and ears.

"Hey, come here!" she shouted in a gruff voice.

She wore dark black lipstick, which left an inky rim on the tip of the cigarette she was smoking.

I walked up to her, and she said, "What's your name?"

I replied, "Prabal."

She said, "Hmm, rhymes with 'trouble.' Well, Trouble, you seem cool. I'm Anu, and I'm going to call you P. Sit down."

I was intrigued by her directness—usually that familiarity would bother me, but she was different.

"Here, you want a cigarette?" she asked as I sat next to her.

I hesitated—I'd never smoked before, but then took it from her and inhaled as she lit it. My mouth and lungs filled with smoke, and I began to cough. I failed the cool kid test. Anu looked at me and in a really low voice whispered, "First timer?"

I nodded yes.

She smiled, then put her arms around my neck and said, "P, I like your style, I like your vibe—I like you." Then she looked into my eyes and said, "We're going to be friends."

My heart skipped a beat. Anu was a badass, feisty like the women I'd known and loved. She instantly became my best friend, which marked a completely different school experience for me. To start, there were other feminine guys at the school—and weird ones, too. While the majority of the students were straitlaced, none seemed threatened by me. If they were, they did not say anything. For the first time ever, I could relax a bit.

Instead of living in a dorm, I now had my own apartment, cook, and driver, which my mom paid for. I was twenty-two years old and living like a trust fund kid. My mother's businesses were finally doing well enough to afford such luxuries. That same year, my sister and Rajesh moved back to Nepal, so I was also on my own—but I no longer needed them as my protectors. I had Anu, who lived with her parents and introduced me to all her friends, and to the Indian club scene, which was where I first spotted Koel on the dance floor. She stood out in her short sparkly silver mini–slip dress, feather boa, massive sunglasses, and chunky platform shoes, channeling an amalgamation of the Spice Girls, one of my favorite bands at the time. Even more enchanting was the fact that she was dancing by herself. Twirling, eyes closed, lost in her own reverie, while everyone watched her in awe. She must have sensed me staring too, as she opened her eyes and looked straight at me, and, with one flick of her head, I was out on the dance floor with her.

"I'm Koel!" she shouted above the music.

I smiled and shouted back, "Prabal. Or P, as Anu likes to call me."

Her face lit up. "I've heard about you!" she shouted, and we wound up dancing together for hours. That night, I found a kindred spirit: feminine, feisty, and fearless. Witty and ballsy. She was how the nuns described Maria in *The Sound of Music*: "People would find her nervy, exasperating, or say she was a lot." I had no idea then that Koel was the daughter of a very influential, well-connected family who owned a magazine called *India Today*. That didn't matter to me—what mattered was I had finally met someone who felt almost like the female version of me. We also became very close.

I finally found my people at NIFT, but the courses were not as inspiring as the fashion world that was beginning to bloom in Delhi at that time. I was taking classes in the basics of patternmaking, draping, sketching—but to be completely honest, I was bored. I wanted to venture out into the world of fashion, not just study it in the classroom.

Several months into school, Koel invited me to the wedding of her friend's sister Kalli. The party was at Koel's palatial house, which was packed with celebrities, famous singers, and Indian high society. At one point in the evening, everyone was playing a Hindi game called Antakshari, where someone picks a song and the next person must use the last word of that song to inspire the next one. I was in the back, observing. Anu knew that I sang—and told me to have a go. At first, I demurred. But then a song ended with a word no one else had a song for but me. That was "Ajeeb Dastan Hai Yeh" ("What a Strange Story This Is")—one of my parents' favorite Hindi songs, which holds rare happy memories of my childhood.

I sang that and became the life of the party.

That night, I met Manish Arora, an up-and-coming designer. I'd heard about him because he had recently left his position as assistant designer to Rohit Bal, the most famous designer in India at that time, to venture out on his own. He was the wunderkind—everyone was talking about him. I was smoking a cigarette when I spotted him and introduced myself. I told him I was a huge fan and that I wanted to be a designer, too.

"Why don't you come meet me in the office tomorrow?" he said.

The next day, he offered me an internship.

Manish was disrupting the fashion industry in India by mixing high and low in unexpected, campy, in-your-face ways. Some people deemed his work in poor taste, but I found it extraordinary. In India, there was so much exceptional craftsmanship, textiles, and embroidery—exquisite, but a bit mundane as everyone was using the same material: glass beads, gold threads, silk flowers, and crystals. Manish would take everyday items that people with lesser means might have access to—plastic flowers instead of silk, plastic beads instead of glass—and use a high level of artistry and skill to work them into his garments. The work was unparalleled. New, bold, subversive. The women who wore his clothes were equally defiant, courageous, and provocative, like Koel, who was a client. Anyone who wanted to derive joy and fun from clothes loved his creations. They were expensive and very tongue-in-cheek. Later, as his fame spread beyond our borders, he was referred to as the John Galliano of India.

I continued classes at NIFT and worked for Manish when I wasn't in class. His mind operated in a magical way that was fascinating to witness.

It was also a crash course in starting your own brand, and the perfect balance to my otherwise boring school. Manish was the mentor I was looking for: the ultimate outsider who made it into the fashion world but refused to kowtow to the system. I loved him as a designer, and the eclectic world that he exposed me to. I became his right hand and did everything from networking to PR to production.

One evening, he took me to a house party hosted by Rohit Gandhi and Rahul Khanna, designers who were also a couple. It was like so many other fancy parties I'd been to in south Delhi—posh, glitzy, good food, great music, and free-flowing alcohol. The only difference was that at this party, I'd never seen so many openly gay men: tall, short, muscular, skinny, chubby, older, younger, masculine, feminine, drinking, chatting, gossiping, dancing, and some, to my absolute amazement, were kissing. Real open-mouth-with-tongue kissing. People in India and Nepal rarely kiss in public like that, let alone two men. Being gay was still illegal, but nobody at the party seemed to care. I envied that freedom and longed to be that way. I did notice that I was the only non-Indian-looking man at the party. I refused to let that dampen my spirits. I sat in the corner soaking it all in, fascinated by this world.

At some point, I went to the bar to get a drink, and when I turned around, there were several guys circling me. One older man, in an ivory kurta and matching shawl, holding a cigarette in one hand and a drink in the other, said, "My, my, aren't you beautiful. And who are you?"

I was so taken back—in the best way possible. That had never happened to me in public before. Then another guy introduced himself and we all started talking. It was so easy. A bunch of campy gay guys with wicked senses of humor immediately welcomed me into their fold.

At some point, I turned around to get another drink, when I saw a man standing right behind me. He was tall and lean with dark James Dean hair and an outfit to match: tight jeans and a fitted white T-shirt.

"Can I get you a drink?" he asked.

I nodded yes.

"Vodka martini with a twist, right?"

I smiled. He'd been paying attention. He handed me my drink and introduced himself.

"I am Vineet Malhotra."

I immediately recognized the name: he was a former model, now a very successful entrepreneur whom I'd read about in magazines. As we started talking, I began having an out-of-body experience because he was just so handsome—and he seemed attracted to *me*. I was also aware that I was not the only person who thought he was hot—many men had been watching him that evening. His attention made me feel special. It was the first time in my life that I felt so comfortable—and safe—in my own sexuality. At one point during our conversation, Vineet took my hand and led me outside where others were hanging out, smoking. He sat on the arm of a white sofa and pulled me close to him. And then, out of nowhere, he kissed me. It was so heady and romantic.

That moment was interrupted by Manish calling my name.

"There you are!" he said in a huff. "It's time to go."

I was Manish's plus-one—and designated driver.

Vineet tugged on my waist and said, "I'll follow you home."

But Manish was throwing a fit.

"I'll come back after I drop him off," I promised Vineet.

In the car, Manish kept ranting, "Ewee. Vineet is verny," which meant he was "not posh." It also meant that he could not speak English well, which was not true. I ignored Manish's comments and dropped him at his home—and then went back to get Vineet. That night was the first time we hooked up. He was the hottest guy in town—and he was attracted to me. It was uplifting! And it was the most adult decision I'd ever made.

Around this time, I decided it was time to come out to my family. I no longer wanted to hide, nor could I. My truth, which I'd kept secret, had been weaponized against me for too long. I no longer wanted to give other people the power to diminish me. Still, the whole process was daunting. I'd heard horror stories about families rejecting their children when they came out—some excommunicated, others ignored, quite a few forced to marry against their own will, and so many just living in silence. In India, I knew so many young men who were hiding their truth from their families. The pain of that deception often manifested in a destructive lifestyle of drugs and alcohol or, worst-case scenario, suicide. When I told my group of friends in India, two of them got up and left without saying a word. I have not spoken with either since.

I didn't have a role model or anyone to walk me through the process. Most of the people I knew weren't even familiar with the concept of homosexuality. I felt so alone. I was also nervous about disappointing my family—again.

I decided to first tell my sister and Rajesh, who were living back in Nepal. During a visit home, I invited them out for dinner. It was a beautiful starry night and our always-easy conversation, aided by martinis, gave me courage.

"I have to tell you something," I finally announced.

I explained I'd been exploring my sexuality more openly in India, and that I trusted that they would understand. My sister grew teary-eyed and then threw her arms around me.

"Of course we understand!" she cried.

I will never forget how safe I felt in that moment: Kumudini had fought for me all my life. This was no exception.

Rajesh looked at us and said, "So what's the big news? He's gay? So what?"

I loved them both for their reactions.

I TOLD MY BROTHER next. He was also living in Kathmandu after finishing college in Mumbai. I did not see him much during his time in India. I knew he loved me, but I also felt I was never going to be good enough compared with him. People back home said, over and over, "Pravesh is so good-looking! Like a movie star. And smart, too. Pravesh is going to be a doctor." When they spoke about me, it was "Prabal? Who knows."

Pravesh had moved back to Kathmandu to keep an eye on my mother. I did not know that then, as my siblings were so protective of me. I now know that my father continued to be volatile and that Pravesh felt he had to stay with my mother in order to protect her.

During that visit to Nepal, I was sharing a bedroom with my brother. That night, after I'd just come out to Kumudini and Rajesh, I decided to also come out to Pravesh. He and I we both lying in bed in the dark. Before we went to sleep, I said, "By the way, I'm gay."

He responded, in his calm, measured way. "Okay. How do you feel?"

"I feel free," I said.

Being honest with my siblings was such a gift.

"How do you feel?" I asked Pravesh.

"Okay," he responded in a very matter-of-fact way. "Nothing changes between us."

I told him I was going to share my news with my mom, but he asked me not to.

"She will worry too much about you," he said. "Not that you're gay, but how you will be treated."

Pravesh and Kumudini both shared with me that a divorce felt imminent—and we all agreed that their separation was the right thing to do. My mother was fine with it, society was not. Everyone wanted to blame her for my father's terrible behavior. The next morning, Kumudini agreed with Pravesh about waiting to tell my mother that I was gay.

"Don't worry her," they said. "Trust us—this is not the right time."

I GRADUATED FROM NIFT and continued working for Manish for another six months. That planted the seed that I could have a career in fashion. He was an outsider and outlier who disrupted the fashion scene and made his presence felt—loud and clear. His courage to challenge the status quo reignited my own. Working for him, I started to understand designers, celebrities, and the business of fashion. I was probably the only Nepali in fashion in India, let alone Nepal. I did not know one person from back home who was doing anything like what I was for Manish. We put on his first show ever, and it finally all made sense. All those years of wearing my sister's clothes and prancing around in my mother's sandals. The makeup and paper dolls, the notebooks filled with sketches of women in dresses. It wasn't because I wanted to be a girl—it was because I wanted to live in a world where one could be free to be whoever they wanted to be. And this fashion world was it. It was the place I felt the most comfortable, most at home, with my own people.

AT THAT TIME, IN 1997, the burgeoning fashion industry in India was magical, even intoxicating. I started thinking that I could start on my own line of clothes in India, or even back in Nepal. Every night was a party.

Vineet and I dated for a couple of months. He'd come over to my place for dinner, or we'd go out to the movies or to parties. He was literally the most handsome guy in all of India, and I was a bit intimidated. He was a twenty out of ten. His best friend was another gay guy, called Sanjeev, whom I had a one-night stand with prior to knowing Vineet. I don't know if it was jealousy or something else, but Vineet said we had to stop dating because it made Sanjeev upset.

I wasn't heartbroken, but I did find it difficult because I'd run into him all the time, out and about at the same parties. He was always with Sanjeev and would come say hello, which was painful. I was still very attracted to him physically, though I never let on. As we chatted, I'd think, "I hope you drown in drinks." But then I'd see him on the dance floor and would be reminded that we were not meant for each other: he was a horrible dancer.

It was around then that I started to notice it was always the same people at these parties. I remember being on the dance floor one night wearing silver velvet pants and a white silk shirt, looking around, and thinking, "Is this it?" Sure, I was having the best time with all my crazy friends, nonstop partying, but on that night, for no particular reason, I thought, "What's next?"

I FELT A SENSE of restlessness. Everyone around me in Delhi was doing drugs—I've never done any in my life. I saw the effect they had on people and was just not willing to risk it. It felt both dangerous and wasteful. In India, there were farmhouse parties where you would drive out to the country to go to big, debauched raves—dancing, drinking, and drugs. I was always the designated driver, and I was growing tired of it. I wanted something more. I quit working for Manish and fantasized about studying fashion farther abroad—maybe Paris? Or New York? But I wasn't sure how to make it happen.

I decided to go to London for a solo getaway. It was my first trip alone to Europe. On my flight, there was a very cute blond, European flight attendant. Halfway through the flight, I ended up in the Mile High Club. For a scrawny kid from Nepal, the only validation I ever got was these deeply physical attractions. I was intimidated by the white world, so to be honest, it was a great jump start to my London visit.

One evening, I went to a gay bar in Chelsea, but no one at the smoke-filled pub seemed to notice me, which made me feel even more lost. I paid for my drink and walked down the fabled Bond Street, passing all the boutiques of designers I had seen on *Style with Elsa Klensch*: Dior, Ralph Lauren, Prada, and more. Chanel's storefront stopped me midstride. There, in the window, was a delicately pleated butter-yellow chiffon dress with a pearl-adorned belt. It was both soft and fluid, and yet immaculately constructed. It beckoned to me the same way my cousin Karuna's tulle dress had done years before. I had an immediate visceral reaction. This time, I did not so much want to wear this dress—I wanted to know how it was made. Simple yet grand: How could all that be contained in one dress? I wanted to be part of a world where that was possible.

BACK IN INDIA, I was still trying to figure out my next move. I decided to go back home to Nepal. I was at the airport waiting for my flight when I saw *The Celestine Prophecy* sitting on the bestseller shelf at the bookstore. Intrigued, I picked it up and started reading. It was about a man who goes on a journey. I purchased it and continued to read on the plane. I can't remember much about the book other than that it tapped into a spiritual side of me that I didn't know even existed. It was almost a signal to listen to the universe.

I finished the book the next day, at a restaurant called the Bakery Cafe in Kathmandu while eating momo Nepali dumplings, and could feel, as I turned the last page, that there was something bigger out there waiting for me. I shared all these thoughts with my sister and Rajesh in Nepal and, once again, Rajesh had a profound impact on my trajectory.

"Go to America," he said.

I did not know then that Pravesh had been back-channeling to Kumudini and Rajesh. My sister told me years later that Pravesh said to her, "Prabal won't listen to me—but he will listen to you. Tell him to leave Nepal." I understand now why he could not tell me directly: I was so tired of being constantly compared with him that I saw him as a Goody-Two-shoes, a perfect being. I never would have listened. He loved me so much and he wanted what was best for me and found a way to do it behind my back.

A few days after my conversation with Kumudini and Rajesh, I turned on the TV. *The Phil Donahue Show* was finishing up and right after that was Oprah. I was riveted. I'd seen Black women on TV shows before, of course, but never as the host. Oprah had her own show! I watched the next day, and the next. That third show was about living your dreams. It was during that episode where I had the epiphany: "Rajesh is right. I must go to America!"

When I told my sister, she started nodding her head emphatically and looked relieved. "Your dreams are too big for Kathmandu," she said. "No one will get you here. Go!"

I told her my plans—to apply to Parsons School of Design for fashion—and watched her face beam.

"You know, Kumudini, I have to give it a shot," I said. "If it's a mistake, then it will be mine and I can live with it. But the idea of living with regret for not trying is something I never want to do."

CHAPTER SIX

Right before I left for New York in the summer of 1999, I learned that my parents were finally getting a divorce. We all knew about my father's infidelities. That was upsetting enough. But then we found out that my father was having an affair with my mother's sister, the one my mother had raised like a daughter. In fact, this was the same aunt who was staying with us when that woman came to the gate when I was a young child, claiming she was married to my father. My aunt witnessed the fight it caused between my parents that same evening. She knew the cruelty my father was capable of—as well as my mother's extraordinary kindness—so the fact that my aunt chose him, behind my mother's back, was a double betrayal. This was the last straw for me.

I would not speak to my father again for more than a decade.

My mother came to the airport to see me off, as she had countless times before, but this time she was unable to hold back tears, which fueled mine. I felt a pit in my stomach as I boarded the plane. I was accustomed to leaving home for school since I was eleven, and yet this goodbye felt different. The distance made this adventure even more daunting—and the added emotional turmoil of my father's news made it that much more painful. The twenty-three hours in flight were a blurry mess of emotions. I was sad to say goodbye to my mother, sister, and brother—but for everyone else, it was good riddance. I was ready for my next adventure and excited for what lay ahead. As an immigrant, I felt the United States was the promised land. While I had found a few kindred spirits in Delhi, I believed New York could finally be a place where an oddity like me might fit in.

When the flight attendant announced, "Fasten your seat belts, we're beginning our descent to JFK Airport," I was overcome with breathlessness. America was a fabled, magical land—a place where dreams could come true. I was ready to realize mine.

As I stood in line waiting to go through immigration, I was both wired and nervous. My excitement for what the future might hold was dampened by the stoic, serious faces of all the immigration officers. What if they pulled me aside? What if my paperwork was not in order? All the stories I'd heard were whirling in my head until a gruff voice snapped me to attention.

"Next!"

It was my turn. I handed over my documents.

"Purpose of visit?" he said, without looking up.

"I'm going to Parsons to study fashion," I said, praying my voice was not as shaky as I felt.

He looked up at me and asked, "You're from Nepal? Wow, you speak English very well."

"Thank you," I said.

"Where did you learn it? In a language school?" he asked.

"No," I said. "I went to an English boarding school for ten plus years in Kathmandu."

"Have you been to the US before?"

When I replied no, he seemed even more impressed.

He stamped my passport, handed it to me, and said, "Well then, welcome to America."

Those words sent shivers through my whole body. I was so excited to finally leave my past behind, to be among all the misfits, to begin the journey of finding myself as all my artistic heroes had—in NYC! Patti Smith, Madonna, Basquiat, Warhol, Debbie Harry. To be part of the welcoming rainbow, to live the American dream.

As I exited JFK, the stream of yellow taxicabs waiting for passengers reminded me of all the movies I'd seen of this fabled city.

"This is my first time in America!" I announced, euphoric as I climbed into the back seat of one. My brown-skinned driver shrugged.

"Where to?" he asked, and I noticed an Indian accent.

"Union Square, Manhattan," I said.

Instead of the visual skyscraper feast I was anticipating, I saw row upon row of low-slung houses and industrial complexes. That disappointment combined with jet lag's drowsiness made me feel suddenly homesick. I dozed off in the bumper-to-bumper traffic only to be jolted awake by my driver shouting out his window. He was talking with another Indian driver in the cab next to us.

"I haven't seen my friend for many years!" the driver said to me afterward, finally smiling. I'd been here for less than an hour and had already witnessed a New York miracle.

"Well, now you met him, you will get to hang out again!" I said.

He looked at me through the rearview mirror, and I watched his smile deflate.

"Sir, what reconnecting, what friendship?" He sounded angry. "Us, immigrants, my only friendship is with this cab. It has seen me through it all. Our tears, our struggle, our pain, and our joy, this cab knows us the best. You know, when my son was born in the hospital, I couldn't be with my wife. I was in this car driving so I could pay the bills. Sir, so no reconnection. This much hi and hello is enough."

This hit me hard. I realized, as we crawled toward Manhattan, that the New York hustle, at least for immigrants with brown skin, was real.

As we approached the Queens Midtown Tunnel, I finally saw the Manhattan skyline emerge over the river, like a glorious crown, glistening in the distance—then everything went dark. And then we emerged into a concrete wonderland of honking cars and buzzing city buses.

I rolled down my car window and drank it all in. A cacophony of scents—part exhaust and part fumes—perfectly blended with the exotic yet familiar smells of delicacies wafting from the roadside vendors and delis. As we drove down Third Avenue, crossing Thirty-Fourth Street, then Thirty-Third, and so on, the scents shifted from caramelized roasted peanuts to salty melted cheese pizza and baked yet slightly burnt pretzels, and I was immediately transported back to that magical night with Sid in Chandni Chowk in Delhi. Different cities, different fragrances, yet similar anticipation. New York City's soundtrack—of blaring sirens, speeding cars, screeching brakes, and shouting people—brought me back to the present.

I was in New York, the place where so many of my heroes had come to realize their American dreams. I was following in their footsteps, and that realization fueled wave after wave of emotion within me: anticipation, nervousness, fear, excitement, and joy. For a brief second, I wished my family could be there with me to experience all of this. I had left all my loved ones back home in Nepal, but in this big, buzzing, diverse concrete jungle, I felt like I was finally home. My love affair with New York had begun.

I SPENT THAT FIRST night with Sonam, a close friend of Deep's who lived in the East Village. We met when we were younger in Nepal, and I reached out to let him know I was moving to New York. I had met him once when I was a teenager and liked him immediately, so when he and his parents moved to America, we stayed in touch. He was my only contact in New York City.

As we walked through Alphabet City that evening, I reveled in the smorgasbord of fashion I was witnessing in real time: from the black-clad moody goths with their dark-stained lips to the colorful spiky hair and metal-studded graffitied punks. Shaggy-haired grunge kids in torn jeans and worn-out plaid shirts coexisted with colorfully and scantily dressed

Spice Girl acolytes and retro seventies bell-bottom disco queens. When I walked past what seemed to be a pack of Hells Angels in their head-to-toe leather, I thought, "Or they could also be a bunch of gay guys inspired by Tom of Finland." Anything was possible here.

It was a thrilling, powerful, eclectic, free-spirited mishmash. I'd never seen so many different-looking people—different races, sizes, sexualities. This was a place where you could express yourself however you wanted without any fear. In Nepal and India, I was always made to feel like a freak. To see so many self-expressive "misfits" in such large numbers gave me palpable relief. Every so often, I'd spot a group of finance bros—drunk and loud—and realized with glee that they were the ones who looked out of place. I could finally exhale. Even more liberating were all the people holding hands, kissing, and making out in the corners—regardless of gender identity. It was everything I had hoped for and more.

The next day, I went to my dorm at Parsons: Loeb Hall is on Twelfth Street between Third and Fourth Avenues. I expected more of an American college with a campus, so I was surprised at how urban it was. My roommate was an Italian guy from Long Island named Carmen. He was a drummer studying music at the New School, reserved but friendly. In the dorm room next to us were a Japanese skater kid with crazy hair and a Black kid with a southern drawl. Straight boys who were all seemingly cool with me. None of them knew where Nepal was, but that didn't matter to me at that moment. I'd never experienced so much diversity in such a small space in my entire life.

I WAS ALSO INCREDIBLY excited to be at a famous fashion school that taught the likes of Marc Jacobs, Donna Karan, and Anna Sui, *and* in a city that gave birth to the gay rights movement—not just in the United States but arguably worldwide. People in Nepal and India did not even talk about homosexuality—so for me, being so blatantly out on the streets was thrilling.

It was the first time in my life when I could dress however I felt on any given day, in public. That was so liberating. I was five feet eight inches and 120 pounds, a scrawny little kid, so while men's sizes were too big, I fit perfectly into women's clothes. I bought blouses from French Connection and H&M that I wore with leather pants and fur coats that I found at vintage stores. For the most part, I got positive reactions. Though, occasionally, someone would pierce that protective bubble with a "faggot" shouted from a car passing by.

That was not the norm: I can still remember going to my first gay bar and seeing men openly flirting with one another, holding hands, kissing, and more. In Nepal, this was taboo. In India, everything was hidden, but here in New York it was all out in the open, comfortable, easy. That was thrilling to me.

One night, I was at Wonder Bar, one of the more popular gay bars in East Village on Sixth Street between Avenues A and B with some students from the dorm. I was still getting used to living in a city where you could go to a place like this to meet and talk to people. We were ordering drinks when an incredibly gorgeous guy across the bar started looking in our direction. He was tall with dark hair and green eyes, and we were all commenting on how hot he was, when one of my new friends, Damien, said, "Prabal, I think he's looking at you."

I looked over at the handsome stranger and he smiled at me. Dustin, one of the guys from my dorm, interrupted this reverie. "I doubt that," he said. "What are the chances that *he* would be into a gaysian?"

All the air left the room. I'd never heard that word before, and its meaning did not register immediately, but I knew based on Dustin's snarky delivery that it was demeaning.

"Let me go and find out for you, Prabal," he added. Without waiting for my consent, he scurried off to speak to the guy.

I was so embarrassed that I couldn't even look over to see what he was doing.

When Dustin returned, he was smirking, "He's coming over to say hello to all of us later."

Damien asked, "What did you say?"

"I asked him if he was a rice queen and if he was into gaysians," Dustin said with a loud cackle.

I finished my drink in one gulp and went outside. I lit a cigarette, leaned back on the brick wall outside the bar, and began seething with anger as I replayed what had just happened. It all felt so familiar. And disappointing. I was trying to calm myself down, as my impulse was to confront Dustin. His attack was so unexpected that it felt that much more shocking. He was in my dorm, and part of my friend group. He was also Jewish, and very effeminate, so it felt like an even greater betrayal. Surely he understood what it meant to be othered—why target me? Also, how could this happen in a city like New York—in the East Village, no less, and at a gay bar! I choked back the tears welling up inside me. I refused to be a victim anymore.

Just then, the guy from the bar came outside and introduced himself. His name was Rodrigo. He had grown up in Queens, the Spanish American son of an immigrant. We chatted a little and I learned that he was a part-time model and worked as a bartender at a bar on the Upper West Side. He had come to Wonder Bar by himself on a rare Friday night outing. I told him that I was from Nepal—and he knew where it was—and that I was studying fashion at Parsons. Then he asked me if I wanted to go get a drink somewhere else. I looked at this beautiful stranger and nodded yes, adding, "As long as the night ends up with me in your bed."

He looked at me, smiled, and said, "Okay, let's do this."

We both went inside to grab our jackets. I then went to say goodbye to my friends.

"I'm going to another bar with someone," I said coyly.

"Who?" Damien asked.

"Rodrigo," I said. Everyone looked confused—except Dustin. I pointed him out, and Rodrigo waved.

"Okaaay, gurrl, go get him," Damien said.

"Be safe," another friend added.

I looked at Dustin as I was leaving and said, "Remember, everybody loves rice."

RODRIGO AND I WENT to another bar before going to his place. It was my first one-night stand in New York City, and it was perfect. I woke up early the next morning. As I was getting ready to leave, Rodrigo, groggy and smiling, gave me a tight hug goodbye.

As I was about to head out the door, he held my hand and asked, "Hey, that guy who came up to me and talked before we spoke, is he your friend?"

"Not sure," I said. "He lives in my dorm."

He looked at me, now wide awake, and said, "You need to get rid of him. He's no good."

I was grateful that he saw what I had felt.

"And get rid of this filthy habit!" he added pointing at my box of Parliaments. "They will kill you."

I nodded and kissed him goodbye.

I never saw Rodrigo again. And I was okay with that. I was so used to the feeling of abandonment by then that a one-night stand felt fine to me. Rare moments of affection had only been confusing and fleeting. By then, I had learned to say goodbye when I said hello. It was a coping mechanism and the only way I knew how to survive.

Out on the street, I lit another cigarette and thought about the sequence of events the night before. That incident at the bar went against all my expectations. America has a PR pitch of being diverse and welcoming. And here I was, among people I thought were new friends, at a gay bar in a city that gave birth to the movement. I was open to all the possibilities of the American dream—walking through this city and seeing men making out or holding hands in public, gay bars—it was my dream come true, which made the racist comments even more devastating. I had let my guard down.

Race was not the only issue: body-shaming was another uniquely American obsession. In Nepal and India, being heavy suggests that you come from a wealthy family. So even though I grew up in a culture where people commented on each other's physical appearances, I was aghast at how people's bodies were referenced in the United States, whether fat or thin. It was always so direct, blatant, and damaging. I was extremely skinny and could never find any clothes that fit. I had this one boatneck sweater from French Connection that I wore often—and loved—but was teased mercilessly for it being a woman's blouse.

"Shopping in the girls' section again, Prabal?" I heard so often I would simply roll my eyes. Imagination was lacking, and insults were the defensive default.

One day, another so-called friend named Joe, a rich white gay boy who was studying fashion marketing, said, "Ew, you're so skinny. What's your waist? A twenty-seven?"

"Twenty-six," I replied.

He said, "Mine is a perfect thirty-four."

I replied, "There is nothing perfect about a thirty-four."

I remember thinking, "What is the definition of perfect? And who gets to define it?" It made no sense to me, especially at one of the premiere fashion colleges.

In another exchange, an acquaintance said, "Why don't you cut your balls off and wear skinny jeans."

That one really stung: I was in New York and still a hijra.

Despite the diversity of my dorm, most of the students at Parsons were wealthy and white. So I stood out, as did a Black student named Desmond. When he showed his collection in class, people would snicker and make affirmative action jokes. Likewise, that whole first semester, I was barraged by microaggressions: My taste was questioned, as were my design choices. But my talent was undeniable.

I'd learned the foundation of fashion at NIFT and was able to build on that knowledge at Parsons. I loved the illustration class and learned every technical aspect—from patternmaking to draping and sewing. But the design concept class was my favorite. There, I learned how artistry and philosophy fueled great fashion. I thought of all the designers I discovered on Elsa Klensch's show—this was what made my idols, like Karl Lagerfeld and Yves Saint Laurent, so great. Their designs told stories and created worlds. I excelled in that class. For our final project, we had to create a collection based on music. The theme was "collision" of cultures. I did "Italian opera meets Nepali classical music" and submitted a collection around the beauty that comes from the tension between two opposite cultures. I was already beginning to try to tell my own story about the East and the West via the fabrics and textiles and embroidery techniques and colors. Women in Nepal and India dress in a very graceful way—reveal and conceal. The way you drape your sari might show a little stomach or an arm. This was so different from the pragmatism of Western design.

We also discussed the concept of quiet luxury. The definition of old money in American fashion is beige and gold and navy—a subtle, colonized idea. Those in power can dictate what luxury looks like. But if you look at my history, my culture, which was never colonized and is older than Europe let alone the United States—it celebrates opulence, colors, and textures. It's the inverse of neutral palettes and blending in. I loved working on that project simply because it meant beginning to integrate the two opposite worlds in which I lived. Somewhere in that collision was my truth.

One day in class, our teacher returned everyone's work but mine.

"Prabal, can you stand up for a second?" she said.

I felt the room grow quiet, and my heart began to race as I nervously followed her direction. I didn't know what to expect. In the past, in Nepal and India, anytime I was called out in class, it didn't end well for me. I was preparing myself for what was to come.

"Your project was quite different from anything I've ever seen," she said. "I'd even say it was radical."

All my classmates were staring at me. I felt a familiar pit in my stomach.

"I want everyone to look at this work," she said, holding up my project. "In my life as a teacher, every few years a student shows up who I know is going to be a star. Prabal, I think that you're one of them."

I was shocked. No teacher had ever said anything like that to me. I was flooded with so many emotions: she saw the potential in me.

After class, I noticed a blond girl named Lucia out in the hallway, fighting back tears.

"What's wrong?" I asked.

"I can't believe she said that in front of all of us!" She was now sobbing. "I put so much work into my project. What makes you so special?"

I was taken aback. The fizzy feeling that had been coursing through my body started to flatten. I looked around and saw other white students nodding in agreement.

Someone muttered, "Yeah, that was so uncool."

Someone else added, "Not fair."

From that moment on, the dynamic shifted in school. The microaggressions became macro.

"Oh, it's very ethnic," I'd hear from more than one fellow student when I showed them my designs.

One of my classmates joked, "Oof, that smells like curry."

I did not let this deter me. I poured my heart into my drawings and ideas and decided to compete in a fashion contest called Fusion, which was an annual event held for FIT and Parsons students. For that, I submitted a design concept and, once chosen, I had to create a collection of eight to ten looks for what would be my first runway show. I was excited: this was my first opportunity to tell my story, from my point of view.

Twenty-five other designers were competing, roughly half of whom were my peers from Parsons. Everyone was talking about their concepts, but I decided to keep mine quiet. I didn't want to give anything away. A couple of days before the competition, the coordinator and organizer, a resident assistant at Loeb named Jimmy, shared the lineup: my collection would be presented last. I was thrilled and honored to make my statement at the end of the show.

FIT went first, and there were some memorable looks, including one dress made with peacock feathers. The Parsons students followed, and again, the talent was undeniable. The level of sophistication, ideas, and execution was solid. I was proud of my classmates, and both excited and nervous when it was finally my turn.

My collection's theme was "Finding Beauty." All the looks were made from discarded materials and found objects that I repurposed to look desirable. I turned old velvet curtains that I bought at an East Village thrift store into an evening gown, and loved the idea of the romances, parties, and fights that sun-faded and streaked fabric may have witnessed in its former life. I used old cans, metallic cleaning scrubs, and even pine cones, which I reworked with spray paint or glitter before stitching them onto found fabrics to become glistening, glittering sculptures. The combination was grace and beauty with a lot of edge and attitude.

Bringing these opposite worlds together was exciting: I used Eastern elements with Western design and played with gender as well, casting two male models and dressing them in sheer fabric. Meanwhile, my female models were strong and independent looking in a variety of sizes. I wanted to deconstruct the rules of fashion and the concept of beauty. I also wanted to make it clear that just because I was from Nepal didn't mean that I made "ethnic" clothes. I wanted to challenge the norm of what fashion could be—specifically in regard to how we look at gender. I wasn't trying to make a political statement—I just wanted to push back against all the norms. It was an unconventional and ambitious collection, and it landed: when my name was announced as the winner at the end of the event, I was stunned. I had finally won something! Alone, on my own. At the same time, I missed my siblings and my mother. They would have been so proud of me.

That evening, everyone involved in the show went out and celebrated. I was enjoying the attention, which continued back at my dorm. My roommates were high-fiving me, exclaiming, "Great job! Congratulations! You rock!"

These were all the mantras I'd been telling myself for years but had never heard from anyone but my mother and siblings. It felt strange and unfamiliar for my peers to be celebrating me. But it made me happy. So much so that I decided to share the news with my classmates back in Nepal. This was proof that I had made the right choice by following my gut and coming to America to study fashion. Oddly enough, I was in a St. Xavier's high school group chat, as was everyone from my grade. I never had anything to say but found it amusing to follow other old classmates. Now that I was in New York, pursuing my dream to become a designer, I decided to post a message about this prestigious award I had won. That would show those boys. I was okay after all.

The very next day, I saw that there was a message in the chat. I clicked on it: "You're a fucking faggot and a sissy we don't care about your fashion." Two or three others chimed in, echoing this sentiment.

Once I got over the shock of the meanness, I wrote back: "All my life, you guys have treated me this way. And I've always taken it."

I went on to list every abusive experience I had at the school, naming the boys who participated. And as I finished the very long list of offenses, I read through it and hit send.

As that message whooshed out into the world, I felt free. I had been looking for apologies and accountability from men who were so damaged that they were incapable of acknowledging that they were in the wrong. Leaving that group chat was my final message to them all.

As MY FIRST YEAR was coming to an end, my fellow students were all talking about internships—making it clear that I had to get one, too. The program at Parsons was two years long, and a summer internship helped set the stage for a job after graduation. This, I was told, was how everyone in New York started their career in fashion. I had no idea where to even begin, so I went to the career center for advice and learned that there was a coveted internship with Donna Karan. She was, at that time, one of the most important designers, the queen of New York.

It was a Monday, so I went home and worked on my résumé and portfolio, and the following day, after classes, I went to the Donna Karan offices at 550 Seventh Avenue, a legendary building that was also home to Ralph Lauren, Oscar de la Renta, and Bill Blass.

"We begin accepting applications tomorrow," the receptionist said.

"I really want this job," I replied. "I don't mind waiting."

I didn't have any connections, or an understanding of protocol, but I did have determination and talent. After a few hours of waiting in the lobby, a well-dressed Asian man appeared. He seemed annoyed. "Intern interviews are tomorrow," he said.

I told him my story—that I was the only person I knew studying fashion from Nepal. How I had come to New York without knowing anyone and I had just won the Fusion contest. And, most important, how much I loved Donna Karan not only as a designer but also because she was a working woman like my mother. His face softened.

"I know that other people are coming to interview tomorrow—I also know that I want this job more than any of them," I added. "And I promise you this, I won't disappoint."

He nodded slowly and then disappeared for roughly fifteen minutes. When he returned, he was smiling. "Okay, the internship is yours."

When my peers heard that I'd landed the position, they saw that I was also ambitious. Call it what they might—I felt I had no choice.

That summer, I rarely interacted with Donna Karan, but it was fascinating to watch her lead this massive company. She'd designed several collections using Nepal and Tibet as inspiration, so I thought there was a chance I would fit in. I wound up doing tedious menial jobs like cutting yards of fabric into inch-by-inch swatches and delivering coffee to boardroom meetings. Still, I was grateful to be in those rooms, watching designers draping, and hearing the conversations. It was also incredibly powerful to see a woman leading.

BY THE START OF my second year at Parsons, New York was officially my home. I could not imagine ever going back to Nepal or India. Damien and I decided to move in together as roommates, and we scheduled our classes around New York's nightclub scene. Beige was a gay party at the Bowery Bar that took place every Tuesday night—a fabulous mix of drag queens and celebrities—so we made sure to have no classes on Wednesdays.

Our first night at Beige, I sashayed up to the bouncer, channeling JLo, Madonna, and Britney Spears with low-slung jeans, oversize sunglasses, and a dramatic scarf. The line went around the block, and every single guy was wearing a white T-shirt and True Religion jeans, trying to look like an Abercrombie & Fitch model. I could not help but think, "These people are so boring and unimaginative! We're in New York! Where is your individuality?"

The bouncer looked at Damien, who's half-Mexican and half-Portuguese, and me.

"You boys have to wait in line," he growled.

"With them?" I responded with exaggerated mock disdain, gesturing at the people in line.

So obnoxious! But it worked.

We got to know Derek, the gruff gay bouncer at Beige, who pulled the rope aside every week when Damien and I arrived. We'd each buy one vodka soda with cranberry and sip it—slowly—until one of the drag queens, who loved us, would give us drink tickets.

BETWEEN CLASSES AND CLUBBING, I spent hours searching for cool clothes at vintage and thrift stores all throughout New York. My favorite shop was called Cobblestones on Ninth Street between First Avenue and Avenue A. That's where I found the turquoise belt and white faux fur coat that both became my trademark. I also started experimenting with making my own clothes. I'd buy XXL men's shirts at thrift stores and then stitch them down to my size with elaborate smocking. Or I would take a boring white T-shirt and layer it with colorful swaths of chiffon, stitched on and then cut in specific spots so the fraying caused a shimmery rainbow effect. I'd find old Levi's and wear them cinched tight with cool, eclectic leather belts.

It was during this period of my life when I learned that how I dressed and showed up was one of the biggest ways I could resist and defy the people who wanted to make me invisible. Fashion allowed me to get my foot in the door—and once I got in, I could hold my own, get free drinks, and learn how to navigate this new landscape. Some days, I'd dress head to toe in white, topped with that fab fake fur coat. Then there was the month I skipped lunch so I could save up for the Gucci glasses during the Tom Ford era. I spent hours scouring thrift stores for the seventies scarves he styled his models with and found a red vintage leather jacket while I was at it.

On Fridays and Saturdays, I'd go to art openings or spend hours browsing books at the Strand. And then in the evenings, I'd head to Suede, another popular gay bar, or a club called APT in the Meatpacking District. Damien and I went so often that we became friends with Jonathan Morr, the owner. I remember one evening, my friends were excitedly whispering and nodding their heads to indicate someone famous had arrived.

"What's up?" I asked.

"Monica Lewinsky is here!" one announced.

"So what?" I remarked. "She can come say hi to me."

I'm sure some friends thought, "What a diva!" But I also knew that I had to create my own fantasy world where I could become famous one day. There were no role models, no road map—though it all felt possible in New York.

We were nearing graduation when I was asked to open the Fusion competition with my own collection, a huge honor. I created fifteen looks for my first ready-to-wear show, which was a stark contrast from the conceptual one I'd done the year before. For this, I wanted to blend East and West with totally wearable clothes. The colors were red, white, blue, black, and beige, with beading and embroidery, but cut in a very modern way. It was my version of American sportswear. I was pleased with the outcome: a well-rounded, polished collection. Cynthia Rowley was one of the judges. After the show was over, she asked, "Are you going to start your own thing?"

I said, "No, I'm about to graduate and I need a job."

"Why don't you come down to my office?"

I did, but there was nothing available at her small, independent company at the time, so I wound up going to a headhunter and got a job working for a mass-market gown company that made dresses that retailed for eighty dollars. It was a polyester hell. The first time I touched the fabric they were using, I thought, "Oh my god! This will give you a rash."

But the people who worked there were kind and thoughtful. They handled the samples with such care, like the gowns were priceless.

"I know this is not Valentino or Yves Saint Laurent," one of my colleagues said. "But somewhere, in the middle of Iowa or Wisconsin, it is someone's prom gown."

That immediately brought me down from my elitist pedestal. It was a moment that humbled and stayed with me. Of course, fashion should be for everyone.

I WAS THERE FOR only two months when Cynthia reached out to say there was an opening in production and that she would sponsor me for a work visa. That would put me on a course to getting a green card, which was something I had already planned to do, the first step toward applying to become an American citizen.

By then, Damien and I had moved into a fifth-floor walk-up on 108th Street and Amsterdam Avenue. On our first night, I heard a gunshot and saw cops chasing someone down the street from my window. The next morning, I went to the corner deli and saw that the cashier was behind a cage. I'd never seen that before. And yet, just a couple of streets over, there were posh doorman buildings and professional dog walkers. The tragic magic of New York is how dreams and possibilities can change from block to block.

Damien and I were both pursuing our dreams. He was waiting tables at Cafeteria, a hip restaurant in Chelsea, and interning at *Vanity Fair* (where he eventually got a job in the fashion department working for style editor Elizabeth Saltzman). At Cynthia Rowley, I worked my way up from production to a design job—and began to see just how difficult it was to make it as a privately owned fashion brand. Cynthia was cool and smart as hell, and she hustled harder than anyone I'd ever known. If there were UPS boxes that no one was moving, she'd do it herself, in heels. She also trusted me to figure out production even though I had no idea how to do it.

This was my deep dive into the behind-the-scenes runway-to-retail process of taking every look Cynthia designed and turning it into an array of different sizes to be priced and delivered to stores in a timely manner. Cynthia was making all her clothes in China, which was also an amazing learning experience for me, like going to business school. I worked day and night and figured out the formula for costing and margins. Before that job, I had never opened an Excel spreadsheet. I also saw how many things she had to do to keep her company afloat—whether it was designing a Target collection or a doing a Japanese licensing deal. The perception of the fashion industry is that it's all fab parties and gorgeous models. I learned quickly that that's only 5 percent of it. The other 95 percent is pure hustle and hard work.

CHAPTER SEVEN

I'd been working with Cynthia Rowley for two years when I was asked to meet the creative team at Bill Blass. They were looking to make a change and were hiring an assistant designer. Bill Blass was one of the top American couture houses and had a formidable reputation for impeccable clothes worn by the crème de la crème of American high society: women like Brooke Astor, Nancy Kissinger, Nan Kempner, and Gloria Vanderbilt. As a designer, Blass was loved and revered by the women he dressed and by the fashion industry worldwide. His brand was one of the three American fashion houses—along with Carolina Herrera and Oscar de la Renta—that rivaled those in Paris. I really wanted to work in couture, and Bill Blass was the perfect place for that.

I first learned about Bill Blass on *Style with Elsa Klensch* back in Nepal. His clothes reminded me of my favorite designer, the late Yves Saint Laurent, that perfect mix of tailored suits and beautiful dresses as collection staples. The only difference was that Saint Laurent was very provocative and elegantly French. Mr. Blass's clothes defined American luxury. There was an easy elegance to his fashion—it was always pragmatic, uncompromisingly meticulous, and undeniably glamorous. Like Saint Laurent, it was clear that Blass loved and revered women. Each piece of his came alive when worn, as did the woman wearing it.

But that was in the house's heyday. It was now 2004. Mr. Blass passed away in 2002 after selling his company in 1999 to Michael Groveman, his chief financial officer, and Haresh Tharani, who oversaw his licensee relationships. At the time of his death, Mr. Blass had more than eighty licensing deals—on shoes, handbags, perfume, home goods, and more. Licensing deals were (and still are) how many designers make their businesses work financially. Michael Groveman became the CEO and in 2000 hired Steven Slowik as designer. But Slowik had big shoes to fill and was quickly replaced in 2001 by his design assistant Lars Nilsson. Nilsson also struggled. The day after his February 2003 runway show, Nilsson was unceremoniously fired, which caused a stir throughout the industry. *Vogue* had recommended Nilsson, and Anna Wintour was not pleased with the way he was treated.

The word on the street was that the brand was in crisis—neither Nilsson nor Slowik could live up to Mr. Blass's talent, wit, or clear understanding of his clientele. As a result, I wasn't really interested in the job. But my rule was to always take meetings, as you never know what opportunities might present themselves. Plus, I wanted to visit one of the most reputable fashion houses in New York! Even if it was in decline.

Call it the arrogance of youth, but I did wear flip-flops to that interview. As I entered the lobby of 550 Seventh Avenue, I had a feeling of déjà vu. It was the same building I'd gone to for the Donna Karan internship. I had learned so much since then and felt ready to ascend to the next level. This building was also the home base to Ralph Lauren and Oscar de la Renta. Seeing these iconic names as I pressed the elevator button for Bill Blass's office made me giddy.

There, a friendly receptionist named Michelle, who was wearing a bright red lipstick, greeted me.

"I love your toe ring," she said with a smile.

She immediately put me at ease. I sat down on the ivory couch in the waiting area and, as my feet sank into the plush ivory carpet, I realized that everything in the room was a monochromatic shade of white. Jean Claude Huon, a handsome Parisian and the vice president of Blass, came to greet me. He was precise and curt, which I assumed was a French thing, until I found out later that he didn't approve of my flip-flops. He introduced me to another man in his fifties who was dressed in khaki pants and a plaid shirt. He looked out of place at Bill Blass, a bit frumpy compared with everyone else who was impeccably dressed and polished.

"Hi, I'm Michael Vollbracht," he said in a very theatrical 1940s film star way. He was the creative director. He reminded me of a friendly uncle. I learned that day that Michael was also a good friend of Mr. Blass and the latest designer brought in to save the brand. He was best known as an illustrator, having worked in-house at Bendel's and then Bloomingdale's, where he designed a bag so iconic that it's now in the Cooper Hewitt museum of design. He also launched his own fashion line in 1978, which was sold in Neiman Marcus and Bergdorf Goodman and was considered a success until the mid-eighties, when he closed it to focus on his illustration work. When I asked why, he responded bitterly with, "I refused to license my name."

He told me that he was working for *The New Yorker* when he was offered the design position at Bill Blass, and that he was excited by the possibilities. He also made it clear that it had been a rocky road.

"You're the one who's been sent to me to mend my ways," he said with a sarcastic smile.

Sensing my confusion, he continued, "You see, Prabal, I'm apparently too old to understand what modern women want. That's what they tell me."

He emphasized *they* and pointed toward the CEO's office, with a dramatic sweep of his finger. "And what *Vogue* said. What did they say? That I was . . . irrelevant and stuck in the past. Oh, the press. You know, Prabal, Halston always said to me, 'Never trust the press.' They're the lowest of humanity. So, what do you think? Do you agree?"

Michael's monologue bewildered me. This was, after all, a job interview.

"Well, if you listened to what everyone said, you'd be a listener. A spectator, and not the player," was all I was able to muster.

Michael looked at me, threw his head back, and shouted, "Ha!" He then pointed at me and said, "I like that answer. I like you."

I smiled politely. I was still confused, but intrigued. This was not what I had anticipated.

"Come on in, let me take you around," Michael said.

As we toured the office, he filled me in on his time thus far with Bill Blass. For his first collection, he put his favorite models from the 1970s—so women in their fifties—on the runway. A very modern and bold move, but clearly too far ahead of its time, as the critics panned the show. The fashion industry is particularly cruel to anything that feels dated. He was clearly gutted by those reviews, as he brought them up several times that morning.

"They called it backward-looking and archaic," he said bitterly. "Why can't older women be considered chic?"

I appreciated his outrage and found myself slowly warming up to the idea of possibly working there. But I wasn't fully convinced until he showed me the tailoring and the flou rooms, where all the clothes were made.

Bill Blass was famous for his handmade bespoke tailoring and dresses—this was where that magic happened. The tailoring room was run by an Italian man named Roberto who had worked at Armani. Everyone else there—all Italian men—had perfected their craft at either Armani, Ferragamo, or Geoffrey Beene, or on Savile Row. All of them wore white lab coats that popped against the backdrop of bolts of dove-gray and ivory-pinstripe silk wool, camel and ivory double-faced cashmere, pale blue and midnight zibeline-finished cashmere. Bespoke jackets and coats in the various stages of construction and completion were on mannequins placed throughout the room, which had a serene, monastic, yet distinctly masculine feel.

Then Michael whispered something to Roberto, winked at me, and said, "Wait till you see the insides of the jacket. That is the real beauty. Real work of art."

He pulled back the lapel of a beautiful simple pinstripe blazer to reveal the bones of the jacket, all handsewn, canvassed, and framed in various forms of silk, cotton, and sturdy linen that transformed the softest wool into a three-dimensional form.

It took my breath away.

"We do it all by hand," Roberto further explained in his thick Italian accent. "It takes days to shape it and bring it to life. No other place in New York does that."

"That's why Bill Blass jackets cost what they cost," Michael added with a dramatic flair. "They outlast their customers."

I was completely in awe. That level of patience, rigor, and precision was something I'd never encountered before. I knew I could learn a lot here.

Then we made our way to the flou room. Compared with the tailoring room—home to structured and fitted tailored garments—the flou room is where all the softer, languid, and fluid pieces like dresses, evening wear, and blouses are made. The flou room was run by an incredibly chic Chinese American woman named Barbara, who oversaw a dozen seamstresses, each at her own station, making magic out of the most luscious silks. All the women wore white coats like their counterparts in the tailoring room, and each had her own sewing machine. Some were hand basting to hold the slippery silks in place before running through the machines, and others ran yards of delicate fabrics with two hands through the rapid-paced needling. The whirring of those machines matched my heartbeat. The trims and scraps in colorful silks and satins puddling on the sides of each seamstress reminded me of a Jackson Pollock painting, but softer, delicate, and lyrical. There were rows and rows of the most gorgeous fabrics, Taroni silks, duchesse satin, and silk chiffons in a symphony of colors.

Then I spotted what seemed like a stunning silk brocade fabric on the patternmaking table, various shades of the softest pinks and luscious reds so layered and rich, I had never seen anything so beautiful and intricate. The patternmaker saw me gawking, smiled, and nodded at me, gesturing to come closer. She lifted the pattern paper so I could see the detail in the embroidery.

"You can touch it," she said. "But, more importantly, also feel it."

She placed her hand on her heart to make her point. This was more than texture. It was emotional. As I ran my finger softly over that fabric, I was completely mesmerized by the intricate details, every inch hand embroidered in silk threads, layered with bugle beads, and then sewn with another layer of crystals in perfectly matching colors, meant to dance gently as the wearer moved. I could feel the play between its exquisite fragility and the strength in the fabric's structure. It was, again, a level of craftsmanship I had never seen before. Yet it reminded me of an old heirloom sari of my mother's that had been handed down to her by her great-grandmother. Delicate yet resilient and rich with history. This was no ordinary piece. It was a tapestry of art. It was breathtaking.

I thanked Barbara and the seamstresses, who had also come to Bill Blass from the best of the best high fashion houses: Chanel, Dior, Valentino, and Ungaro. As I walked through and watched these women of various ages and races turn fabric into art in real time, that Chanel dress in the Bond Street window popped into my mind.

"This was how that was made," I thought.

At Parsons, I'd learned the fundamentals of fashion—from design theory and concepts to basic sewing and garment construction. It was a rigorous process of looking at an inspiration, dissecting it, and then coming up with my own ideas about how to make something new.

At Bill Blass, I saw that I could elevate that learning into an art form. So when I was offered the job as design assistant, I said yes.

DESIGN ASSISTANT WAS A step back from my position at Cynthia Rowley, where I had worked my way up to associate designer, but this was couture at its finest. I was happy to downgrade to design assistant—as I imagined that I'd move up the ranks to associate designer, designer, senior designer, and finally to design director, Michael's title. Bill Blass was a prestigious house, and I wanted to be in the luxury space. This was my entrée.

I grew up in a very similar world of high society back home in Nepal and India. I was used to the type of people that Bill Blass dressed for galas and parties in America. Glamorous, wealthy, educated, often superficial but occasionally fun, and mostly secluded and out of touch with reality. They liked to mingle with their own kind. Bill Blass catered to the top 1 percent of American society. The company was similarly white—from the boardroom to our clients. Mr. Blass was a designer who dressed the First Ladies of the White House, like Barbara Bush and Nancy Reagan; to the first ladies of American society, including Babe Paley, Slim Keith, C.Z. Guest, and Lynn Wyatt; to the first ladies of the silver screen, like Elizabeth Taylor, Jane Fonda, and Faye Dunaway; to the first ladies of media, like Barbara Walters, Diane Sawyer, and so on. This was a slice of New York society and America that was not easily accessible to many who looked like me—queer and brown and Nepali—regardless of a similar upbringing.

I knew this would be the first brick I laid for the luxury brand I wanted to build someday. I knew that as a minority, to play in the luxury world where the rule books are written by the majority, I had to learn the rules first and fast. And there was no place better than Bill Blass. It was not only an honor to be working at one of the great American couture design houses but also an opportunity to learn from the back rooms with the tailors and the seamstresses. It was also a crash course in America. A certain segment of America that was not readily accessible to people like me. Bill Blass also agreed to take over sponsorship of my green card—so it was more than just an amazing job. It was my path to becoming an American citizen.

As DESIGN ASSISTANT MY job was to support Michael Vollbracht, however necessary. He would do sketches—of gowns, coats, blouses, skirts—and I'd bring them to the patternmaker and assist in draping with muslin on a mannequin to get an idea of what the drawing would look like as a three-dimensional garment. Those pieces of muslin were then used to create the paper pattern—which was a technical recipe, an unspoken language of symbols that was both mathematical and scientific. So many seamstresses are immigrants, often first-generation, for whom English is not their first language nor is it the means of communication in their daily lives. I'm still in awe about how a sketch becomes a three-dimensional piece of wearable art: I found the whole process romantic.

Once the pattern was made, I helped find the right fabrics for the piece. This was where I learned the difference between chiffon and silk, cashmere and wool. I started to see how and why different fabrics behaved in specific ways—how one draped this way or fluttered that way. The craftsmanship that went into building a jacket, dress, or gown was so precise and meticulous that some customers had blazers and jackets for more than three decades that still retained their shapes. I worked with the best of the best mills—in Italy and France—including Lesage, which Chanel now owns.

I had read about couture dresses costing north of $100,000 but had never seen what goes into making them. One of the first pieces I encountered was the most exquisite hand-embroidered jacket made from silk threads and thousands of bugle beads that, when hand stitched together, looked like the most intricate brocade. It cost $85,000 and was just one of many precious items that I saw being constructed in those rooms. Another piece that stands out was a chiffon gown, in an ombré of pastels, that began as twenty-five plus yards of fabric. It was cut on a bias, then hung for several days while the pieces took the desired shape. Only then was it meticulously hand basted and handsewn before being finished on the machine. All that fabric not only looked weightless on the wearer, it also made her appear as if she were floating on a diaphanous cloud.

The seamstresses were reserved with me at first, but they slowly started to open up. I was constantly asking questions: Why were they were cutting a fabric a certain way? What were they were thinking when they sewed a piece so perfectly? How did they have the patience? Did they meditate? Or get into a zone? Or was the sewing and basting the meditation? I was most intrigued by how they felt once they saw their finished creations on a client. Was it as wondrous for them as it was for me?

As a result, I spent most of my time in the flou room, watching in awe as the seamstresses worked. For someone who had left family behind in Nepal, finding home with these women was a blessing. They reminded me of my mother and sister, kind and gentle, but also tough. They had also come to America from different parts of the world to make a living, and each had a remarkable story. There was not one American-born seamstress in that room. They were Nigerian, Indian, Chinese, Korean, Spanish. Elona, who was in charge of quality control, was a Holocaust survivor. Her job was to check the garments before they were shipped to either stores or to clients to ensure that all these impeccable pieces adhered to the quality standards set by the house—flawless. The women would bring food for lunch and share it with me. It was my home away from home. In so many ways, we were all connected by this notion of the American dream. Our stories sounded similar, and so did our struggles. They were decades older than me, and I was so moved by their resilience and determination. It also reconfirmed my belief about women's strength—mostly uncelebrated but always unshakable.

IF PARSONS WAS MY foundation in fashion design, and Cynthia Rowley my MBA, Bill Blass was my PhD. I learned basic design tenets for a luxury line like "keep the money on the table"—meaning exquisite embroidery should be at the neckline, not the hem, so it can be seen at the lunch or dinner table. And yet, understated luxury was also very Bill Blass, so a wool coat could have the most luxurious silk lining, or a silk cape could be lined with fur. Through the sales team, I learned which stores matter (Saks, Barneys, and Bergdorf Goodman) and how trunk shows are their own economy, which made going from city to city (Palm Beach, Dallas) to sell to very specific high-net-worth clients valuable.

My desk was near the PR department, so I also got to see how important press was to the success of a brand. Anna Wintour and *Vogue* reigned supreme, as did dressing celebrities for premieres, magazines, and galas. As part of my job, I went to all the events that we dressed our clients for because Michael refused. Michael hated that part of his job, so I happily volunteered. I loved to go out on the town. This was how I met former First Lady Laura Bush and became close friends with her daughter Barbara, as Bill Blass dressed both women for the Snowflake Ball.

American high society reminded me of high society in India and Nepal in terms of wealth and class—the only marked difference was skin color and the type of gowns women wore. But what struck me was how myopic Americans were—they knew very little of the world beyond the United States and Europe, whereas the people I met in Asia's upper echelons were extremely cosmopolitan. The other thing I found fascinating was that for all this talk of feminism in America, these high-society women were as trapped by the patriarchy as those in Nepal and India. There was a stunning hypocrisy—this idea of independence felt like an American marketing ruse.

I was always one of the very few people of color at any of these events—and fully aware that my access was simply because of my position at Bill Blass and that two of my dearest friends—Barbara Bush and Maggie Betts—were also clients. Barbara had introduced me to Maggie, and we immediately hit it off. She was confident and cool, and one of the very few biracial woman I'd ever seen in high society. Her father, Roland Betts, was friends with George W. Bush, which was how she knew Barbara, and her mother, Lois, was one of the few Black socialites on the scene back then. Maggie invited me to dinner at a French restaurant on Lafayette Street, and on that first date, we became fast friends.

Bill Blass often sponsored tickets to galas, so I'd dress Barbara and Maggie and take them as my dates. For the Guggenheim gala one year, I dressed Barbara in a sparkly black dress and Maggie in a stunning black tuxedo. Robert Jonathan Barnes, a pseudo-socialite I knew from my Parsons days, was also there. When he saw me with my stunning dates, he said, "What are *you* doing here?" in a snide, surprised way.

"Maggie and Barbara invited me," I said, annoyed by his disdain, but not surprised. I never liked him.

But then Maggie corrected me. "That's not true!" she countered. "Prabal invited us! We are his dates."

I appreciated her sticking up for me, but Robert's comment flung me back to his twenty-first birthday, five years prior. A few of my Parsons friends had been invited to his party on the Upper West Side, so I tagged along. Barbara and Maggie were both there, though we had also not yet met, as was Jessie Silverstone, a Black socialite who had been adopted by a wealthy white family. Someone had put together a video montage for Robert where everyone was saying something about him for his birthday. I can't remember what Jessie had said in her tribute, only that Robert did not like it, as he stood up and yelled, "You fucking n——!"

I was stunned and immediately looked at Jessie—who was even more taken aback. But then I scanned the mostly white room and realized that no one else seemed to notice. Or, if they did, they didn't seem bothered. That was even more terrifying than the comment itself. I saw the hurt in Jessie's eyes and was about to say something but felt one of the friends that I'd come to the party with tug my hand—he was shaking his head no. I looked over at Jessie and saw that she kept quiet, too, as if it didn't happen. It was eerie.

I turned to my friend and said, "I have to go."

It was disturbing. But it was in line with the racism I encountered in these lily-white spaces, where people would say things like, "You're beautiful. I don't even think of you as Asian." Even more ridiculous was when whoever hurled the insult would follow it up with, "Oh, lighten up! You know I love Asians!" Or, "I love sushi!" Or, "I love Indian food!"

I cannot tell you how many times someone has said to me, "I'm normally not into Asians but you're attractive."

My response has always been, "Well, too bad I'm not into douchebags."

The surprise that I'd see on their face made me realize how clueless they were. Utter obliviousness is the privilege of being the majority. Encountering this kind of racism was a shock to me, as I'd come to this country with this delusion that it was founded on freedom for all. This was the heyday of Condé Nast, the company responsible for *Vogue*, *Glamour*, *WWD*, and *Vanity Fair*, all of which had dedicated socialite pages and society reporters, as did Hearst's *Elle*, *Marie Claire*, and *Harper's Bazaar.* It was a white haze of glory, glamour, and skinny blonde "it" girls, all celebrated in these pages, which gave the impression that the only way to succeed in the fashion world was to celebrate the white, Waspy, Eurocentric ideas of beauty. As one of the few brown people in the haute couture, luxury fashion space, I was also in a unique, and awkward, position as I witnessed this world as an outsider.

STILL, I HAD A lot of admiration for the women we dressed—many were strong and opinionated. And many were neglected by their husbands, so it was always helpful to have a handsome salesperson to make them feel good. This was the height of NY society galas and ladies who lunch. They dressed for one another and seemed stuck in a world of seeking approval or setting unrealistic goals.

At Bill Blass, we were catering to the richest of the rich. Our clients would come in and look at the clothes on the models and then charge them on multiple cards so their husbands would not catch them. Or they'd say, "I have a $50,000 allowance to spend this month—I still have another $30,000 to go!" Some would buy expensive coats and carry Hermès bags—and then would sell those bags and put the money in a private bank account. One woman in her eighties would come in and spend so much money on clothes she'd never wear, simply because she did not want her stepsons to get the money.

There was so much that was unsaid. No one talked about politics, and I was even more shocked at how many women and men in this moneyed world were secretly gay.

Bill Blass himself was a gay man from Indiana who designed clothing for the ultimate WASP. He never came out publicly, but everyone in the fashion world knew that he was gay. It was hardly a secret. There was so much passing going on in these ultrarich circles, which was something I simply could not do. I'm brown, clearly Asian, and very effeminate. I could not pretend to be anyone other than myself.

It blew my mind that in a city full of queer people of all races who were unapologetically out, these uptown galas and events were so blindingly white and uptight. There, whenever I stepped outside for a cigarette, I was inevitably hit on by some married white man, always a few drinks in. I slept with many of them—they'd either take me back to their apartment or pay for a hotel. After our tryst, each would say some variation of "let's keep this between us," "this is our secret," or "no one can know about this, to be clear."

By THEN, I HAD moved into my own apartment on Mulberry Street in Chinatown. I was making a good salary and had a company card, which I used for lunches and dinners. Damien was working in the fashion department at *Vanity Fair* and had moved to his own apartment in the East Village. We were living our best lives.

It was summer 2004 when Damien asked if I wanted to do a summer share in Fire Island.

"What's that?" I replied.

He explained that it was a weekend beach community for gay men an hour and a half outside the city.

"Sounds like heaven!" I said.

I mentioned it to Michael, who agreed. "It is a gay heaven, one of the very few places in the world where you can be sexually free."

I was even more intrigued to experience this fabled place!

We rented a large house in the Pines with five other friends, all of whom worked in fashion: Yuki was at *Harper's Bazaar* working as fashion editor Brana Wolf's assistant; Miguel was at *Details* magazine as a fashion editor; Adam was working at KCD, a major fashion publicity firm. Yuki, Miguel, Adam, and I had all bonded over being people of color in the fashion world. There were also two white men in our group: Dustin, who was at *WWD*, and Sam Spector, a freelance stylist.

We arrived by ferry that July, and as soon as I stepped onto the network of boardwalks, I was in awe: everywhere I looked, there were beautiful men, mostly wearing bathing suits, walking to the beach, barefoot, sun-kissed, sandy, holding hands, laughing. Interlaced in the salty air was a promise of maybe meeting your future lover.

On our first night, we all went to a bar for "tea," or the first cocktail of the evening. There, I saw Ken Brown, a friend from Parsons who was half-Asian but could pass as white. I was so happy to see a familiar face—until a thin-lipped white guy he was with named Ryan announced, "Oh, the gaysians are here!"

Ken was visibly embarrassed—as was I. I scanned the room and realized, yet again, my friends and I were the only brown people in the shockingly white scene. Sadly, Ken never hung out with us again that summer, but I did not let that get in the way of having fun. Still, whenever we would show up for tea, or any of the parties that took place that summer, someone would announce, "Oh, the fashion house has arrived!" often followed by a thinly veiled racist remark like, "Everyone is so tan!" "Did you forget the sunscreen, boys?"

I always shot back, "Wait a minute, did we just enter a Spam factory?"

I FOUND THE RACISM ridiculous but infuriating. It was everywhere—in my private and professional worlds alike. As was sexism. Both seemed to be profoundly American attributes—especially in fashion. This was the era of Russian models and skinny girls, and when I tried to cast Liya Kebede, a very talented Ethiopian model who looked stunning in Bill Blass clothes, for a runway show, management was dismissive. I asked Michael why we were not hiring her, and he said, "She's not quite right."

"Do you mean not white?" I responded.

I found out later that one of the owners didn't want Black models on the runway representing the brand. As a brown-skinned man, I knew what it meant to be invisible. But I also knew that it was possible to elevate beauty in all its versions, as Yves Saint Laurent had always done. He used Black and brown models on his runway in France. Why couldn't we do it in America?

Another young woman who came in for a fitting was clearly suffering from an eating disorder—she was so emaciated that you could see her skeletal frame beneath her skin, which was carpeted with hair that looked like peach fuzz, the body's attempt at insulation in the extreme stages of anorexia. I found it so disturbing that I called our casting director.

"We cannot use this girl," I said. "You need to call her agent. She clearly needs help."

"Oh, Prabal, please," he said with a laugh. "Stop being such a hero. Look at French *Vogue*, look at *V* magazine. All the coolest magazines have these girls on their covers or in editorial."

As upsetting as his response was, it was also true. Even I was becoming accustomed to the size preference of the fashion world. The industry liked emaciated models—the argument was that the clothes looked better on bodies that functioned as hangers. They wound up using that model, and I was branded a troublemaker. This reputation didn't help me when I finally complained to human resources that Michael Vollbracht was being verbally abusive and making unwanted sexual advances.

EVER SINCE I STARTED my job, Michael had avoided looking at my face whenever I asked him questions. He'd answer me as if he were talking to someone over my shoulder. It happened so often that I finally asked Jean Claude if Michael disliked me.

"Prabal, Michael doesn't look at you because he thinks you are way too beautiful," Jean Claude explained in his thick French accent.

I thought he was joking. But then, a few months into the job, Michael invited me to Patricia Field's Halloween party as his plus-one. I was excited—this was when *Sex and the City* was at its peak popularity and Patricia Field was the downtown doyenne who had become a household name as the series costume designer. Her Halloween party was legendary. It was at her loft on Bowery, just above Houston, and packed with characters from the downtown club scene. I went dressed as a football player, and there, sandwiched among throngs of people, Michael grabbed my ass and kissed me. I was so shocked that I froze up.

"I'm going to find the bathroom," I shouted above the chaotic din.

The crowded room felt more like a mosh pit as I made my way to the nearest exit, ping-ponging off people as they danced to the blaring music. All these memories—of Edon Richards, of those boys in high school, slamming me against bathroom walls and forcing themselves on me—were swimming in my head as I thrashed my way through the costumed characters and looked for the exit. The room was spinning, and I started sweating so much that I felt as if I might faint. Finally, I spotted the door.

Once on the street, I started running. My feelings toward Michael were primarily sympathy. He'd shared with me that he lost many dear friends to AIDS in the eighties. "Every time the phone rang," he said, "I was scared to answer because I knew that it was either a good friend who had tested positive, or someone calling me to say another friend had died."

That conversation haunted me.

He was especially angry about the Reagans and all the rich people who had the power and influence to slow the ravaging impact of that disease—and did not do more. Some of whom we now dressed at Blass. I understood his anger, but I also knew it wasn't going to get him, or me, anywhere. As horrible as his behavior was toward me, I felt sorry for him. Still, that did not make up for his abuse. Almost daily, he'd yell at me about something he thought I'd done incorrectly at work. And then, the next minute, he'd regale me with stories of his encounters with Elizabeth Taylor, Ava Gardner, and Joan Crawford in his heyday. In his youth, he was a very good-looking man who had left Kansas City to study at Parsons before going to work for Geoffrey Beene, where he hobnobbed with the most famous celebrities. And yet he lamented that high society never fully embraced him.

"Prabal, these rich people do not give a fuck about people like us," he'd say. "Especially a person like you! Gay and Asian? Forget about it. And the change you talk about—on the runway with diverse models—it will never happen. This industry does not give a shit about that."

I was constantly walking a delicate line of setting boundaries with him, and not wanting to be fired. Once, in the office, after I ignored another one of his advances, he hissed in my ear, "Where's the joy in your life? You just need a good fuck up your ass."

"No, Michael," I replied calmly. "What I need for you to do is back off so I can do the work that you aren't willing to do."

ONE YEAR INTO MY JOB, I finally got fed up and complained to human resources. Their response? Become closer to him. As if being nice to your tyrannical boss would solve the problem. It was a complicated situation, as I was waiting for my green card and Bill Blass was my sponsor. I felt stuck.

I also rationalized that I'd been through a lot worse, and I knew that I could handle it. So when Michael invited me back to his apartment one evening for a drink, I said yes.

He lived on Twenty-Third Street between Sixth and Seventh Avenues in a three-story carriage house. It was eclectically decorated with arts and artifacts, his own paintings, and towers of fashion and interiors books. It was a visually thrilling space, with knickknacks at every corner, but reeked of loneliness. He made me a drink and prepared some snacks for us to enjoy while we watched *Charade* starring Audrey Hepburn and Cary Grant. I was excited, as I knew Hubert de Givenchy had designed the costumes. The film was sublime, a study in fun fashion. Up until the moment the credits were appearing on the screen, it had been a perfect evening. Michael taught me so much about fashion, history, and films, and I was grateful for his tutelage.

But then, right when the film came to an end, he said, "Prabal, come join me in my bed."

I politely declined and watched as his face went from pleasant and longing to agitated and angry. The title music was still playing when he jumped up and slammed off the recording. He asked me one more time to come to bed, this time more forcefully.

I said no, and added, "Michael, I have respect for your talent and for your perseverance. You have taught me a lot—and I'm grateful. But this behavior must stop."

That was the end of the night but the beginning of an even more nightmarish time for me in the office. I stayed my course, defiant but not disrespectful. He did not like it, and kept looking for ways to challenge me. He hired a straight white man named Scott as design assistant, which was my title, and announced, "Prabal needs some competition."

I bit my tongue. By then, I was staying in the job only for my papers and for the women in the flou room. My fashion family. I believed in them and the clothes they were making.

CHAPTER EIGHT

I'd been at Bill Blass for almost three years and had done six collections with Michael Vollbracht when we learned, in December 2006, that the company was being sold for $70 million. The buyers, NexCen, were known for mass-market consumer products—they had also purchased the Athlete's Foot—and had no concept of fashion, let alone haute couture. The new execs would literally toss gorgeous gowns that took weeks to make around like they were bags of garbage. The way they handled these beautifully made clothes left my colleagues and me in complete shock. The only saving grace was Bob D'Loren, the new CEO, who seemed committed to making Blass a success. He was impressive. His team was not.

Soon after the acquisition, Bob asked for a meeting. I was still working as an assistant designer, and still waiting for my green card. My relationship with Michael had continued to deteriorate. On a good day, he would sulk, pout, or be passive-aggressive. On a bad day, he'd hurl words, or objects, at me. For a lot of people, this would have been severely traumatic, but I had faced this behavior throughout my life. In school, at home, and in the world. My sense of calm may have aggravated him even more. The other design team members he had hired "to put me in my place" were straight, white, and benign. Within less than a month, they always realized that I was not the villain Michael had depicted me to be, nor was he the monster. We were all pawns of this ever-demanding, hamster-wheeled fashion industry where one bad review could wipe out months of hard work.

Michael had faced this from the minute he arrived at Blass. While some of the criticisms were valid because his collections sometimes felt archaic, the way it was doled out to him was ruthless.

Bob wanted to know how it was going, and, in particular, why the design team was having so many issues with Michael. I was diplomatic in my answers, not mentioning Michael's volatile and erratic behavior, until I realized that Michael had told Bob that I was the problem. My survival instinct kicked in: I calmly delivered a blow-by-blow account of all the issues past, current, and in the inevitable future. Issues not just related to Michael but also to the entire management team, their mismanagement and lack of vision.

"What do you suggest?" Bob asked.

"Look for a courageous, talented new creative director who understands the modern, changing America and isn't afraid to tell that untold story," I said. "Invest in a few crucial areas—hire top-tier team members, marketing, and smooth the relationship with *Vogue*."

I saw Bob's face soften into surprise.

"I appreciate your candor," he said.

Soon after that, Michael was let go, and I learned that Bob had planned to fire me based on Michael's accusations. He changed his mind when he heard my side of the story.

Now came the big question: Who would be the next creative director? A lot of names were floated, like Proenza Schouler, Phillip Lim, Derek Lam, Thakoon, Thom Browne, Richard Chai, and Peter Som. All up-and-coming designers with their own fledgling brands who were several years ahead of me in the industry. I, too, aspired to have my own label one day—but had not ventured out on my own like they each had. So I was thrilled when Bob and the new CFO called me in for another meeting—to ask me what *I* would do as the creative director.

I had so many ideas, and such respect for the brand. I had also spent countless hours in the archives, soaking up Mr. Blass's elegant style, his point of view, his love of detail and structure. I understood that I was a wild card—and yet I also knew I could do the job better than any one of the others being considered. I knew the brand's DNA inside and out. I also believed the only way to move the brand forward was to go beyond the Upper East Side. The landscape was changing; stylish people no longer resided only on the Upper East Side. They were in the Meatpacking District, Tribeca, the Lower East Side, Brooklyn. I knew that I could connect both worlds with ease, as I had done all my life. I also knew the brand's heritage, its history, and its dedication to craftsmanship. I believed that we could reclaim its relevance—and I'd have the support of the design team as well as all the seamstresses and tailors. I wasn't arrogant enough to ask for the job—but when Bob and the head of PR and marketing asked me if I was up for the challenge, I said a calm and resolute yes.

Soon after, I was called back into Bob's office to discuss that possibility. He knew that I was loyal and that my heart was in the right place. He just wanted to make sure I was ready for the pressure that came with the position. I assured him that I was, and from that moment on, our meetings started with, "When Prabal becomes the creative director . . ."

One day, he added, "Prabal, you do have to get Anna's blessing."

I knew that was crucial—and that it was up to me to get a meeting with her.

"Does she even know who you are?" Damien asked later that night when we all met up for drinks. She did not.

I had met her a few years prior at the screening of the documentary *Seamless*, which focused on a competition that the Council of Fashion Designers in America (CFDA) and *Vogue* had set up post-9/11 to help emerging designers. It was a moving, poignant story about a group of young designers struggling to launch their own lines. At the postshow screening party, I saw Anna across the room, getting ready to leave. I was with Damien, as well as Victor, Hanuk, and Treena, new friends who also worked for Condé Nast magazines. When I announced that I was going to tell her how much I enjoyed the film, which she had produced, they all jumped as if I had given them an electric shock.

"Are you fucking crazy? Why would you want to talk to *the* Anna?" Hanuk said.

"You can't just walk up to her!" Brian exclaimed.

"Protocol!" Treena chimed in, exasperated by my boldness.

But the documentary made me feel seen and gave me hope that perhaps I, too, could make it as a designer, one day. As I watched the closing titles, I thought, "This was why I came to America."

For the first time, I saw a glimmer of hope as to how it could happen for me. I gulped down my vodka soda and walked toward her.

She was putting on her jacket when I said, "Excuse me, Anna?"

She turned around and looked at me with a gentle smile. She seemed genuinely curious as to what I had to say.

I told her how much I'd loved the documentary and the work *Vogue* and the CFDA was doing to support young designers.

"It gives me hope," I explained.

"You should apply for the competition next year," she said.

"One day I will," I responded. "Right now, I'm working."

"Where?" she asked.

"Bill Blass," I said.

"Good luck there," she said. "I hope you do something on your own. Very soon."

"Me too," I said. "Perhaps I'll be ready in a few years."

"You seem confident," she replied. "You will know when it's your time."

"It's a dream of mine to launch my own brand someday," I blurted out. "I came from Nepal with that dream."

She looked me straight in the eye and said, "Then don't let anything stop you."

With that, she walked away.

When I returned to my friends, they all wanted to know, "What did you say?"

I told them that I expressed my gratitude to her—but I did not tell them the dream part. I wanted to keep that to myself.

Now, three years later, I had a reason to meet Anna. But getting a meeting with her was a daunting task. Why would she make time to meet me, an assistant designer at a troubled fashion house? And what was I going to say? All these paralyzing, self-sabotaging thoughts started to surface. Fortunately, by now I was practiced in quieting my mind. I asked myself, "What's the worst-case scenario?" *Vogue* will say no to the meeting. Or perhaps, if I meet with her, Anna might say no to my becoming the creative director of Bill Blass. I could live with those rejections. I had to try. It was the beginning of the future that I had dreamed of.

Damien's coworker at *Vanity Fair* was Alexis Bryan, a beautiful, smart, and funny woman who had a direct line to Anna. I shared my plight with her, and, the very next day, I had an appointment at *Vogue*. There was hardly time to be nervous! I wanted to get this right. For the tailors, seamstresses, and everyone in the back room who had been rooting for me. For my design team, who knew what I had endured with Michael. And for my friends, who had heard the endless stories. Above all, for myself, to prove that I could indeed do this. I wanted to impress Anna and everyone at *Vogue*. I wanted to take Bill Blass to the future.

I woke up that morning, had my coffee, called my mother, who wished me well, and then got dressed in a dove-gray wool suit, crisp white shirt, and a slim gray tie with black leather shoes—not my usual dress, but what I imagined the world thought Bill Blass's creative director should wear. As I walked into her office, Anna got up from her desk to greet me and said, "Prabal, nice to meet you."

I knew better than to remind her of the time we first met at the *Seamless* premiere. I was always hopeful, but not arrogant or delusional. I knew I could do amazing things as the creative director for Bill Blass—I just needed to convince her. I told her my whole story, starting with Nepal. I knew the odds were against me, but the fact that she even took the time to meet with me felt huge. As I got up to leave, she said, "Prabal, just keep doing what you are doing. It's okay to wait for your moment."

I was not sure how to interpret that, so I simply thanked her for her time.

THE MORE I THOUGHT about the future of Bill Blass, the more confident I was. Bob asked for a proposal. "Bill Blass is American luxury—but it's a changing world," I wrote. "The geographical demarcation between Upper East Side and Lower East Side is getting smaller and I want to represent that."

I was setting myself up to reinstate Bill Blass to its former glory. So when I saw the designer Richard Chai come into the office one day, followed by Thakoon, I was deflated. Jean Claude assured me that they were just going through the motions. The following week, I was called into a company-wide meeting at the NexCen headquarters to discuss the transition. I was excited. This was the moment I'd been waiting for. Bob was there, as were several board members, our CFO, and the PR team, including Caitlin, who was our liaison at Paul Wilmot, a big PR company that had been hired to do the announcement. She and I had become good friends. Her boss Paul was there, too.

After everyone took their seats around the conference room table, Paul asked, "So, when are we announcing Peter Som?"

A wave of humiliation washed over me. As I scanned the faces around that table, it was clear that everyone knew—but me. I felt nauseated, almost seasick, like the whole floor beneath me had become a stormy ocean. I felt my palms getting sweaty and the tears behind my eyes. I repeated my mantra, "Grace under pressure," several times in my head before switching to "Don't cry."

I had believed them when they said the job was mine. I trusted that they were telling me the truth. Once again, I had let my guard down.

Caitlin was sitting next to me. I knew if I looked at her, I would burst into tears. Did she know, too? If so, how could she keep this from me? I stayed composed through the meeting, but as soon as it was over, I fled the building, hailed a cab, and then finally, in the back of that yellow taxi, I began to sob. And all I could think was, "When am I ever going to be good enough?"

When I was finally able to pull myself together, I went back to the office to pack up my things. That was it. I had to quit. Nothing else made sense.

Meanwhile, my phone was ringing nonstop—I knew it was Jean Claude calling. I did not pick up. Next thing I knew, he and the vice president were in my office. They apologized and said it was top secret—they had wanted to tell me but couldn't. No one but they and Paul knew. They also blamed it on *Vogue*.

"They thought you were too green," Bob said.

"So why didn't you guys just tell me that?"

He just shrugged his shoulders and looked at me apologetically.

THAT NIGHT, I DEBATED what to do. As much as I wanted to call my mother for advice, I was too upset to admit yet another story of my failing. And the truth was that even though I wanted to quit, I knew it was a bad idea—I was still waiting for my green card. If I left, I would no longer be eligible unless I found another sponsor. I'd dedicated five years to Bill Blass and had such high hopes of where I could take the brand. I had begun to imagine what I would do at the helm, and it was so exciting. This news was like being pushed off a peak. I fell hard. And while it was painful, I knew it was neither the end nor the beginning of me. I reminded myself that I was used to rejection, and I turned to my old mantra: "Something good will come of this."

My mother had taught me how to persevere through difficult moments with grace and grit. To not become a victim, but instead make the most of a situation. The following day, I went back to work and announced, "The only way I'll stay is if my title becomes design director," I said. "And you triple my salary."

They agreed to it immediately. They couldn't afford to lose me, so I had the upper hand. No one was sure if Peter Som would be the right fit. And they knew my loyalty to the brand. I saw this on their faces as I was making my demands.

"And, I want you to make the announcement in *Women's Wear Daily* when you're making the Peter Som announcement," I added. "You have one day to think about it—otherwise I'm going to leave."

They looked surprised and shocked.

"I'm not sure we can make that work," one of them said.

"Either make it work, or I am out," was my response.

The next day, the president said, "We can give you the salary, but Peter Som's team is saying no to the design director title, and no to the announcement in *WWD*."

"Okay, I'm leaving then," I said.

A few days later, there was an announcement in *WWD* that said Peter Som was the new creative director and Prabal Gurung was staying as the design director.

Nothing was going to come easy for me. And yet, nothing was impossible.

I WOUND UP DESIGNING the first collection as Peter Som was just starting and needed time to acclimate. I decided to use the frivolous, irresponsible Daisy

Buchanan as my muse. She was the opposite of the women I loved. I wanted to hold a mirror up to what I saw happening at that moment in fashion: skinny white girls in pretty party dresses. This was 2007, a time when socialites like Paris Hilton and Lauren Santo Domingo were as famous as any Hollywood celebrity. *Vogue* had a page that celebrated whomever they decided was the current "It Girl," and the website Socialite Rank rated socialites based on the number of parties they'd attended and what they wore. To me, Tinsley Mortimer was the modern Daisy Buchanan. And so I decided to present to the very white world of Bill Blass a runway filled with one skinny white girl after another. That was the world we were living in—and celebrating. It was my tongue-in-cheek way of critiquing the fact that everywhere you looked—in magazines and on television—being blond, thin, and rich was considered beautiful. I found it all so limiting. I wanted a collection that magnified that to an extreme. I wondered if anyone else would even notice.

I sent twenty white, skinny models down the runway with the same long blond hair, curled at the bottom. Very *Stepford Wives*, curious to see if anyone would notice the homogeny, or dare to ask the question, "Is there more than this?"

In all of the reviews, there was no remark on the celebration of whiteness. And while barely noticed by the press, who were waiting for Peter Som to make his mark, this collection sold well in stores.

On his first day at the office, a woman from Peter Som's office arrived before he did. Jane was a petite brunette with a very Long Island accent and gruff voice. She was arrogant and self-important, which I didn't necessarily mind until she took off her jacket and threw it toward me, expecting me to hang it for her.

I simply gave it back to her and said, "There's the hook. You can hang it yourself."

Jane glared at me, and I returned her gaze steadily. I was not going to be intimidated. That set the tone immediately with her.

I GOT THE SENSE that Peter and his team were not thrilled about my being there. He was not a screamer like Michael, but he would make cutting comments about how Bill Blass clothes were "old." I swallowed my pride and did what was right for the company—which meant supporting him and his vision for Bill Blass.

The new owners wanted someone to please their white audience and cater to their established customers, which was why they hired Peter. I kept thinking of all the customers they were ignoring. Peter colored within the lines and honored the Waspy Bill Blass tradition. His first collection got good reviews. People liked that the change wasn't too radical. Celebrities started to wear the clothes, but there wasn't enough time. The losses were simply too great to make up.

Peter was designing the next pre-fall show for 2009 when the company started to sell the archives to make money. They were selling all the pieces that Mr. Blass had made over his lifetime—to private clients, in public sample sales, and to vintage stores.

People said, "It is just clothes! What is the big deal?"

Selling the archives is like giving your family heirlooms to strangers. This was the brand's history, the foundation, the backbone. Every single piece in the archives had a story—not just of the fashion, but who wore it, when, and to what historical event. Some of these pieces were made by the women and men who were still working there. It was heartbreaking. The women in the flou room were in tears. It was a nonstop funeral, the beginning of the longest, most painful death. There were rumors that we were going to close, but we kept showing up at the office waiting for that dreadful moment.

One cold, rainy spring day, we had just presented the new collection to the buyers at Bergdorf Goodman, and the reaction was a polite nonchalance. I could read between the lines. They didn't like it. I braced myself for the finger-pointing that would inevitably follow. The design team would get the blame for the lackluster reaction. If it was a great collection, the creative director would get the praise. If it was not well received, we'd be in the line of fire. I kept my cool, always—I was the one who had to relay the news to the design team. But first, I needed some fresh air. As I pressed the elevator button, I felt the exhaustion hit me. I was worn out by all the infighting and frustrated that no one could see the limitless possibilities of a brand like Blass.

I also had no idea what to do next. It was June 2008. I had finally gotten my green card in late 2007, and was free, at long last, to look elsewhere for employment. Unfortunately, it was now the height of the recession. I was meeting with headhunters but the feedback I was getting was a mix of:

"He's not the right fit."

"He's not talented enough."

"He doesn't understand America."

As the elevator made its way down, I could feel everything weighing on me.

The rain was steady, and I sought refuge beneath the scaffolding outside 550 Seventh Avenue. Eight years had passed since I first stepped foot in that building. I had learned so much about the fashion industry and the craft itself, and knew that I had more to offer. It sickened me that Mr. Blass's legacy was under threat. As I lit a cigarette, a few rogue raindrops splashed on my face.

Midtown just south of Times Square was always a jam-packed hustle of people coming and going. The honking and yelling added another layer to the intense loneliness I was feeling. I wanted Bill Blass to succeed so badly that I had put my own personal life on hold, and I sensed that the end of Bill Blass, or at least my time there, was imminent. I was lost in these thoughts when I heard a familiar voice say, "Are you okay, honey?"

It was Roopal Patel, one of the fashion directors at Bergdorf Goodman who had just come out of the appointment at Blass. Our paths had crossed during these sales meetings, fashion shows, and at some New York charity galas. I remembered the moment I first laid eyes on her: a woman of Indian descent who grew up in America. She was eloquent, soft-spoken but concise. We were at an uptown charity gala for New Yorkers for Children, which she was cohosting, and I marveled at how graceful she was—a beautiful brown woman in an elegant, ruched gown with a long train. Roopal's ease at navigating this uptown, utterly white world struck me. While we were not close friends, she always acknowledged me even though I was not the main lead at Bill Blass—most buyers focus their attention on the creative director. I was very fond of her—which was why I decided to tell her the truth.

"No, I'm not!" I blurted out.

I shared my struggles at Blass, and how frustrated I was with the management for not having the vision to take it to the next level when I could see such a clear path. I told her about my impossible bosses, the challenges we were all facing internally, and how I could not seem to land another job anywhere. This was perhaps one of the very few rare moments where I was vulnerable and open with someone who was not a close friend or trusted ally. But somehow in her I found comfort. Maybe it had to do with our shared background, or maybe she reminded me of the women in my family. Whatever it was, I bared my soul to her that day.

"I'll ask around about jobs at other places but a real question to you," she said with a very serious but kind expression, "Have you ever thought about starting your own brand?"

I looked at her quizzically.

"I'm serious," she said. "Start your own thing. You're talented and charismatic. You have what it takes to make it. So go for it."

I was so moved that I couldn't respond. This made her smile.

"And when you are ready, I'll take a look," she said. "I cannot promise anything, but I will definitely be there for you."

I mumbled words of gratitude. After we parted, her words stayed with me. Starting my own brand was of course the dream—but one I imagined would take a few more years. It was the beginning of the recession, the worst time to launch anything new. But then again, I had nothing to lose.

CHAPTER NINE

Bill Blass's last collection, Peter's third, was presented in June 2008—but it was too late. The company was hemorrhaging money and, once again, up for sale. Peter left, and I spent that summer interviewing for positions I did not get. Some colleagues found new jobs, others decided to retire early—or leave New York entirely. There were tearful long goodbyes and promises of "see you soon," though we all knew that was lip service.

Everyone in the industry was abuzz about Bill Blass and his legacy. Our massive office space began to feel more and more like a morgue. The once buzzing corridors were now silent. Every so often, there were rumors about another possible buyer, and those of us left would think, "Maybe there's hope after all?" There were a few seamstresses remaining, there for the clients we still had, and I decided to maintain the attitude that things were going to work out. The job market was dismal, and I felt I owed it to the company that had sponsored my green card.

Rather than sitting around worrying, I began to design a collection. I wasn't sure if it would be for Bill Blass, or perhaps for my own line. I began playing with this idea: if no one would hire me, I could become my own boss. My attitude was, "Do I become a victim of my situation? Or do I do what makes me happy?"

As a kid, I derived joy from dressing up in my sister's and mother's clothes. In school, it was sketching. Now, I played with fabric. I was in the design studio when I started draping a striped, two-toned red silk duchesse satin made by Taroni, an Italian company founded in 1880, on a mannequin. The fabric reminded me of saris back home. Playing with fabric, imagining what it could become, was the only way for me to shut out the outside chatter and noise. That solitude—me, fabric, and my ideas—was my therapy. As I was working, that red silk started to come to life: as a knee-length, asymmetrical dress with a sculpted bow on one shoulder. I stepped back to look—and was wowed by its elegant simplicity and daring.

"This is the beginning of something," I thought.

That dress made me realize, ten years after arriving in New York, that I was ready to launch my own label. I felt energized. Hopeful. Even excited. This was why I came to America. I did not know that was possible as a child back in Nepal—but I found a way to express my creativity, through fashion, in New York. This magic making on a mannequin was what I'd been searching for. And I refused to give up on my dreams, or on my mother, who had supported them from the beginning. I also could not give up on that scrawny, six-year-old self who had so often felt so alone but somehow mustered the strength to survive and thrive.

Later that evening, I met up with my old Parsons pals, Damien, Shaun, and Sam, as well as new friends from the fashion industry, Brian, Victor, and Hanuk. We were all in our late twenties, on the ascent in our careers. Over drinks, we poured our hearts out to one another about how we did not know what our futures would hold. We all came to New York to make our dreams come true. What would happen? Who among us would become the next editor in chief at *Vogue*? Or run their own fashion line? Become a stylist to celebrities? We never spoke about love or finding a partner—we were all focused on our careers.

"I'm thinking of starting my own line," I announced that evening.

"Do it," they all said, raising their glasses.

Afterward, I started to walk home toward Chinatown, lost in these thoughts. I had designed a few other pieces in the studio that were promising—and I was excited to go back to work the next day, to keep draping and dreaming.

It was close to midnight, and the soundtrack of New York—horns blaring, trucks hissing, subway steaming—was on full blast. Right on the corner of Houston and Wooster, I ran into Ashish Singh, a classmate of mine from St. Xavier's Godavari. He came to New York for his business degree and got an investment banking job on Wall Street. Though he and I were never close, I felt proud and happy for him. I feel that way about anyone from Nepal, as any individual's success was a collective win for us all.

When Ashish first arrived in New York, we hung out here and there, but then he changed his name to Ash and developed a finance bro swagger. He was trying to blend in. One night, he invited me to dinner at his home with a mostly Nepali group. I was chatting with a woman who clearly had a crush on him, and when she found out he and I went to St. Xavier's, she said, "Oh my god, you guys are *so* different."

Then she asked me for the seventh time, "And you work in the fashion industry?" I nodded yes, annoyed. "You know, a friend of mine was a teacher in St. Xavier's Godavari," she continued. "Edon Richards, do you remember him?"

I froze. Right at that moment, Ashish joined the conversation and said, "Oh yes, Edon, he was great."

Shocked, I said, "You know Edon Richards was problematic, right?"

Ashish patted my back and said, "Oh, come on. . . ."

And when I was about to explain how so, this girl dismissively said, "Oh, please, we don't want to hear about it."

Soon thereafter, everyone decided to go out dancing. As we were getting ready to leave, I overheard another finance bro, Suresh, say to Ashish,

"Oh, dude, I don't want to go where that faggot is going. I hope he's not coming with us."

Ashish just laughed, and I realized that he never stood up for me. I went home and started to distance myself from him. No animosity, no anger or hard feelings, just disappointment.

That was almost eight years ago, so when I ran into Ashish that evening, I was just happy to see him. We hugged each other and started to walk down the street together. He told me about his achievements since I last saw him.

"Wow, I'm so proud of you," I said. "You really did it, Ashish. This is so inspiring. Congratulations!"

"Thank you, Prabal," he replied. "That means a lot. I came from Nepal and, dude, I'm living in New York, making tons of money. I'm a catch, you know I am."

We both started to laugh. I shared with him my recent experience with Blass and how I was thinking of starting my own brand. He stopped, looked at me incredulously, and said, "Prabal, when was the last time that a guy from Nepal came to New York and made it as a fashion designer? When? Can you tell me?"

I was thrown off by his tone, but responded calmly, "There hasn't been one for sure. But I will change that."

"What makes you think *you* will make it in this competitive, dog-eat-dog city? Who is going to buy Prabal Gurung clothes? Have you thought carefully about it?"

"If all I did was think, Ashish, I would still be in Nepal," I said. "I came here because I wanted to become a fashion designer. I wanted to make a name for myself, and I want to pursue that. Is it hard for you to believe that perhaps, just maybe, I could make it?"

"Prabal," he said. "Do you even know what it takes to make it in this city? It's connection and more importantly money. Tons and tons of money. Find another job or maybe go back to Nepal. It might be possible there since you know people and you have a family. But honestly, I just cannot imagine Ralph Lauren, Calvin Klein, Donna Karan . . . and, um, Prabal Gurung? I just don't see it happening."

His sarcastic callousness stunned me, but I didn't show it. Then he looked at me and said, "You seriously think that you will have a name like that on a store?" We were now on the corner of Wooster and Spring in Soho, and he was pointing at Chanel.

I looked at him and just smiled. I didn't say a word but knew that was a sign: I would start my own brand and call it Prabal Gurung.

THAT FALL, I WAS relieved to learn that Bill Blass had finally been bought by a Korean tie company. They were going to shut down the couture and ready-to-wear sections and reestablish the brand at a mass-market price point—which had also happened to Geoffrey Beene and Halston. Selling very expensive couture to a handful of people was not sustainable—whereas selling jeans, T-shirts, bags, or perfume to millions was big money. It was disappointing, but at least Mr. Blass's name would live on. Maybe not in the way he had envisioned it, but forward, nonetheless.

As I packed up my office, I selected some old patterns that were otherwise being thrown away, as well as Bill Blass's vintage whiskey flask and his Rolodex with the who's who of New York society in his heyday written on small index cards in perfect penmanship. All the fabric was being sold to jobbers—people who buy extra fabric, dirt cheap, and sell it at places like Mood Fabrics and other stores in the Garment District. I asked Bob if I could buy some of my personal favorites—he insisted that I take them for free. By then, I had already designed that one-shouldered dress, and a dozen other looks as well. I took the rest of the Taroni red on red silk duchesse satin, and another bolt of ivory silk with a black border, as well as camel, black, and navy-colored double-faced cashmere, the color scheme for my first collection.

The hardest goodbyes were to the seamstresses and the tailors, some of whom had been there since the company's inception. They had helped me make each of the outfits I would go out into the world with, on my own. And I felt ready—because of them. I learned more about couture from them than anyone and am forever grateful.

I WAS STILL LIVING in Chinatown, paying $5,000 a month for a three-bedroom apartment with a backyard, and had grown accustomed to town cars and expensive meals out. It was a lifestyle I could no longer afford. That November 2008, I moved into a tiny studio in the East Village, on the ground floor on Third Street between First and Avenue A, right in front of the Hells Angels. It cost $1,250 a month. Damien lived on the second floor. I had $20,000 in savings and immediately signed up for unemployment, which I used to hire Tyler Rose, my assistant at Bill Blass. He was a sweet, hardworking, and talented kid.

My new space was so tiny that I'd wake up from bed, stretch my arms, and touch the refrigerator. I bought a bookshelf from Ikea to separate the bedroom from the living area and used the kitchen table as my desk. I still had a gym membership through Bill Blass so I would wake up, make coffee, go to the gym, shower, and then come back to "my office," where Tyler would meet me. I'd sketch, and he would tape the best designs to the whiteboard we installed on the wall. He also helped source fabric samples and embellishments. We set up two dress racks in the living room, and Tyler would take samples back and forth to our beloved tailors and seamstresses who had set up their own small shops in midtown. The collection started to take shape.

My friend Dustin came over often to see the progression and that same afternoon offered to help produce and cast the show. He also suggested that we reach out to Caitlin to do the PR. She had left Paul Wilmot and was doing her own thing. So I sent her a picture of the red dress, to pique her interest, and she came to meet me in my apartment the next day.

"I'm in," she said.

Once I knew Caitlin would handle the press and communications, I could breathe. With her, Dustin, and Tyler on board, my dream was becoming a reality. Caitlin put me on the fashion calendar, which was the bible in the fashion world, and how all the editors knew what to expect at fashion week. It was late November 2008, and we planned on presenting the first Prabal Gurung collection in February 2009.

While I admired what other designers were doing, I felt there was a story that was not yet being told. There were contemporary price point designers—like Rachel Comey, Alexander Wang, and Phillip Lim—who sell a T-shirt for $80, a pair of jeans for $200, or a dress for $400. And then there were Oscar de la Renta and Carolina Herrera, who made $10,000 gowns or $6,000 suits. The former dressed the downtown kids, the latter the ladies who lunch and go to galas. One was street, the other uptown chic. I wanted to launch an American luxury line that connected the two and addressed the void I saw at Bill Blass between style and substance. Back then, if a woman cared about clothes, she was considered superficial, ditzy. I knew that this was simply untrue—beginning with my mother, my sister, all the way to Anu, Koel, Maggie, and Barbara.

I called my first collection "A Thinking Man's Sex Symbol," where "East Meets West, Style Is Substance." The clothes I designed were proof that dichotomies can coexist and can defy expectations. They were very much a combination of Mr. Blass and me—I couldn't really escape it. The epitome of luxury American sportswear—understated but refined. The palette for my first collection was black, white, beige, and gray, as well as cobalt and crimson, very much inspired by the Newa people of Nepal, who live in the Kathmandu Valley. They have held on to their roots and are known for their artistry. Plus, Kumudini had married Rajesh, who was Newa, and in some ways this first collection was an homage to him, her, and my mother.

Once I had completed nineteen looks that I felt were strong, I needed to find a stylist who could help me present each look. A professional tastemaker who could help me decide that one look would be chicer with flats, whereas another might need a stiletto. So many decisions go into a presentation: A chignon? Messy long curls? Red lipstick? Or black? Shimmery makeup? Or matte? Which model for which dress? Styling a collection is an arduous process from the tips of your toenails to the top of your head.

In mid-December, Tiina Laakkonen reached out to check in on me. I met her through Peter Som, as he brought her to Bill Blass to style his collections. She had worked with Karl Lagerfeld at Chanel and had impeccable taste. I loved working with her at Bill Blass and was delighted when she invited me to her favorite Japanese restaurant, Omen Azen, in Soho for dinner. There, over sushi and sake, I told her about my collection and watched her eyes sparkle as she asked me questions about the launch and delighted in my answers.

"Basically, it is a celebration of style and substance," I said finally.

"I'll help you," she said.

"Tiina, I don't have money to pay you," I explained.

By this time, I had spent all my savings—and was literally going on dates to get free dinner. The seamstresses from Blass who helped me make the pieces said it was their gift to me. I wanted to pay them back but had run out of money. Their generosity, love, and belief in me were the only reasons those samples came to life.

"I'll do it for free," Tiina said. "I don't even know what you're creating, but I believe in you."

Tiina was one of the most prominent stylists working at that time. She had worked with *British Vogue*, *Vogue*, *The New York Times*, and countless other publications. She was styling Bottega Veneta, one of the most successful and tasteful brands at the time, and was known for her impeccable taste and uncompromising point of view. Her belief in me gave me the encouragement to really push myself.

Once Tiina signed on, everything started to happen in rapid speed.

Damien was still at *Vanity Fair*, which meant he left for work at 9:00 a.m.—so he let us use his apartment to style the collection: we had two racks of clothes and one pair of shoes and a fit model who was Tyler's friend. We worked, putting together looks—Belted? Stilettos? Hoop earrings? Nude lip?—then we would take a Polaroid of the final look and tape it to the wall downstairs in my studio. After three days, Tiina and I were looking at the entire collection, a series of Polaroids, when she looked at me, smiled, and said, "It's incredibly chic."

She was not the only angel to appear in my life. When Bill Blass was closing, I met one of his clients, Amanda Fuhrman, at a sample sale, where she wound up buying several pieces that I had personally designed. We kept in touch, and in January 2009 she reached out to ask, "What are you up to these days?"

She invited me to have a drink with her fiancé, Glenn, and over a glass of wine, I shared the painful demise of Blass. When I finished, she asked, "What's next for you?"

I told her about my journey from Nepal to this moment, launching my own line.

Her eyes lit up.

"How wonderful!" she exclaimed. "Where will you show?"

That was one piece I had not yet figured out.

"I'm still looking for spaces," I said. "Perhaps a restaurant? I really don't know yet."

"Glenn has an art gallery," she said. "Why don't you just do it there?"

Things were falling into place. Now that we had a space, the FLAG Art Foundation in Chelsea, we needed press, so Caitlin and I reached out to my friend Adam, who was working at KCD, which specializes in fashion. Everyone there knew me from Bill Blass, and they were all willing to help. I contacted MAC for cosmetics—and the company generously offered to sponsor the show. Then Bumble and Bumble agreed to do hair. And because I had a relationship with Manolo Blahnik at Blass, they loaned us shoes. It was all about relationships and trust. The glorious thing about the New York fashion scene is that when you get the right person on board, everything falls into place. I had Tiina, and then KCD. The stars were aligning.

My friend Sam let us use his apartment for castings, and the great James Scully, a casting director I had worked with at Bill Blass, agreed to cast my show. He had worked with Tom Ford and Stella McCartney, and his influence was crucial. Slowly and surely, I pieced together the most important players in each respective field from PR to styling to casting to hair and makeup. It was all word of mouth, friends coming together, a belief in each other and in me. It was also what New York celebrates—humanity, ambition, and grace.

WHAT I HAD IMAGINED all my life was slowly coming to fruition—it was thrilling but also terrifying. Could a boy from Nepal with a new take on American luxury even have a chance in a market monopolized by predominantly white designers? To stay positive, I hyped myself up. I repeated my mantras. I had draped fabric and sketched dreams and turned them into small miracles that began to fill my studio, one dress, one jacket, one blouse at a time. I've always been my own self-motivator—this time was no different. I also thought, "Worse comes to worst, I can always work at a restaurant."

By then, so many people had come on board to help me that I didn't want to let anyone down. I knew what I had created was good. It had a perspective. But would it resonate? Tiina gave me so much confidence. After we put the finishing touches on the presentation, she said, "I think you should have Cathy Horyn look at it."

Cathy was the fashion critic for *The New York Times*, known for her formidable and often brutal point of view. In those days, her review could launch, or ruin, a designer.

Meanwhile, I was completely broke. My unemployment checks barely covered Tyler's salary. I was bringing home leftovers from my dinner dates to have for breakfast. I wasn't selling my body for sex—not that there's anything wrong with that—but my head was entirely into launching this collection. No distractions. I also never asked any of my friends, or my mom, for money. I wanted to do this on my own.

Plus, I had Caitlin. She was able to get Eric Wilson, who also wrote for *The New York Times*, to come to my apartment to see the presentation. All the looks were hanging on the two racks, the Polaroids taped neatly to the wall. I was nervous, but there was still a small part of me that felt my designs might resonate with him. Perhaps it was my wishful thinking.

After I walked him through the collection, explaining my philosophy and inspiration, he said, "I'm going to let Cathy know about you."

And then, right before he walked out the door, he said, "Do yourself a favor and don't bring anyone else here."

I looked around at the apartment and understood. While I had cleaned the apartment as much as I could, it was still a tiny hole-in-the-wall studio, the antithesis of luxury. The cream-colored front door was covered with scuff marks, the foyer reeked of mold and rust, and the once ivory wall-to-wall carpeting in the hallway had turned gray over the years. I shuddered to think that I had also shown the collection to Lauren Santo Domingo, a contributing editor at *Vogue* and swan of the Upper East Side social scene, whom I'd met at Bill Blass. She showed up in a Zipcar the day before and tried on several things in my tiny studio.

"Darling. It's fucking fabulous," she said. "Anna's going to love it."

I heaved a sigh of relief. Everyone knew that if Anna Wintour liked your collection, then doors would open for you. Meanwhile, I was talking to my brother, sister, and mother daily, sharing all the details of this heady time. They were all so excited for me.

"It is finally happening," Kumudini said. "And I'm coming to see it!"

"What?" I may have even screamed with excitement.

"When you left Nepal, you said, 'Don't come for my graduation, come for my first show,'" she reminded me. "We made a pact. I haven't forgotten."

Knowing she'd be there meant the world. She was my rock.

Oprah Winfrey was also part of my daily routine. I watched her show religiously, recording it if I could not be home in time. That was another form of therapy. She made me a better person. I intuitively knew my worth and what I was capable of, but when you're constantly told you're worthless, you start to believe it.

Ever since I had arrived in New York, there was an overwhelming feeling that I did not fit into the fashion world, nor could I ever be part of high society. Not belonging was my life's theme. Oprah did several shows on intention and believing in yourself that impacted me. I still had to give myself daily pep talks to convince myself that my clothes would find a place in the luxury space. Oprah helped me hone this practice: finding and trusting that inner confidence is always the biggest obstacle.

THREE NIGHTS BEFORE THE DEBUT, I was struggling to do just that. I was alone, curled up in a ball in my studio apartment, panicked. What if those headhunters were right? What if I had no talent? What if no one came? Or if those who did were not impressed?

And then I got a text from my mother. "Are you free to talk?"

This was strange—we always spoke in the morning. Worried something was wrong, I put my own insecurities aside and called her immediately.

"Mami, is everything okay?" I said as soon as I heard her voice on the other end of the line.

"What is this I have been hearing?" she asked.

"About what?" I said, confused.

"That you are gay?"

My heart stopped beating and my breath slowed down.

"Who told you this?" I asked, not defensively, more surprised.

"That does not matter—what matters is that someone told me—and it wasn't you."

She was not angry, more hurt. I realized that by trying to protect her from my own truth, I had kept a secret from the person who loved me the most.

"Mami, it is true," I said quietly. "And it is also true that I should have told you. I am so sorry."

She had no time for apologies—just questions.

"Do you have a boyfriend? Are you in love?" she asked.

"Not yet," I said. "But I do hope to find love one day."

There was a brief silence. I thought I heard her sigh. And then she said, "I hope you do, too. And when you do, I will throw the biggest wedding Kathmandu has ever seen!"

All my anxieties—about people finding out I was queer back home, about my upcoming show—dissipated in that moment. Rather than respond, I started laughing, and she joined me, the two of us relishing that thought. We spoke a bit longer, and when I hung up, I lay in my bed in the quiet of that East Village room. I looked at the Polaroids on the wall and at the gowns, which were all on hangers, filling the room like old friends. I imagined the strong women I knew and loved wearing them—my mother, sister, friends.

This gave me courage—and hope.

KUMUDINI ARRIVED THE DAY before the presentation, which helped with my nerves. And then, the day of my debut, I felt a strange calm. My sister came with me to the gallery—Tiina was already there, helping me dress the models. Hair and makeup were happening on the second floor. Downstairs, we set up platforms in the gallery, where the models would stand, because this was a presentation, not a runway show.

Caitlin arrived beaming. "People are starting to arrive!"

One by one, I reviewed each model before they walked downstairs to take their positions. Tiina was there, smiling. As the last model left, she gave me a hug and said, "Look at them! You should be so proud."

I was.

I joined everyone downstairs and watched as people started to trickle in. At first, it was junior editors, assistant buyers, and a few curious fashion people. I walked them all through the collection and explained my inspiration. Then my friends began to arrive—Maggie, Barbara, Damien, Yuki, Sam, Dustin, and so many more. In my head, I was so grateful for their support, but I was also panicked. We had invited every publication, all the major editors, including Cathy Horyn and Bridget Foley, the editor in chief of *Women's Wear Daily.* About an hour into the show, assistant editors started texting their bosses, who began to show up.

My first interview was with Meenal Mistry from Style.com, a powerful online fashion website that everyone followed.

"What's the show about?" she asked.

"A woman as a thinking man's sex symbol," I responded.

Looking back, I realize how sexist that sounds! What I meant at the time was that there has always been an idea that women who love fashion were whimsical and even ditzy. I wanted to break that notion, and introduce another perspective, which was that women could be unapologetically feminine, smart, independent, and strong—not either-or.

I was surrounded by women in my life who looked great, loved fashion, and were also doing incredible things. This collection was for them. Smart. Sexy. Feminine. Bold.

When Cathy Horyn showed up toward the end of the presentation, I did a double take to make sure I was not hallucinating. She was here. It was as if I had conjured her. We had a long talk about the collection, my inspiration for it, and my background. I walked her through each look, explaining the fabrics, how and where each piece was made, and how my time at

Bill Blass brought me to this moment. She seemed both interested and reserved, occasionally nodding but mostly stoic. She was neither cold nor warm, but very attentive, and that was enough for me. When I finished walking her through the collection, she nodded and said, "Thank you. Good luck with everything."

As she was putting away her pencil and notepad, she said, "You should be proud of yourself. Very proud."

Bridget Foley had also come to see the collection and asked me a lot of questions. After I walked her through the collection, she said, "Congratulations."

It was tempting to try to decipher Cathy's and Bridget's comments—to closely analyze whether they liked the presentation or not. But I decided to just be in the moment and allow myself to take it all in.

My debut show was coming to an end. I looked around at all my friends and colleagues who had collectively believed in me: Glenn and Amanda, Dustin and Sam, Caitlin, Tyler, and Tiina. My dear friend Zoe Saldana was also there. She had just moved to Los Angeles from New York to shoot the first *Avatar* film—but flew back to New York for my presentation. We met during my time at Blass, and I dressed her when no one else seemed interested because she was not a movie star yet. We had spent countless days talking about our future over cigarettes, martinis, and coffees. We promised each other that I'd dress her for her first premiere and she'd show up for my first presentation. She made good on her promise, and I told her I could not wait to make good on mine.

I felt so blessed to be surrounded by people who had been cheering for me all along. I wanted them to know what their belief in me meant. How each gesture of kindness had changed my life. No matter what happened next, I felt like I was on my destined path.

THAT NIGHT, GLENN AND Amanda hosted dinner in Chelsea, and all my friends came, as did Kumudini, who was so proud.

"How do you feel?" she asked.

I shrugged. I honestly didn't know how to feel.

She looked at me, tears in her eyes, and said, "I'm so proud of you. The collection was beautiful, it was perfect."

She gave me a hug and said, "Now, don't overthink it. Go and enjoy yourself."

I just looked at her, gave her a hug, and whispered, "Thank you so much for being here."

And then I added, "I miss Mami."

We both looked at each other, and tears started to roll down.

We decided that we didn't want Mami to come because I wasn't sure how it was going to turn out. I didn't want to disappoint her. But at this moment, we both realized that she should have been there.

DINNER WAS A DREAM. There were a few speeches, lots of cheers, laughter, dancing, and drinks. I will never forget that night. The fairy lights twinkling at the table reflected how I felt: Hopeful. Grateful. Illuminated.

I was incredibly happy with how things went—beyond my wildest dreams. And yet, I knew friends who had tried to launch their own collections and had not been successful. I prayed for a mention in *Women's Wear Daily*. A paragraph. A sentence. A start. Enough to keep going, to sell enough pieces, which would give me the money to design the next collection.

BY THE TIME KUMUDINI and I got home, it was 3:00 a.m. and we were so exhausted that we passed out. Then, around 5:00 a.m., we woke up and called our mother and brother on a group video chat. I let Kumudini explain the whole night because in our family there is no one better than my sister when it comes to telling a story. As we were chatting, I started getting a lot of texts and messages.

"Mami, hold on one moment," I said, and looked at the stream of messages lighting up my phone.

"Congratulations!"

"So proud!"

"You did it!"

At first I thought, "Oh, they must have really loved the show!"

Then one text read, "Have you seen *Women's Wear Daily*?"

"Mami," I said back on the video chat. "Let me call you back—friends say that my show got mentioned in *WWD*!"

Mami had no idea what *WWD* was, though she could tell it was important.

We hung up and my phone kept buzzing, now with messages from industry people who had never given me the time of day.

Another text commanded, "Go get *Women's Wear Daily*. Now!"

Kumudini and I got dressed and hopped on the subway to Pax, a deli in Bryant Park that got *WWD* delivered early. We ordered tea and waited for the morning truck to arrive.

"Prabal, I always knew you were meant for this big a playing field," Kumudini said. "You were always restless, itching to do something more than what life had offered you back home, and look at you. This is a good start—but remember that it is also only the beginning."

She sounded just like my mother.

At that moment, I saw the truck pull up, and a guy hopped out with a stack of magazines. He plopped the pile down by the cash register, and as I approached, I saw a flash of red on the cover. I asked for a copy of *WWD*, and once it was in my hands, I let out a giant gasp.

The title was "Drama Class," and below was a stunning shot of my sculpted red cocktail dress with the dramatic floppy bow, the very first dress I designed at Bill Blass that inspired the entire collection. The caption read:

> **There's a fresh crop of new designers in New York who are creating beautiful, well-executed clothes. One bright star is Prabal Gurung, whose glamorous fall collection, presented on Thursday evening, combined the fashion vernacular he had learned at Bill Blass with his own self-assured style. These were clothes for sophisticated women, created with considerable élan.**

We were in the thick of fashion week, and *WWD*'s covers during those seven days always went to well-established designers like Marc Jacobs, Ralph Lauren, Calvin Klein, Michael Kors, Carolina Herrera, Oscar de la Renta, Donna Karan, or Anna Sui. I'd never seen a new designer on the front page.

I started to tremble, right there in the middle of Pax deli at 6:30 a.m. Memories quickly resurfaced in my mind: me dressing up in my sister's clothes, my parents fighting over it, paper dolls, Mami doing my makeup, my aunt jeering and taunting me, boys from St. Xavier's bullying me . . . it all came back to me in rapid succession. I was so overwhelmed and emotional that I could not stop crying. I hugged my sister and wept into her shoulder.

"You did it, Prabal!" I could hear her whispering in my ear. "You did it."

CHAPTER TEN

That same day, my cell phone did not stop buzzing from the congratulatory texts, and my email inbox was suddenly deluged with party and event invitations. I knew not to get too swept up, as I'd seen this happen to other designers who had been hailed as the next big thing, only to shutter their label before they even made it to the next collection.

I'd encountered so much failure in my life. It made me more resilient. Stronger. Smarter. It taught me to manage my expectations when things didn't work out. This was new territory—I was being heralded as an overnight success. In an ideal world, I would have made a business plan, complete with a sales plan and production schedule, and my branding and marketing all mapped out. But I was a creative person with no real business sense beyond what I had learned at Cynthia Rowley and Bill Blass. My biggest priority was to sell the line to select stores, namely Bergdorf Goodman and Barneys, as they represented high fashion, luxury, and ultimate chic. Once either bought your line, it signaled that you were a designer to watch. That would lead to more interest, more sales—and a chance for my brand to make it in the cutthroat competitive fashion world.

I knew that I needed more press. Ideally, a mention in *Vogue* as that, too, was another rite of passage for any new designer. By then, I'd asked Caitlin to join me as the vice president of communications and PR for a minority stake in the company, as there was no way I could pay her. I was still collecting unemployment, which I used to pay Tyler, and had spent every cent of my savings launching my brand. Caitlin and I both knew that in order to succeed—and make it to the second collection—we first had to sell this one to as many stores as possible.

Caitlin was a terrific partner. Kind, thoughtful, and fun, she came from a wealthy family but had also worked her way up in the PR world and was well respected. She reached out to *Vogue*'s market editor, Meredith Melling, who invited us to bring the collection to *Vogue*'s office. We were thrilled! There, at the legendary Times Square building, we set up in a conference room where several market and fashion editors came to have a look at the clothes. Everyone was thoughtful, kind, and encouraging. I left feeling hopeful that we'd at least get a mention.

Meanwhile, I had also reached out to Roopal Patel, who led the Bergdorf buying team, following up on the promise she had made that rainy afternoon at Bill Blass.

Her response was immediate: "I'd love to come see your collection."

We now needed a proper place to show the line, as I knew better than to invite any potential buyers to my Third Street studio. The woman who ran the licensing for Bill Blass outerwear was a friend—she offered the Blass showroom in the Fur District on Thirty-Ninth between Eighth and Ninth Avenues, which was walking distance to all the factories where my collection had been made.

Tyler and I spent the morning of the Bergdorf presentation running back and forth, slaloming around honking cars and hot dog carts, carrying garment bags filled with samples from the factory to the large room where we set up a few clothing racks in one corner. Caitlin brought flowers in an attempt to make the space a little more elegant. As we were hanging the pieces, the fit model called to say she was sick—which meant I had to scramble to find a size 6 friend to come model the clothes for Roopal and her team. I immediately thought of Alice, a tall, lanky, lesbian architect friend from Parsons who had modeled in my shows there. She rarely wore any dresses, and did not enjoy the experience at all, but looked amazing in all my designs. Desperate, I called her and was so relieved when she agreed to help. She arrived minutes before Roopal and her team, who were thankfully running late.

"Lovely!" Roopal said as Alice emerged wearing the first look of the collection. I saw different members of her team smile, nod, and scribble notes down as each outfit was modeled.

As they were getting ready to leave, Roopal gave me a hug and said, "Congratulations on a very strong first collection."

I was hopeful.

The following day, she sent an email that said, "We love what you are doing, but we're going to wait until the next season."

I was crushed. That same day, Caitlin received a similar email from *Vogue*: "We want to wait and see what comes next."

All the adrenaline that had propelled me through the last few months was starting to fizzle. But then, I received an email from Princess Deena Aljuhani Abdulaziz, a Saudi American businesswoman who had married into the royal family and owned a high-end boutique in Riyadh called DNA. She had read the *WWD* cover story and wanted to come see my collection. I felt like a yo-yo, ricocheting between highs and lows. That night, Caitlin and I went for a drink to strategize.

"If we don't sell to someone, it's over," I said.

"Bergdorf was our first pass," Caitlin said. "There are other possibilities! We'll find a way."

I toasted to that and insisted on paying the tab to thank her for being such a supportive partner.

"I believe in you," she said with a smile.

The waiter took my card and then came back a few minutes later.

"I'm sorry, sir, this was declined."

"Tomorrow is another day!" Caitlin said as she handed the waiter her card.

I appreciated her optimism but did not feel it myself. That night, I cried myself to sleep. The next morning, I woke up at five and went to the gym to work out—my morning ritual—followed by coffee at a café and breakfast back in my apartment. Afterward, I called my mother, the best part of my daily routine.

I told her about Bergdorf Goodman and *Vogue* both passing.

"Be patient, kanchu," she said. "You are off to a great start. Pace yourself."

There was no time—nor any money. Plus, I was literally running to keep up with all the calls, appointments, invitations, and my rising panic. *WWD* cover aside, if I could not sell this collection, there would not be another one.

On the morning of Princess Deena's appointment, Tyler and I transported the samples to Caitlin's childhood home, as her parents had offered their Sutton Place town house as a fallback showroom. It was far chicer than the Garment District, and a better match for our brand. We invited the princess to meet us there, on the garden floor of the gorgeous four-story brick home just blocks from the East River. When we arrived, Caitlin was already there, placing bouquets of flowers on the fireplace mantel, elegant touches to an already stunning living room. Tyler and I carefully hung each piece on black velvet hangers.

"This is more like it," I said, scanning the beautiful room, feeling hopeful again.

Zarena, our fit model, was the next to arrive. A gorgeous Black woman, she reminded me of the models Yves Saint Laurent used in the seventies:

strong, powerful, stunning, chic. She represented everything I wanted my collection to be at that moment. Then Princess Deena buzzed. I greeted her at the door and thought, immediately, that she lived up to her reputation of having impeccable taste. She was dressed head to toe in Azzedine Alaïa, carried a Chanel bag, and wore a perfume that reminded me of my part of the world—jasmine and neroli.

"Show me your dream," she said with a radiant smile as she entered the room.

Zarena proceeded to walk out in each look.

"Ooh la la!" Princess Deena cooed.

"Stunning. Love."

My breath grew easier with each affirmation. Her enthusiasm *was* contagious.

As Zarena emerged in the last look, Princess Deena turned to me and said, "I need to buy your entire collection."

She asked me for the line sheets, which describe each item, the date it would be delivered, the wholesale price, and the suggested retail price.

"I will be in touch," she said, kissing both cheeks before she left, leaving a trace of her perfume after she was gone.

"Wow!" Caitlin shouted as Tyler and I began laughing, giddy with relief.

"Sounds like that was a success!" Caitlin's mother had just entered the living room, her smile matched ours—until I saw it shift to concern.

"Please tell me you did not give the princess water out of a plastic bottle!" she added, horrified.

Caitlin and I looked at each other, then at the Evian bottle on the coffee table.

"We did!" I gasped and went to give her a hug. This was something my mother would have said—and had the same effect. We never served water in a plastic bottle again.

The very next day, Nicholas Mellamphy came to look at the collection for The Room, a posh store in Canada that was known for taking chances on up-and-coming avant-garde designers. He also placed an order.

I WAS BEGINNING TO breathe again. But while we were on a roll, these were boutiques, placing small orders. I needed a department store to pick up a large quantity in order to generate enough money to both make the clothes for the stores *and* design my next collection.

And then Bloomingdale's reached out. While they were more mass market, and not the pinnacle luxury store I was hoping for, I was happy that they wanted to see the collection unsolicited. Their buyer came with her team and was brimming with excitement. "This is exactly what we want to do at Bloomingdale's!" she said as Zarena came out in each look. "It's perfect."

This was great news, but also complicated. It was spring 2009, when Barneys and Bergdorf were the pinnacle of high fashion, whereas Bloomingdale's was the tier below. I knew that if I said yes to Bloomingdale's, Barneys would use that as an excuse not to work with me. Fashion is that competitive. Bloomingdale's wanted the entire collection, so before we responded, we emailed Julie Gilhart, the head buyer at Barneys, inviting her to come have a look. She asked that we bring the collection to her.

Once again, Tyler and I schlepped all the samples, neatly folded in garment bags, in a cab to her office, where Zarena met us. Julie's reception was rather cold.

"A fit model is not necessary," she said.

She seemed uninterested from the moment we arrived, a tone that she maintained throughout our presentation. As she flipped through the pieces on the rack, she was forthright: "I just don't think this is right for us."

I was both devastated—and confused. Was she talking about herself? Barneys' clientele? There was no time to worry, as Saks was also coming to have a look back at Caitlin's parents' town house. There, they asked a bunch of production and distribution questions, a good sign, but then segued to: "The price point is a bit high for us."

"Bloomingdale's has already made an offer to buy the collection," I said, perplexed. If they could afford it, then why not Saks?

The rep responded, "Well, if you sell to Bloomingdale's, then we won't be able to carry it."

I stayed quiet, but my mind was racing: if I didn't sell to someone, then I wouldn't have money for my next collection.

I was very grateful to go back to Bloomingdale's to say, "We'd love to work with you."

They placed a $70,000 order, which meant I was able to fund my next collection.

USUALLY, THE TERMS ARE net thirty or sixty, meaning you get paid thirty or sixty days after you make and deliver the order. But Bloomingdale's understood that as a small, independent start-up brand I needed a deposit up front to buy the fabric and commission the factory to fulfill the order. And while it was far cheaper to work with factories abroad, it was important to me to make everything in New York. I had relationships with the people who made my clothes, plus I wanted to give back to this country that gave me this opportunity. It also meant that I had more control over the quality, as I could pop into the factory to check fabric, answer any questions, and make sure every detail was perfect. Plus, all the people working at the factory were like me, immigrants—as were the factory owners. It reminded me of the flou room at Bill Blass. It felt familiar.

With the money from Bloomingdale's, I felt confident enough to begin sketching and dreaming and draping the next collection. I based it on the YSL Rive Gauche perfume bottle that sat on my mother's vanity. I thought back to watching her transform into my version of Wonder Woman. A process that started with makeup, hair, and sari, and always ended with a dab of that floral scent—a mix of magnolia, honeysuckle, and sandalwood—on her clavicle and behind her ears before she went out into the world. It was the last layer of feminine chic that cloaked a strong, spirited, intelligent woman. I wanted to channel that empowering feeling, and used the cerulean blue bottle with the black YSL logo as my inspiration. As I sketched and dreamed—in my studio, at cafés, on benches in Washington Square Park—Tyler helped me source fabrics in deep cobalt, emerald green, and coral pink to bounce off neutral creams, white, and black, doing for me what I did for Michael and Peter at Bill Blass. We installed an inspiration board on the wall of my studio, and began to pin ideas—a swatch, a photo, a beaded trim.

THAT APRIL 2009, MY dear friend Zoe Saldana wore the red one-shouldered minidress with the floppy bow from my first collection to her *Star Trek* premiere in Berlin. It was her first big blockbuster film, and she was photographed, looking exquisitely beautiful, wearing a Prabal Gurung dress. She was a friend, making good on her promise—I was so grateful. That led to more press and more interest in my brand. More stylists started to reach out to borrow samples for their celebrity clients, another vital step in a fashion brand's vitality, as the ripple effect leads to more press and ultimately more sales.

Case in point: on June 27, a friend texted, "Are you on Twitter?"

"No, why?" I responded.

It was the beginning of the social media platform, and while I had an account, I was not active.

"Demi Moore is tweeting about you."

I logged on immediately and saw that she had worn a black-and-white dress from my collection that her stylist had selected for a Bulgari perfume launch. Her manager snapped a photo of her, which Demi posted with the comment, "Wonderful young designer to look out for Prabal Gurung!"

I was stunned. Demi was a super-duper star—not just in the United

States but beloved globally. The same guys who had bullied me in India and Nepal had posters of her from *Ghost* or *Striptease* in their dorm rooms. She was dating Ashton Kutcher, who was more than a decade her junior, and was Hollywood's highest paid actress, as she had insisted that her paycheck match her male counterparts'. She was a powerful, beautiful badass who defied every patriarchal expectation of how a woman should behave. The incarnation of my dream woman—style and substance—with more than a million Twitter followers.

My very first tweet ever was to thank her. Within seconds, I got more than five hundred followers, and I realized the power of social media. I had still been wondering, "How the hell am I going to pull off the next collection?" Yes, I had money to at least make the clothes for the show itself, but I needed to buy all the buttons and trim and pay the fabrics mills, the zipper vendor, the shipping companies, the models, assistants, phone bills, credit card bills . . . as well as afford my own rent and groceries. And then Demi Moore pointed her magic wand at me. Twitter became my lifeline, and my business center. With every celebrity tweet, I got more followers, more inquiries from editors and stylists, and, most important, sponsors began to reach out, wanting to be part of my next show. Bumble and Bumble offered to do hair again, MAC said it would love to do makeup, and a well-known beverage company offered us $50,000 in exchange for being our brand partner.

In a matter of months, I went from being a "new designer" to a "designer to watch" to a "designer worn by A-list celebrities." First Zoe, then Demi, and then Rachel Weisz wore another look from my first collection. The celebrity seal of approval leads to more press, more opportunities, more sponsorships, and eventually, the hope is, collaborations with retailers.

FASHION IS ABOUT CLOTHES, but it is also about perception. So when Adam Glassman, the creative director of *O, The Oprah Magazine*, reached out to ask if I would like to submit a dress idea for Oprah for her December holiday issue, I said yes without hesitation.

It was a wonderful time, but also a period marked by great cognitive dissonance. I was still doing all of this from my studio apartment, relying on monthly unemployment checks to afford rent and groceries.

That same month, the clothes from my first collection were finally ready to ship to the stores that had ordered them. I went to the factory for the final review and walked between the racks of cashmere coats, ivory cream silk blouses, black trousers, and red dresses. I was overcome with emotion. These items, conceived from sketches, were going to stores in New York, Dubai, Toronto, and beyond, to be purchased and worn by strangers. Those women, whoever they may be, would also be choosing me—my vision, my story, my point of view.

This, I thought, was the American dream.

And then I also noticed that every single item had the same off-white label with the black lettering that read PRABAL GURUNG. For a moment I panicked: It should read Rana, not Gurung. My mother was the reason I was able to do any of this. I had seriously considered changing my name—and went as far as discussing it with my siblings. They were hesitant. In Nepal, Rana is a posh name with a problematic history, so they did not think it was a smart move. But I wanted to pay homage to my mother, and to fight a patriarchal system where the woman takes the man's name. This time, the patriarchy won.

I went to thank the seamstresses and other production people for all their incredible work. Before I could utter a word, they all stood up and began clapping.

"You did it!"

"Congratulations!"

I hugged everyone, and walked into the madness of midtown, where no one had any idea who I was or what I had just experienced. There, on the corner of Thirty-Eighth Street and Eighth Avenue, I bought a slice of pizza and sat on a city bench to let it all soak in. I did it.

BACK IN MY STUDIO, I was working on my second collection, which would show at the same gallery. I was also working on that dress idea for Oprah—I envisioned a riff of the one-shouldered red dress that landed on the *WWD* cover, but longer, with two sleeves. No one but me knew how meaningful this potential Oprah opportunity meant. Next to my inspiration board for my new collection, I had a vision board for my career. That was my daily reminder to keep striving and pushing, to never rest on my laurels or take anything for granted.

It read:

> **Start a brand. Get in a few stores. Make a growth plan. Dress Oprah. Michelle Obama. Gloria Steinem. Get in *Vogue*. Apply for CFDA/Vogue Fashion Fund. Win CFDA/Vogue Fashion Fund. Go to the Met Gala. Become the creative director of Chanel. Start a foundation.**

As I began to design Oprah's dress in the quiet of my studio, I meditated on the miracle of this assignment. Oprah had taught me how to manifest my dreams, and here I was in my small East Village studio, still living on unemployment, but making a dress for *her.* I bought more than ten yards of a deep red silk faille and started to drape it with help from Doo Ri, one of my beloved seamstresses from Bill Blass. She was a petite Korean woman with the softest voice and a spine like steel. We worked side by side in her midtown workshop so I could show her the nuances of how I wanted the gown to look on Oprah, the same way my mother wore her saris. Graceful, flattering, elegant, and bold.

Once it was finished, I sent it to Chicago, where I was informed, several weeks later, that Oprah had worn it for the December cover. It was still summer and would not be on the newsstands until November. I imagined she tried several designers and refused to believe anything until I finally saw it. Still, it was gratifying to share these updates with my mother during our daily morning chats.

"Mom, Demi Moore and Oprah like my dresses!" I said one morning that late summer 2009.

"I'm very happy for you," she said. "You have worked hard for it—so enjoy it. But remember, if you're this excited about your success and recognition, then you'll be equally disappointed by your failures or challenges. Try to find a middle ground, a place where you can observe success and failures, joy and sorrow with the same kind of calm, grace and equilibrium. Be able to enjoy it, and be present, but not let it take over your ego. Because once the ego comes into play, then you are doomed. The best thing to do is to practice gratitude because it allows you to be fully present, in the moment. And then look ahead and ask, 'How is my life a service to a greater cause?'"

I let her wisdom sink in. My mother has always been my ballast. We chatted a little more, and then, right before hanging up, she added, "All these actresses are great. But what about the current First Lady of America? Michelle Obama? She represents everything you talk about! She's beautiful, graceful, and equal to her husband. Dressing her would make people understand what you are trying to do—that should be your goal."

I may have laughed. Michelle Obama was, after all, on my inspiration board.

"When that happens," my mother said by way of goodbye, "then let's talk."

My mother kept me grounded. Meanwhile, other people were talking about me as if I were an overnight success. There were rumors that I was a trust fund kid from a wealthy family, implying I had used money and connections to get to where I was. No one seemed to understand how long or hard I had been working for this. Now, I was getting invitations to parties, club openings, and fashion events, where people who had disregarded me in the past were suddenly interested in talking to me. Former Parsons classmates and industry acquaintances who had dismissed me or said my clothes smelled of curry were saying how they had always believed in me.

I tried to ignore the praise and focus on the next collection. Fashion at the time swung between women as hypersexual or very dumbed down. I felt strongly that style and substance were not mutually exclusive—and wanted to make clothes that were beautiful and made a strong statement about the women who wore them. Smart and sexy. Hyperfeminine but subversive. I wanted to ask the industry, "How are we looking at women? As one-dimensional or as multitudes? As objects or as independent, smart, opinionated people with very specific points of view?" I was still mystified that fashion was not more focused on asking, "Who are these women we're dressing? Why are we not talking about their achievements? Who cares whom they are married to?"

I believed then, and now, that a confident woman unnerves the patriarchy. I saw the absolute power in women embracing their femininity—from my mother to Oprah. This was why I loved Michelle Obama, the First Lady of America, a Black, Harvard-educated lawyer who also loves fashion. I wanted to create a fashion ecosystem where women like Michelle, Oprah, Demi, and my mother could be their most fabulous selves. Back then, if you called a woman a serious person, that was a signifier for "she doesn't really care about fashion." I wanted to change that.

MY SECOND SHOW TOOK place at the FLAG art gallery on September 9, 2009. Due to the success of the first presentation there, we had three times as many RSVPs. Cathy Horyn came, as did Bridget Foley from *WWD*, and Sally Singer, *Vogue*'s creative director, who invited Ikram Goldman, a stylist to many luminary women. She also ran a legendary store in Chicago called Ikram.

After the presentation came the showroom appointments. We had moved the showroom from Sutton Place to Caitlin's apartment on Twenty-Sixth Street near Bryant Park, which was where I met Sally Singer and Ikram Goldman. As the two were perusing the collection, Sally pointed to a long white draped matte jersey gown and said, "This would be perfect for *her*—maybe Prabal red?"

Ikram nodded, and wound up placing an order for her store, as well as pulling the white dress and another floral silk organza sheath dress for "one of her clients," she explained.

IN LATE OCTOBER, CAITLIN called. "Are you sitting down?" she asked, giddy.

My heart skipped—and I thought, "Is Barneys finally interested? Has Bergdorf reconsidered?"

"I have the December issue of *O, The Oprah Magazine* in my hands," she said.

"And?"

"*She is wearing your dress!!!*"

"Our dress!" I replied.

Tyler ran out to get a copy, and there was Oprah, looking like a goddess in my bespoke red gown, standing next to Ellen DeGeneres, who was wrapped in Christmas lights. I gasped. Oprah wearing my dress on the cover of her magazine was the metaphor for the American dream. It was a validation of my courage to live my truth. That moment was bigger than any opportunity that could be monetized.

Then her team asked me to make her another dress, for an event. Caitlin and I flew to Chicago to deliver it, and I spent the entire trip preparing myself mentally to meet a woman who had changed the course of my life. Instead of feeling nervous, or stressed, I focused on how grateful I was. This was way more than dressing a celebrity. This was the woman who had motivated me to live my impossible dream. She made me a better person—

and was someone I had manifested to both meet *and* dress one day. Both were happening at this singular moment.

At Harpo Studios, a young woman brought us back to Oprah's dressing room, which I had seen glimpses of on TV—the rows of dresses hanging on racks opposite an entire wall of shoes. Everything was so mesmerizing—and colorful and joyous! Just then, Oprah emerged in the black-and-white dress I'd made for her.

"Ta-da!" she said, with a wave of one hand. "What do you think?"

I was speechless. She was wearing no makeup and her hair was pulled back into a bun—and she was luminous! As beautiful as I had imagined her to be.

"Stunning!" I said.

"Your work is beautiful," she said. "How long have you been a designer?"

"I just launched my collection in February 2009, so less than a year!" I stammered.

She almost gasped, and said, "Wow! Well, congratulations!"

The connection I felt to her at that moment was so strong that I felt compelled to say, "Oprah, I must tell you, my journey to America started because of you."

I told her about how I'd never fit in growing up in Nepal, and how everyone in my extended family and beyond had written me off as a failure.

"And then I saw your show on living your dream, and it was the inspiration I needed," I explained, tears welling up in my eyes. "I decided to come to America, with no family or friends—to study fashion—because of you!"

She never once broke my gaze.

"You taught me to trust my inner voice," I said, now fully crying. "Your show made me a better person. It not only kept me moving forward but it also healed me from all the people in my life who have tried to hold me back."

My heart was beating so fast I thought it might jump out of my chest—and then I saw that she, too, was crying.

"Thank you for sharing, Prabal," she said.

That afternoon confirmed that I was on the right path. All my mantras and hard work had gotten me here. For so many years, I had to fight to be seen. And now, I was dressing the woman who showed me that manifestation along with intention, tenacity, and ambition works.

My spring 2010 show debuted in fall 2009. And I was already at work on my third collection, fall 2010, which I would present in February 2010. Timing in fashion is very *Alice in Wonderland*. By then, we had expanded to selling the line to roughly fifteen stores, but it was still very hand to mouth. Each order placed gave me just enough money to keep it going—but barely. Still, I wanted to do a runway show. My previous shows had all been presentations, where the models stand still. Having models walk a runway means the editors, stylists, buyers, and celebrities who come see your show get to view the clothes in action. It's an announcement to the industry that you are serious. It's very theatrical, and incredibly expensive to produce.

I was still figuring out where and how to do a runway show when I spotted Fern Mallis at the Boom Boom Room, a club on the eighteenth floor of the Standard Hotel, which had replaced Bungalow 8 and Beige as the latest hot spot. On any given night, you might see Madonna, Lindsay Lohan, or Beyoncé milling about. I remember being tired that night, but had pushed myself to go as I knew that I might run into someone—an editor, stylist, or potential investor—who could help move the brand forward, as well as celebrities I might want to dress.

Fern Mallis was the head of fashion at IMG and former executive director of CFDA, where she started 7th on Sixth—which produced the biggest runway shows during fashion week. She was a legend.

I spotted her at the bar and went to introduce myself.

"I know who you are," she said. "I've heard a lot about you!"

I was amazed that she recognized me.

We chatted a bit, and then she asked, "What do you want to do next?"

I knew that it was the last year of 7th on Sixth, which she still oversaw, so I decided to go for it.

"I'm doing a runway show for my third collection, and have always dreamed of doing it at Bryant Park," I said. "Because it's the last one, I'd really love to do it there. It would be great for me—but it would also be great for you to support a young, independent designer from Nepal."

She looked at me and smiled broadly.

"Wow, you have balls to be so forthright!" she said. "And just for that, I'm going to say yes."

MY THIRD SHOW WAS my love letter to New York. Specifically, to the Lower East Side, where I was still living. I called it "The Speed of the City" and as my muse chose the architect Zaha Hadid, a woman who designed buildings that looked like waves and defied linear expectations. Her work reminded me of all the women I admired—defying stereotypes. This collection had sharp, careful tailoring in a gritty city palette of black, bottle green, and antique gold. Positive reviews of the show led to *Vogue*'s fashion editor Mark Holgate calling me.

"We want to do a story on you," he said.

"Finally!" I thought.

Being in *Vogue* was Anna's stamp of approval, which opened doors and led to even bigger opportunities—not just retail but also investors, which I felt I needed to grow my business. I would have been happy with just a mention, so when I saw that my story was a page and a half, I was overcome with gratitude. It was not just a vote of confidence for me, but for everyone who had believed in me—from the beginning. Caitlin, Doo Ri, Tyler, Amanda, Tiina, Damien—the list was long. Also, as head of an independent small brand, I knew that I could take that story and create a career map.

As anticipated, that story led to more opportunities, including sales appointments in Paris that spring, which was thrilling, as branching out to Europe had always been part of my plan.

I WAS IN PARIS presenting my third collection to buyers in May 2010 when my phone started to vibrate. I looked down, and all these texts were flooding in: "Oh my god, congratulations!"

Someone sent me a link, and when I clicked on it, I saw Michelle Obama at the Smithsonian National Museum of American History, wearing the floral silk organza sheath dress that Ikram had pulled from my second collection for "one of her clients."

I must have gasped out loud.

"Is everything okay?" someone asked.

I showed the image on my phone, and everyone in the showroom burst into applause. People were hugging me as my phone began blowing up with text after text after text. Then, as if by magic, the phone in the salesroom started to ring: a new buyer saw Michelle Obama in a Prabal Gurung dress and wanted to know if they could make an appointment. That was just the start. The power of that moment felt like another miracle. The phone did not stop ringing all afternoon—people who had never returned our calls were suddenly interested in carrying the collection.

Back at the hotel, I called my mother.

When she picked up, I said, "Hi, Mom, can we talk?"

I was trembling as I shared the news.

"I'm very happy for you," she said. "And very happy for her. As I've said before, take it all in, enjoy it. But remember, from now on, your success is no longer your own."

This time I was a bit flummoxed. She had asked me to dress Michelle Obama. And I had done it. I expected her to be overjoyed. To say, "Kanchu! You did it!"

But, of course, that was not my mother's way. She had never responded to any news—good or bad—in an overly emotional way. True to form, she continued very calmly:

"From now on, you're representing your country—and also the continent," she said. "This is for thousands of people back home in Nepal, and millions throughout Asia. It's for people like you who want to pursue art but don't know how to. It's for those who've been bullied, and called names, who've been told that they can't amount to anything. It's for all the misfits who are never welcome anywhere. This is for them."

I suddenly understood and wanted to say, "It's also for all the mothers who trusted their instincts and allowed their children to follow their dreams and realize their potential."

Instead, I remained quiet.

"Remember, our success is a testament to our characters—and a test of your character," she said. "So, what are you going to do with it?"

THE NEWS OF MICHELLE OBAMA wearing my dress traveled like wildfire. Soon, I was getting messages from old classmates and relatives in Nepal, people who had unabashedly mocked me and my dreams to become a designer.

"We always knew you could do it!" the emails and texts read.

I was so grateful for my mother's advice. Don't be distracted by the attention. Stay your course. I was also deeply moved by the news reports that I was the first person from Nepal—as well as South Asia—to dress an American First Lady.

This was a reminder that it was time to embrace my roots. For so long, I had been hiding behind the whiteness of the fashion world. Dimming my vision, assimilating my innate sense of style to appease a white audience. My work at that point was derivative of Bill Blass, albeit infused with bold colors and shapes draped from saris. A nod to my Nepali roots, but subtle. I was making beautifully constructed clothes and giving them my own twist. But now was the time to truly reconnect—with my heritage and first home and the shapes and hues that inspired me to become a designer in the first place. Michelle, Oprah, Zoe. All of the women who inspired me were women who wanted to wear what I was making. And they all reminded me of my original muse: my mother.

On the morning of April 26, 2010, I awoke to a buzzing phone.

The stream of texts pouring in read, "OMG! CONGRATULATIONS! YOU DID IT!"

I clicked the link a friend sent and slowly saw the First Lady's face appear and as the rest of her image downloaded, I caught a glimpse of the "Prabal red" at her neckline, and then my dress filled the screen. Michelle Obama was walking into the White House Correspondents' Dinner, holding President Obama's hand, wearing my dress. I was blinking back tears as I thought, "Of all the racks of clothes to choose from, she selected this dress, which I had, once again, specifically draped to resemble my mother's sari."

Michelle was the epitome of style and substance, and she was married to a man who was beginning to redefine patriarchy. His slogan during his presidential campaign about the audacity of hope epitomized why I wanted to come to America. And the Obama White House was so much closer to my own idea of what it meant to be American than anything I'd ever seen. By choosing this dress, she was choosing me.

That same day, I got an email from someone at *Vogue* inviting me to the Met Gala pre-party cocktail hour. Going to the Met Gala was another item on my vision board. The event started in 1948 as a fundraiser for the Costume Institute at the Metropolitan Museum of Art and has since grown to become one of the most famous and glamorous fundraisers in the world—thanks to Anna Wintour, who has been the host since the midnineties. It always takes place on the first Monday in May, and *Vogue* controls the coveted guest list.

Every year there's a theme, and in 2010, it was "American Woman: Fashioning a National Identity." Joining Anna Wintour as cohosts that year were Patrick Robinson and Oprah Winfrey.

What most people don't know is that there are several tiers of invitations to the Met Gala. This invitation was exclusively for the pre-party cocktail hour. It meant I could walk the red carpet, but I couldn't attend the dinner and after-party. Hilary Rhoda's stylist had selected a black-and-red minidress from my third collection for the young model to wear, so this invitation meant that I could walk Hilary up the famed red carpet to the Metropolitan Museum of Art. This was the next step in realizing my dream: not only to get invited to the dinner but also to host my own table.

And I had been manifesting it since my time at Bill Blass, where I had always advocated that the brand should be represented at the Met Gala, but Michael loathed the idea. After he left, I reached out to Lauren Santo Domingo, who was hosting the after-party that year, and asked if I could bring Zoe Saldana to that as my date.

Zoe and I had become close by then—she had done only two small films, but I knew in my gut that she was going to be a superstar. She was a wildly elegant, gorgeous, and funny Dominican girl from the Bronx who was determined to make it in Hollywood, where there were so few Latinx roles. From the moment I met her, I adored her. She reminded me of myself.

Lauren said yes, and I dressed Zoe in a beautiful Bill Blass ball gown and myself in a tuxedo. We had dinner at a chic restaurant—a Dominican girl and a Nepali boy—on the Upper East Side, where we stood out among the crowd of Upper East Siders. There, everyone commented, "You look so beautiful! Where are you going?"

"The Met Gala," we said, smiling.

It was all very magical.

That evening, over dinner, we talked about our dreams—and heartaches. She was filming *Star Trek* and had been cast in *Avatar,* but neither had come out yet. I told her I wanted to leave Bill Blass and launch my own namesake line one day. That was the night we made our pact: I would dress her for her first red carpet appearance, and she would come to my first show. And then we headed to the Metropolitan Museum of Art for the after-party, where I saw all the usual suspects—socialites, editors, models, celebrities—whom I always ran into at all the galas. Some of them had become good friends over the years and some remained acquaintances. All polite, nice, sweet, but once again, every person except for Zoe, the actress Joy Bryant, very few others, and me were white. I wasn't disheartened or dejected. Though I do remember coming back home that night and thinking to myself, "Is this ever going to change? Is white America the only America to be represented in this haute couture high fashion space?"

Being invited to any portion of the Met Gala gives you access to the most exclusive curation of creative people—designers, movie stars, artists, and musicians. I was still in the early stages of building my brand, so having a moment on the red carpet with Hilary Rhoda wearing my black, white, and red sculpted minidress that was a hybrid of old-school couture meets the new modern world was huge. In a sea filled with gowns and trains, she looked young and hip and totally glamorous.

When we arrived at the Met that evening, I took a deep breath. The stairs leading up to the museum were lined with photographers. I took Hilary's arm and we began to ascend, surrounded by the sounds of clicking cameras and different names being shouted interlaced with the syncopated pops of flashes. I focused on each step, one foot in front of the other, thinking how far I had come from playing with paper dolls to sketching in notebooks to getting on that plane to Parsons . . . and now making my way toward the pinnacle of the fashion world. I was halfway up the stairs when I heard a photographer shout, "*Prabal!*"

I was shocked, as I did not expect anyone to know who I was. And yet, as I turned and posed, it also felt totally natural, like I was meant to be there.

Once inside the museum, I began weaving through the glamorous crowd and recognized so many faces, from Taylor Swift to Sarah Jessica Parker. I was mesmerized, just soaking it all in when I heard someone else shout my name:

"*Prabal!*"

This time, it was Oprah Winfrey, standing with Anna Wintour. I walked over to her to say hello.

"He was in my closet a couple of weeks ago," Oprah said with a big smile. "And Michelle! She looked amazing! Congratulations, you must be so thrilled."

I was! Particularly because she was saying all of this in front of Anna.

"I'm so proud of you, Prabal!" Oprah added. "You're doing it! You're really doing it!"

And then she gave me a tight hug. It was the most generous and loving moment. We chatted a bit more, and then I started to wander through the crowd—saying hello to the people I knew, including magazine editors and a few famous designers. I felt like Cinderella at the ball, caught up in the magic of it all. When people started to move toward the dining room, I realized that the clock had struck midnight for my fairy-tale story. As much as I wished that I could follow everyone in, my invitation limited me to the cocktail party, not the dinner. I did not want to face the red carpet again. People were still arriving, and I thought it would be best to slip out unnoticed. I pulled a waiter aside and asked discreetly, "Is there a back exit?"

He looked at me, confused, and I explained. "I'm not going to the dinner."

He nodded and said, "Follow me."

I did, and as he pushed open a back door he said, "It's going to happen for you."

I was so touched by his vote of confidence, this total stranger. His kind words felt like the hug I needed at that moment. I thanked him, and as I walked into the spring evening air, I could hear the paparazzi behind me. I turned to see the red carpet, the cameras snapping, the stars still arriving, fashionably late.

CHAPTER ELEVEN

For all the accolades and fanfare, the reality was, at this moment, I had four employees and was selling my clothing line to roughly twenty stores, which meant the sales from one collection would barely cover the cost of designing the next one. I was not sure how I was going to keep going: there was so much to learn, and my success, while thrilling, catapulted me in ways I was not prepared for. Stores were willing to take a chance on me when I first launched, but now wanted net terms—and I still did not have the money to pay for production up front.

Cash flow for any company is always an issue, but for an independent brand like mine, it is more magnified. The flow from design to sales to production is constant. If there's any interruption—a late payment, returned clothes, a fabric mill mistake—the whole cycle can be disrupted. I needed a financial buffer in order to keep the label going, so I started applying for awards and grants available to up-and-coming designers, like the Ecco Domani Fashion Foundation award, which I was thrilled to win. Established by the wine company under the leadership of industry insiders like former CFDA cochair Marylou Luther and *Vogue*'s Sally Singer, the Ecco Domani Fashion Foundation award came with a $25,000 grant. Winning was both prestigious and pragmatic.

I'd also been approached by the CFDA to apply to its Fashion Incubator, a two-year program created by Mayor Michael Bloomberg in 2009 in conjunction with CFDA that gives emerging designers mentorship matches with industry legends like Carolina Herrera and Diane von Furstenberg, educational seminars, networking opportunities, and affordable office space. That application process was arduous, but in a good way, as it forced me to create the business plan I should have made before I launched my label: it asked for production costs, sales projections, employee growth charts, and more.

When I learned that I was one of ten designers selected for the two-year program, class of 2010–2012, I felt a wave of relief. I was tired of always having to borrow spaces and ask for favors. Damien's lease was coming up, so this meant that I could finally move my office out of his East Village studio to a professional workspace on Thirty-Ninth Street between Seventh and Eighth Avenues, in the heart of the Garment District. It felt like a new beginning.

My new office space was one of eight cubicles on the eighth floor. We hired a sales rep, so our company of five moved into the space, which we split into four sections: a showroom, our office, PR and sales, and a design space. White curtains doubled as movable walls, which we could open or close depending on what was happening on any given day. Simple and clean. I left my manifestation board at home but otherwise moved everything else work related to this new space.

It was so satisfying to have everything in one place, where we could invite prospective buyers, models for fittings, and editors for desk-side visits. We used one of the walls as our inspiration board, where Tyler and I would pin up what the next collection would look like, and then our showroom, while small, had enough room for three metal racks with the current season clothes displayed, and three small chairs for visitors. It was one step above scrappy.

After I unpacked my sketchbooks, pencils, mood boards, fabric swatches, and books, I placed Mr. Blass's Rolodex on my desk, next to my computer.

Every so often, I'd flip through it for motivation. Practically every card had a recognizable name: a brilliant, creative person whom he considered a friend. I aspired to have his professional life one day. He set a high bar.

Next to that, I placed a black-and-white photo of my mom and me at age four. It was taken in Singapore, and in it, she's wearing a cropped blouse and skirt, and I'm looking up at her. That photo made me feel safe and grounded, reminding me of her unwavering love and belief in me.

We were still settling in when I got another email—this time from *Vogue* editorial encouraging me to apply to the CFDA/Vogue Fashion Fund. This competition, which was separate from the Fashion Incubator program, was also on my manifestation board. It was the most prestigious award in the industry—and it came with a huge cash prize. I first learned about it when I watched the *Seamless* documentary five years prior while working for Bill Blass. That was also the first time I met Anna. I remembered her saying, "If you're confident enough to talk to me, then I'm sure you're confident enough to know when it's your time."

It was my time.

I also knew that hundreds of designers applied, and from that only ten were selected to compete. That application was more intimidating than the Fashion Incubator: in addition to a business plan, I had to also submit a portfolio. That was a daunting and rigorous process that once again forced me to think about the road map for my brand. The questions were, "What's your vision? What's your voice? What story do you want to tell?"

As competitive as the fashion industry is, there's also camaraderie. My friend, the high-end jewelry designer Monique Péan, had done the competition the year before and guided me through the entire process. She truly wanted me to succeed.

MONIQUE'S DESIRE TO HELP me was in stark contrast to so many other people who were circling me at the time, as the fashion industry also attracts people who want to be part of what they see as a glamorous and "fabulous" playground filled with beautiful people. After my second show, these "investors" came out in droves, surrounding and sniffing around me and my business. I lost count of the number of texts I received with promises to connect me with this or that potential investor, some claiming that they were going to be the "next LVMH!"

I'd also often hear, "I want to make you the next Calvin Klein or Ralph Lauren." Both designers are excellent at what they do, but neither has anything to do with my journey. So I also dismissed those investors, who did not even bother to ask me what I wanted.

Instead of feeling flattered, the interest put me on guard. When I was at Cynthia Rowley, there was a group called Pegasus that was making a lot of investments into designers. Cynthia had a bad feeling about it and steered clear—but other designers she knew were not so savvy. None of their lines exist today—but hers does.

I UNDERSTOOD I HAD to pay extra attention to my intuition about whom not to trust, something I had developed since I was a child. Still, I'd always take meetings with anyone interested, as I believe you never know what you might learn.

In those early days, I'd ask a series of questions to give me a window into the way they thought:

"Why do you want to invest? What drives you? How do you envision the world?"

I met with all types: the finance bros with model girlfriends who loved the glamour of the fashion industry. The rich kids who thought fashion was cool, and had trust funds but no business sense. Anyone who promised to "make me rich" got crossed off my list. I knew how hard it was to survive the fashion world—especially after seeing what happened to a legend like Bill Blass. That was my cautionary tale. I saw how much money was poured into that label, and how badly it was managed. For every business that succeeds and grows, hundreds have failed. I knew that I had to find the right people to partner with. I needed an investor who had not only the infrastructure to grow the company but also the patience to support my long-term vision. I needed a partner who could see the value of my brand for its social, cultural, and human impact. Someone who believed in the power of fashion to make people feel seen, validated, and celebrated—especially in the luxury sector, which still was an entirely white upper-echelon world.

I wanted to build a brand that represented a new idea of America. One where dichotomies could coexist: style and substance, femininity and power. I wanted to create the world that I saw on the streets of New York City, which was so incredibly diverse and colorful. But when I described this vision to potential investors, they all seemed flummoxed. They did not know what to make of it. Some looked at me like I had ten heads.

A FORMER EDITOR AT *Harper's Bazaar* set up one meeting with an investor who had amassed his fortune buying and reselling estate jewelry. I respected her, so I agreed to meet with him. "It's like high-end luxury recycling—and doubles as a 401(k) for the people I'm helping out," he said, describing his business.

"Where do you find your clientele?" I asked.

He began to name-drop all the places he traveled, from Cannes to the Hamptons, as my friend hung on his every word. She was clearly buying his do-good sales pitch, but his shifty eyes and pompous demeanor gave me pause.

"Have you ever built a company from scratch?" I asked.

He changed the subject.

"How is this philanthropic? Who's benefiting?"

He started rattling off all the galas he attended, as if buying tickets made him a hero. I quickly surmised that he was all hot air.

"I have the money to make you a star," he said more than once.

I politely declined and said I wanted to build my business on my own. His laugh became more of a sneer: "Okay then, good luck! You won't survive more than a year or maximum two without investors."

Later, I found out that he preyed on the elderly and took terrible advantage of them and that he was trying to legitimize his own Ponzi scheme as a real business.

Another time, a private equity guy named Lucky introduced me to a potential investor who wanted to own my brand but clearly had no idea how to build a company. I kept on asking him why he wanted to put his money in fashion, where the return on investment was so low, and he'd never answer directly. There was no passion, no story except how he "wanted to invest in a fashion brand." One day, I suggested we go for drinks: after he downed a few, he finally revealed that the amount that he was going to invest was far less than he originally promised and that he wanted to impress the woman he "hoped" would become his third wife, as she loved fashion.

I WAS BEGINNING TO DESPAIR, when Steven Kolb, the CFDA CEO, called.

"Congratulations, Prabal!" his voice boomed into the phone. "You made it to the final round of the CFDA/Vogue Fashion Fund!"

That meant that I was one of ten designers selected to compete for a $500,000 prize. My heart began to flutter as I stammered, "Seriously?"

"Yes!" he said and then explained next steps: I was invited to present five top looks from my collection that best represented my brand to that year's panel of judges: Steven Kolb, Diane von Furstenberg, Jeffrey Kalinsky, Andrew Rosen, Anna Wintour, Julie Gilhart, Sally Singer, and Jenna Lyons—the smartest and most powerful minds in the fashion industry.

To prepare, I printed out headshots of each judge and taped them to the wall of my East Village studio, which meant I'd wake up every morning to all the judges staring at me. My morning routine shifted: I'd make coffee and role-play fielding possible questions, looking at each headshot as I made my case.

On the day of my presentation, I brought the five looks I had selected to represent my brand to Vogue's office at 4 Times Square. They provided the models, and as I dressed the girls, I rehearsed what I wanted to say to the judges in my head.

"Prabal, you're up!" a voice snapped me from my reverie.

I walked into the conference room, where I saw the judges were all sitting behind a long table, facing me.

"Good morning!" I said, though my heart was pounding so hard, I worried the judges could not hear me above its thuds.

One of the judges then motioned to the timer on the table, and asked, "Are you ready?"

I nodded, knowing that meant I had eight minutes to speak. The clock was set, and I began: "My collection is American sportswear with couture ideals."

I first showed the red dress that wound up on the cover of *WWD*, followed by the one Michelle Obama wore to the White House Correspondents' Dinner, and then the black-and-white feathered dress that Demi Moore chose to wear to the Bulgari event. With each look, I told the story of how I came up with the concept, and what it meant to see my clothing on these iconic women. I also included a look from the third collection that I had just finished and one from the upcoming collection that I was currently working on. That spectrum of choices, I explained, showcased how Prabal Gurung could take a woman from morning to evening, or business to cocktail to gala attire.

"What's your vision for the brand?" someone asked.

"I'm dressing a woman who has style and substance," I said, looking directly at Anna Wintour, then at Jenna Lyons, and finally at Diane von Furstenberg, who were all nodding along vigorously. "I want to celebrate women who love art and creativity and who are also running a company."

I could tell it was resonating.

Other questions included, "How did you start?" and "How do you plan to grow?"

"Who is your ideal woman?" someone else asked.

"I want to dress women of all ages," I said. "Intelligent women who love fashion. They're not mutually exclusive."

"Who is carrying your line?"

"Bloomingdale's and Saks," I said.

"How are you financing this?" another asked. "Is it family money?"

"No," I said, laughing. "How I wish it was!"

I explained that I had used all my savings—and was still receiving unemployment.

"What would you do if you won the prize money?"

"I'd pay my factories and vendors," I explained. "And add two resort collections to grow my business."

At that point, I'd been able to do only two shows a year—fall and spring—simply because I could not afford to do more. Those shows, which happen in February and September, are commercially important for brand messaging, positioning, and image making. But those collections hit the stores during the shortest selling windows. Pre-collections, which happen in June and December, have the longest selling seasons, as the retailers don't put things on sale as quickly, which means they have a longer chance to sell at full price.

"If I could start over again," I added, "I'd focus on the pre-collections, establish my brand and DNA, and the sales aspect—and then show in September and February."

The judges seemed impressed with my answer—several were nodding their heads knowingly. By then, I had completely lost track of time. My heart began beating so hard, I could barely hear anything but its pounding.

"Sorry, did I miss the bell?" I asked.

"No," someone said.

"Do you have any more questions?" I asked.

All the judges shook their heads no.

"Do you have anything else to ask?" Anna said finally.

"I will ask those questions when I win the award," I said with a smile.

I was not being arrogant: I truly felt that I deserved to be there. And yet, as soon as I left the room, I broke out into a full-on sweat. I didn't realize until that very moment how much this all meant to me.

FOR THE NEXT SIX MONTHS, all the designers were judged on a variety of challenges. We had to do a workingwoman's outfit for Ann Taylor, and then we were flown to Los Angeles to do a runway show for celebrities. It was fashion's version of *Survivor.* And yet, throughout, the judges were consistently kind and caring. Each came to look at my fourth collection, which I was getting ready for the competition's grand finale.

"Hi, darling!" Diane von Furstenberg arrived at my incubator office with her typical dramatic flair. I offered her a seat and then watched, in horror, as she sank to the floor. The chair was broken. There I was creating a luxury line—and one of fashion's great icons was inches above the floor. I was speechless.

"Well, I'm now back to earth!" she exclaimed with a laugh, so seamlessly kind and gracious. After I helped her to another, more stable chair, she started our conversation by saying, "You are so handsome! And so talented."

I will never forget that. She made it clear that she liked me and what I was doing.

"Enjoy the process," she said. "You're fabulous. Don't worry about anything."

I showed her a few samples I was working on for my next collection, and she turned to me and announced, "Change your name to just Prabal. Like Madonna or Cher. And embrace your roots. That's where your power comes from."

Another day, Anna made an appointment to come see me. The meeting was supposed to be at 9:00 a.m. But everyone in the industry knows Anna always comes early. I was there by 7:30 a.m. to prepare, and sure enough, she arrived at 8:30 a.m. I was excited and nervous. If Anna believes in what you're doing, anything is possible. As I walked her through the collection, she was silent, nodding from time to time.

Finally, she said, "This is so well made. Where's your factory?"

"New York," I said. "The same one I worked with at Bill Blass."

Again, she nodded. Then she pointed to a dress and said, "This should be strapless."

Decisive and intentional.

"It's beautiful," she added.

My heart swelled in my chest. It was not yet 9:00 a.m. and already an unforgettable day.

"How is it all coming together for the show?" she asked.

I shared with her that I was having a hard time getting models.

"There's one designer who has a hold on all the models I'd like to use," I said, reporting on a perennial issue for new designers.

"Prabal, I understand that happens," she said. "But at the end of the day, your clothes need to do the work—not the models."

That grounded me. Of course, she was right.

I showed that fourth collection in September 2011 and called it "Beauty Undone." It was directly inspired by the brilliant bold colors of my childhood in Nepal. I was feeling homesick for Kathmandu's blue sky, saffron yellows, and brilliant poppy reds that you would see everywhere in Nepal. I played with sculptural draping and added paillette embroidery alongside strategic cuts and athletic racer-back details to highlight a woman's curves and celebrate her essence. I also continued to explore the idea of beauty. What does it mean? To whom does it apply? This collection was my homage to Miss Havisham, the brilliant antihero in Charles Dickens's *Great Expectations*, which was my favorite book growing up. It dissected the conventional meaning of beauty and offered a new definition, where imperfections were celebrated, and flaws revered.

Before the show began, Anna Wintour came backstage to check on me. That was the first time she had ever come to my show—the equivalent of the queen arriving. This was her way to show her support—it meant that she believed in you.

"How are you?" she asked.

"Chaotic!"

She laughed.

Karlie Kloss opened the show in an off-the-shoulder red silk taffeta dress that had a cinched waist and flared skirt that ended below the knee. I could feel the positive energy from the crowd reach me where I was, behind the stage, where I made sure each model was ready before sending her down the runway. I used all the highest quality fabrics—Taroni silks, duchesse satin, and organza layers—but gave them a disheveled edge in crimson hues with iridescent metallics. The idea was to present something structured—and a bit messy or undone. My color palette was informed by the East: the pinks, the reds. Coming undone versus the perfect package. I was starting to show different aspects of women, their unabashed desire to love and be loved and how their sexuality can be unnerving.

At the end of the show, I ran down the aisle to take my bow and saw Anna sitting on one side with Hamish Bowles and Carolina Herrera, all fashion demigoddesses and demigods. Across from them were Maggie Betts, Damien, Sam, and Adam—friends who had become family.

The following day, several looks from the collection ended up on the cover of *The Daily Front Row*—with a photo of me and the title "A Star Is Born." This was the last day of fashion week, and that magazine was a roundup of the best shows. This was pre-Instagram, and this publication was the arbiter of the "who's hot, who's not" in fashion.

While I was grateful for the recognition, I was also wary of the language being used. I've always been cautious about how the industry deifies designers, especially young, emerging talent. It felt dangerous to me, like a siren song calling a ship toward a treacherous rocky shore.

Throughout the day, friends called to congratulate me, and later that night, I saw a well-known PR executive at a fashion party. He spotted me and shouted across the packed room, "The star has arrived!"

I knew he was happy for me, but I also knew this kind of attention was a slippery slope. I approached him and said, "Thank you very much, but can you do me a favor? Going forward, can you share your thoughts with me privately? I appreciate you so much but don't want that kind of attention."

He looked at me, smiled, and said, "You got it." Then he added, "No other designer has ever said that to me, Prabal. You're special."

I knew that I needed to manage my ego and expectations, as the CFDA/Vogue Fashion Fund ceremony was taking place two months later, in November. In between, I still had to sell to stores and keep the business going. The prize money could literally make or break me.

THE NIGHT OF THE AWARDS, the runners-up were announced first: Eddie Borgo, a jewelry designer, was the first name to be called. And then my name was called next. I may have sighed: I wanted to win, but I was also grateful and relieved to have made it that far. And the $100,000 runner-up prize would be a lifeline for my brand.

Equally thrilling: Karl Lagerfeld, my fashion hero, handed me the award. I had to hold back all my tears as I scanned the audience, filled with so many familiar faces—famous designers, models I had come up with, editors who had supported me. All the judges, who had chosen me, including Anna, who was beaming. It was a moment I will never forget.

"This means a lot for a boy from Nepal," I said to the crowd, who erupted in applause.

I gave a speech about living the American dream, emphasizing that I was representing not just myself but my country. People were nodding their heads, perhaps as amazed as I was. This was a dream realized. Afterward, Anna introduced me to Karl. He put his hand on my face and said, "You look like a movie star."

I was trembling when I said, "Thank you so much! You have no idea what this means to me—to meet you! Your work is so inspiring."

Karl Lagerfeld was a multi-hyphenate genius: in addition to having his own line, he was the creative director at Chanel, where he staged the most fantastical and divine runway shows. Under his vision, Chanel had become chic and cool for nineteen-years-olds as well as ninety-year-olds. He made the kind of stunning, elegant clothes that I aspired to make one day.

As we were chatting, people began swarming around him, asking for photos. That was when he pulled me aside and said, "Just keep doing what you are doing. All these fashion people, don't listen to them. You're very talented—trust your instincts."

TWO DAYS LATER, I was invited to breakfast at Diane von Furstenberg's place to celebrate the end of the competition with the judges. I was up early, as always, and decided to walk. I left my apartment on East Third Street and headed to Houston, walking past gay bars where I'd had trysts and restaurants where I'd gone on dates for dinner. I took a right on Fifth Avenue, walked north through Washington Square Park, and got emotional thinking of how many outfits I had sketched sitting on those benches that circled the fountain. I continued up Fifth Avenue, through the arch, and past Parsons, where my American fashion journey began.

That walk gave me the necessary time to reflect: When I started my label, I downplayed what came naturally to me. My first collection was inspired by the Newa people of Nepal, which showed up in the color palette. It was a hint versus a declaration, as I did not want to be labeled an ethnic designer. All those snarky "smells like curry" comments from Parsons still stung.

But I was also beginning to understand that even if I wanted to assimilate, I wasn't able to. While I could channel Jane Birkin in the South of France, why would I? That was not my story. I had been living in America for more than a decade, as a first-generation immigrant. My reference points were Bollywood movies, the Himalayas, Kathmandu's chaotic markets, and monks wrapped in saffron gowns. I couldn't reference Boston, Massachusetts, or Greenwich, Connecticut, as those were foreign places to me. Besides, wherever I showed up, it was as a queer, brown man from South Asia. I could not hide my roots.

I was also seeing how invisible Nepal was to so many Americans. People had no idea where it even was on the map; wedged between the two juggernauts India and China, it's often forgotten, invisible. I knew what that felt like.

I turned left on Fourteenth Street, and as I prepared myself mentally to meet the judges in this final moment, I felt in my bones that I was heading in the right direction. Just as the street turned to cobblestones at Tenth Avenue, I saw the DVF store, a glass box on the corner, filled with her colorful, joyous, and sexy designs. Her apartment was in the same building, above the store.

All the judges were there, and everyone was so warm, so celebratory.

"How do you feel?" Anna asked as we all took a seat in Diane's living room.

She then handed me the check for $100,000.

"I cannot begin to tell you what this means to me and my team," I said.

"What will you do with the money?" someone asked.

"I will design a pre-collection this year for sure," I said. "And I will take a trip to see my family back in Nepal."

Diane beamed. "That sounds exactly right," she said.

"Anything else?" Anna asked.

"It occurred to me that we open our doors and hearts to European designers during New York Fashion Weeks," I said. "But I don't see the reverse happening."

I had noticed this trend: all the European designers come to New York during fashion week, and our community welcomes them with open arms, hosting dinners and parties to introduce young designers, especially to the American market.

"When was the last time the fashion world in Paris opened their doors for new American designers?" I asked.

There was a perception that Paris is couture, and America is sportswear. I, however, wanted to change that and create a world where both were possible—and to develop my brand globally.

"Intriguing," Anna said. "Thank you for bringing that up."

That meeting planted several seeds: I'd work toward getting Prabal Gurung sold beyond US borders. I also knew that my new platform—as a Nepali fashion designer—could help shed light on the beauty, culture, and history of the country that made me a designer.

It was time to go home.

CHAPTER TWELVE

The flight from New York to Kathmandu was almost twenty-four hours, not including the three-hour layover somewhere in the Middle East. I didn't mind how long the journey was. I needed that time to transition from one reality to another. I knew I was getting close when I saw the snow-covered peaks of the Himalayas through the airplane window, poking through the cloud carpet, a rugged sky crown. The bright blue sky was layered with the soft floating cumulus wisps interrupted by jagged white glimmering shards of mountain, soaring and grounded at once. Peaceful and silent, and the opposite of the colorful and loud chaos that awaited me at the airport.

Whether one flies business or economy class, there are no VIP passport lines or luggage valets at the Kathmandu airport. There's not even an assigned baggage carousel, just towering piles of luggage, people circling and grabbing. And yet everyone is pleasant, smiling.

In Nepal, there is a saying: "Bhai Halcha Ni."

Translated, it means "So be it. It will all work out."

As I waited for my bags to appear, I noticed so many people were like me, returning home. Mostly migrant workers with sun-weathered skin, lugging Saran Wrapped suitcases that I imagined were bulging with gifts from abroad. The economy in Nepal depends on these men and women sending money home, which means women living without their husbands, and vice versa, for decades. I left my family because I could not see a future for myself in Nepal. I was privileged enough to be able to chase my dreams and become a designer, versus the migrant workers who are forced to leave to make a living so their families can survive. For them, their dream might be getting a better education for their children, or building a house in their village. My leaving was out of desire, theirs out of necessity.

I made my way through customs and walked through the doors into the airport lobby, past the jockeying taxi drivers and families reuniting. Amid the throngs, I saw my mother and sister, waiting for me. Two beautiful beacons in the chaos.

THE FOLLOWING DAY, I was in standstill traffic on my way to the city center when I asked the driver to let me out of the car.

"I'm going to walk," I said to the driver.

"Are you sure?" he responded.

People swarmed the sidewalks; beggars were knocking on car windows, and a lone cow wandered through the street.

"Yes," I said as I flung open the door. I wanted to wander and get lost in the crowd.

It was a muggy day. Cable wires crisscrossed the gray sky, punctuated by the occasional monkey or crow perched here and there.

I was on New Road, the financial hub of Kathmandu, which also leads to the royal palace, built many centuries ago. My destination was Kathmandu Durbar Square, the biggest marketplace in this ancient city, which surrounds a three-story temple that dates back to the third century. On my way there, I noticed that most of the fashions sold in the stores and sidewalk stalls were bootleg designers, imported from Hong Kong. I walked past a guy in fake Levi's, a Tommy Hilfiger T-shirt, and slippers instead of shoes. I saw proof of globalization and colonization in his "American" clothes. Cheap knockoffs that symbolize American culture and are made in terrible conditions in Chinese factories are preferred to traditional Nepalese handmade clothes.

At the market, pickles, mangoes, and lychee nuts were being sold alongside knockoff Fendi sunglasses, fake Prada handbags, and statues of Hindu and Buddhist gods and goddesses that tourists often purchased as souvenirs. It was a well-known fact that the statues sold here had a fraught history. Some were made by artisans in the Kathmandu Valley. Some were stolen from temples across Nepal. Some were mass-produced in factories in China. It was almost impossible to know. Incense smoke filled the air. I marveled that the cobblestoned streets beneath my feet were so many centuries old that this area had been made a UNESCO World Heritage Site. "Who else walked before me? What are their stories?" I wondered. And yet, the juxtaposition of the ornate temples and majestic palace that served as backdrop to vendors selling counterfeit and stolen pieces of our history and culture to European and American tourists was almost more than I could bear.

In the middle of the market, there was a vendor selling concert T-shirts of artists that were popular decades before. These were not vintage collector's tees, but rather mass-produced ones from China. I saw the faces of Michael Jackson, Guns N' Roses, Bruce Springsteen, Tiffany, Samantha Fox, and Modern Talking, a trendy German pop duo, printed on a rainbow of different colored backgrounds muted by a layer of Kathmandu dust.

Growing up, I had collected these shirts: I had several of Madonna and Boy George, one of Charlie's Angels, a Backstreet Boys, and a Britney. As I browsed through the racks, I was reminded of my favorite one, Madonna's *True Blue* album cover. It is a profile picture, taken by the legendary fashion photographer Herb Ritts. In it, her hair is platinum blond, cropped short, and her head is thrown back. She reminds me of a mix of James Dean and Marilyn Monroe. Majestic rebels and pure glamour. I loved it.

Then, in the market, I spotted a white tee with just Madonna's eyebrows and her eyes staring defiantly back at us with the slogan, Who's That Girl. I suddenly remembered buying that T-shirt on the narrow streets of Thamel in Kathmandu with my own pocket money because I loved it so much. I also remembered the first time I wore it.

I was in seventh grade and had been invited to a boy's house, a rarity. When I arrived, there were a half dozen guys already there, in his living room, talking about porn. One of the guys started teasing me about my Madonna T-shirt and started saying, "He is that girl." He then began touching me, pinching my nipples. And then another guy followed me into the bathroom, where he pulled down his pants and demanded, "Give me a blow job."

When I refused, he became irate. I left on my bike, crying.

I left Nepal because I was tired of being desired and discarded, all at the same moment. How could people be attracted to and repulsed by me at the same time? How could any tourist, traveling through this ancient city, buy a piece of it as a souvenir?

"Are you Prabal Gurung?"

The question snapped me from my traumatic memory. I looked up to see a woman in her thirties wearing a salwar kameez standing in front of me with an older woman who may have been her mother. It was not the first time on that trip someone had recognized me. News of dressing Michelle Obama and Hollywood royalty like Demi Moore got picked up in the local Nepali papers. I'd been written about in *Vogue* and many other magazines, and yet, there I was, sitting in front of one of Nepal's oldest palaces, in a market that had also been around for centuries, wondering, "What's my purpose?"

I smiled at the two women and nodded yes.

The older woman's face lit up. She was dressed in a polyester vermillion sari, with a cholo shirt made from Dhaka material, and had a nose ring and a Potay necklace, which married women wear. Her face was tanned, weather-beaten, and her silver hair was pulled back in a messy bun, signaling the end of a long day.

The younger woman asked, "Can I take your picture?"

After she snapped the shot, the older woman took my face in her soft hands.

"We've heard a lot about you," she said, locking eyes with me. "You have every wish from each and every one of us."

She then touched the top of my head in a blessing.

The younger woman asked, "Do you want a picture?"

And the elder one said, "No, this is enough."

I put my hands in namaste and then held her hand and said, "Thank you. Thank you so much."

"This is my granddaughter," she said. "My son has gone to Saudi Arabia." That likely meant he was a migrant worker.

"We've not seen him for years now," she continued. "We don't hear too much from him—but he's doing well, I think."

I noticed the young girl's face softened into sadness. Her grandmother's eyes stayed locked with mine, where I saw the loss and longing in them, too.

"You've made us very proud," she said, now squeezing my hands. "We all want our children to make us proud. You are not only your mother's son, you're every Nepali woman's son."

I was so overcome with emotion that I put my sunglasses on to hide my tears. Fashion can be such a calculating world; it often felt like people praised me only when they wanted something from me. This woman wanted nothing from me except to offer her blessings. She reminded me of my mother, the sacrifices she made for me to live my dream. I said goodbye and began to walk, but I had to stop and sit down as I realized that moment was worth so much more to me than any magazine mention or celebrity wearing one of my dresses. This total stranger understood what I was doing. She saw me. After all the years of abuse, ridicule, and humiliation, I never even imagined how badly I needed to hear those words: that I was every Nepali mother's son.

I didn't care who recognized me or not, I sat in the middle of that market and let my tears wash away that traumatic memory of seventh grade and so many other times when I was told I'd never fit in.

It was there, in front of an ancient temple, where I realized that my purpose was much bigger than just making clothes. The tension between the fabulous and often superficial world of fashion and its very real impact—on workers, on the environment, and even on the people who wear the clothes—is a dangerous tightrope walk.

People often say, "Fashion is not art, it's business." I believe that it's both. For most of the industry, fashion is about money and profit. But for me, it's also a form of creative expression. After all, what's the purpose of art? To make people feel things. To challenge and question the status quo. That's what I wanted my fashion to do. My constant quest was, "How do I continue to make people feel seen and validated in an industry measured by how much money you make and how many stores you sell in?" This woman, mother to a migrant worker and a total stranger, who would likely never buy a Prabal Gurung dress, understood what I was doing in a way that made me realize that I was not just a designer: I was a storyteller. Our clothes tell stories about our world and ourselves. I wanted to make clothes that could tell a new story—clothes that defy the existing narratives about what's possible for our world, for me, for the people who wore my clothes.

BACK AT MY MOTHER'S HOUSE, she broached a difficult topic in her direct, no-nonsense manner.

"Prabal, everyone talks about you in Nepal now. Your success is a big source of pride for your father. I cannot take all the credit for it."

It had been more than ten years since I last spoke to my father. I still hadn't forgiven him for marrying my aunt, or for treating my mother so badly all those years. We were having dinner, eating my mother's delicious home-cooked food. My brother and sister were there, nodding in agreement.

"Your name is in all the papers," she continued. "As soon as I saw that, I knew it would cause problems. Your father would go around saying that you don't talk to him anymore."

I understood that she was being extra protective—not of him, but of me.

"The more you hate him, the more you're harming yourself," she added. "It's not about forgiving him—it's forgiving yourself."

My immediate response was, "No way."

I looked at my sister for backup, but she was shaking her head. "Mom is right."

My brother also agreed, so I felt I had no choice but to go along with it.

KUMUDINI AND PRAVESH ARRANGED a lunch for our father and me, and both joined me. I was, truthfully, dreading it. I still loved my father. He was an extremely brilliant man. His mind worked a mile a minute. He was a voracious reader, with an avid interest in sports, music, politics, and Hindi films. Charming, affable, and sharp. People—including my mother and siblings—have often told me that I both look like him and *am* like him in so many ways. I've always struggled with this. I know they're comparing me with his good qualities, but I also knew what cruelty he was capable of. That scared the hell out of me.

"What a good-looking guy!" my dad said as we approached the table where he was waiting for us. He looked softer than I remembered him, his jet-black hair now streaked with gray. "With a face like that, you could charm the world!"

He was laughing, and I did not say what I was thinking: I do look a lot like him.

We all took our seats, ordered lunch, and let our father regale us with his boisterous stories.

"I go to the department store and people say, 'Gurung? Is your son Prabal Gurung?'" He was hitting the table for emphasis, still laughing. Then he got quiet and looked straight at me.

"Sometimes you're born with luck," he added.

I smiled and nodded, but beneath my amenable facade, I was gritting my teeth and counting the minutes until I could leave. My mother had never once used the word *luck* in describing me or my accomplishments. Nothing about my father had changed. He knew nothing of my struggles, or pain, much of which he was responsible for.

He then looked at me teary-eyed, and said, "You did it! I was not sure anything was going to happen—but you pulled it off."

It was exactly what I had always thought I wanted to hear my father say to me. But at that moment, I felt nothing.

BACK IN NEW YORK, I started to meet regularly with Caroline Brown, the president of Carolina Herrera, with whom I was matched through the CFDA/Vogue Fashion Fund. The conversation I had with Anna and the other judges back when I received that life-changing check led to the organization's first "Americans in Paris" event in 2012. I knew that to grow a luxury brand, you had to get in front of international buyers. And so I was thrilled to be invited, along with a dozen other up-and-coming designers, to show my line at a dedicated showroom at the Palais-Royal during Paris Fashion Week.

That was where I met Franca Sozzani, *Italian Vogue*'s editor in chief, who came to see my collection. I was nervous. I was still wondering, "Is my work good enough? How will they react?"

"You know, this is unique," she said. "You have a unique voice."

I told her my background, and at the end of our chat, she said, "I especially love the part when you talk about Nepal—don't be afraid to show your roots."

I WASN'T AN AMERICAN citizen yet—I still had only a green card, which made traveling to Europe challenging. Shortly after the Americans in Paris event, KCD, the fashion PR firm, suggested that I do an event in London. Elizabeth Saltzman had recently moved there after years as *Vanity Fair*'s fashion director and offered to host a dinner for me. I loved the idea of going back to London, where I had spotted the Chanel dress that inspired me to go to Parsons in the first place. But the British embassy flat-out rejected my request. When I called to inquire why, they would not tell me.

"Can I give you anything to prove what I am doing?" I asked.

"No," was the curt reply.

This was the day before I was meant to get on the plane, so I had to break the unfortunate news to KCD and Elizabeth Saltzman, who had apparently already made a life-size cardboard cutout of me for the event.

I also wrote to Anna to share the disappointing news. Within fifteen minutes of my hitting send, someone from her office called and said, "Go to the embassy, call this person, they'll have your visa ready."

I jumped in a cab and called the embassy to say I was on my way, as it was late in the day. They assured me that the embassy would stay open until I arrived. Once at the embassy, the very same people who had told me it was impossible to process my visa were now fawning over me. I left with all the paperwork necessary and was on the plane to London the very next day. The power of Anna.

THAT TRIP RESULTED IN sales to Harrods, Selfridges, and other UK stores. And then the Duchess of Cambridge was photographed wearing a dress I designed during her royal visit to Singapore. I found that so meaningful, as

I had recently learned that the Nepali people who serve in Singapore's army and police force are not allowed to become citizens. Likewise, the British Army had a unit called Gurkhas, a Nepali force who were treated in a similar manner.

We can fight for these countries—and die for them—but don't have the same rights as their citizens. I hoped that the Singapore government would take note that Kate Middleton chose a Nepali designer.

IN JUNE 2011, I received the Swarovski Award for Womenswear Designer of the Year at the CFDA Fashion Awards.

As a result of all the buzz that had been building, my company moved our office out of the incubator cubicle to a new space in the same building. We now had eight employees and had outgrown the space—and Bergdorf Goodman finally picked up our line.

Grace Coddington and Nicki Minaj came to my spring 2012 show, another well-received collection that opened more international doors—and an invitation for me to interview for the creative director position at Dior. I was flown to Paris to meet with LVMH, the conglomerate that owns Dior, Louis Vuitton, and more. Simply being considered for these jobs was a dream. I could not imagine working with no worries about resources, where I could design without limitation: the highest mountain peak in the fashion world.

WHEN SARAH JESSICA PARKER wore a look from my Miss Havisham collection on a press junket for her movie *I Don't Know How She Does It*, I sent flowers to thank her. I loved *Sex and the City* and what it did for fashion, but more important, for how it represented smart, hilarious, successful women in their thirties and forties talking openly about sex, relationships, work, and life. The show had a global impact.

That was the beginning of a very special friendship. She went on to wear five different pieces from various collections to different events—a huge honor from a fashion icon. Suddenly, I was seeing stories all over with headlines like "Who Is Sarah Jessica Parker's New Favorite Designer?"

The flowers I sent her turned into an email exchange, which developed into a friendship. To me, she is the perfect muse—smart, wildly talented, gorgeous, and curious. In fact, she's the only American friend who has ever asked me, "What does Nepali food taste like? Where can we find it?"

"The best restaurant is in Queens," I said.

"Let's go!"

A couple of days later, I picked her up at her West Village home, and we went to Thakali Kitchen, a go-to place for my Nepali friends and me that has sadly since closed. I ordered for us: momo (our version of dumplings) and chicken curry (which came with rice, vegetables, and lentils).

As we were waiting for our food, two Nepali girls stopped by our table and asked, "Are you Prabal Gurung?"

I said, "Yes."

They then turned to SJP and said, "Do you mind taking our picture?"

She smiled and said, "I'd be delighted!"

A little while later, as we were eating, the girls returned and said, "Wait, are you Sarah Jessica Parker?"

DESPITE ENJOYING ALL THE accolades and recognition, I still found myself circling back to the same questions: "Is this it? What is my purpose?"

I kept hearing my mother's voice: "How will you make a difference?"

I love making clothes, but I also wanted to do more. I had run away from Nepal to India and then to New York, and I found myself plagued by the same restlessness. So I asked my siblings to start a foundation with me. It had always been on my bucket list, and I knew that with all the awards and praise, I needed something grounding.

My siblings agreed, and together we created Shikshya Foundation Nepal. We started by supporting the educational needs of twelve girls, the children of prison inmates in Nepal. Our core belief has always been that if you really want to change the world, you have to empower women, and that starts with empowering girls.

The foundation has, since then, grown to support children from other equally challenging backgrounds, and it has been incredibly rewarding to see some of these children grow into artists, engineers, and medical students. Often, they're the first of their family in their respective fields.

When I wanted to become a fashion designer, I did not have any role models to aspire to who came from a similar background. From that, I learned the challenges and responsibilities of being the first. At Shikshya Foundation, we especially want to encourage Nepali children to dream big and pursue a career in the arts. Since we started Shikshya Foundation, it has become one of the major contributors to furthering arts education in Nepal.

THAT SUMMER, I WAS in Fire Island with my friends, once again surrounded by predominantly white gay men. I was hooking up with people, but it did not feel good. I was lost and confused. One night, I was at a club and saw a guy I knew named Jeffrey. He was dancing, singing, laughing—I'd never seen him so free.

The next morning, I saw him again and asked, "Jeffrey, I noticed a difference in you—what have you been up to?"

I thought that he might have met someone and fallen in love. Instead, he said, "Prabal, I started seeing a therapist. It has freed me."

It wasn't an answer I was expecting at all—and I thought, "I want that."

Therapy is such a Western concept. I had never even considered it until that moment. Intrigued, I went to meet with Jeffrey's psychologist and started telling him my story, including the sixth-grade sexual assault, the physical abuse, my father's violence, the racism I had encountered in New York. It felt strange to divulge all these memories. For years I had been doing the opposite, burying as many of them as deep as I could. Dislodging them was painful.

"Prabal, in this space you're allowed to let it all out," the therapist said. "These experiences don't define you. You define yourself."

TO DO THAT, I felt compelled to go back to Nepal.

Ironically, this moment coincided with my finally receiving an invitation to apply for American citizenship. In September 2013, I took the US citizenship exam in downtown Manhattan. My interviewer was a Black woman, whose kindness immediately put me at ease. She asked me what I did for a living, and I told her that I was a fashion designer.

When she asked, "Who's the current president of the United States?"

I answered proudly, "Barack Obama."

He was one of the reasons why I was so proud to become an American citizen. The first Black president of the United States. It filled me with hope. She smiled. I aced the test.

"Congratulations!" she said as I was leaving. "And by the way, Michelle looks really great in your clothes!"

My heart swelled up in my chest.

A few weeks later, I got the official invitation for my United States naturalization process, where I would be sworn in as a citizen. The ceremony took place at the Ceremonial Courtroom on Pearl Street, where I took a seat among dozens of immigrants from Southeast Asia, Africa, Latin America, and beyond. Brown and Black people were the majority that day, and we all were willing to give up our allegiance to our native countries to become citizens of this new home. This was the America I wanted to be part of, a place where I felt I truly belonged.

A large screen at the front of the courtroom blinked on, and President

Obama appeared. "It is an honor and a privilege to call you a fellow citizen of the United States of America," he said with a warm smile. I was so moved, I started to well up. He spoke of the privileges of citizenship—and the responsibility. "I ask that you use your freedoms and your talents to contribute to the good of our nation and the world," he said. "Always remember in America that no dream is impossible." I felt his words deeply.

"You can help write the next chapter in our great American story."

That line was like a lightning bolt for me. I was still Prabal Gurung. And I was also an American citizen. I got to keep my identity—President Obama's request was that I use it to contribute to the narrative of the United States. As I walked out of the building, my head was swimming with ideas of all the ways I could do that. Out on the street, I was surprised to see Damien and a few friends waiting on the sidewalk, waving an American flag. They burst out into hurrahs and applause.

"Welcome to America!" they cheered as they wrapped the flag around me like a cape, reminding me of my childhood when I would run around pretending to be Wonder Woman.

My next trip to Nepal was my first with an American passport. In therapy, I was beginning to understand how I thought I was running away from Nepal all these years, but I was just running away from the pain I experienced there.

I needed to separate the place from the experiences. It was important to begin healing some old wounds. I decided the best way to do this was alone, in nature.

At St. Xavier's, going on Himalayan treks was part of the school experience. We'd pack everything we needed for a fifteen-day hike, including tents and food. It was a profound way to be in touch with Mother Nature, to understand how insignificant we humans are in the grand scheme of things.

Right before this trip to Nepal, I called my siblings to let them know I had been seeing a therapist, which was already having a powerful impact on me. To begin, I realized that I had been pouring so much of myself into my work that I had never allowed myself to even consider a love life. I wanted to make it happen, but I didn't know how. All those painful experiences—from the secret relationships to the egregious abuse, as well as witnessing the violence in my own home—made me deeply distrustful of intimacy, to the point that I could not even imagine someone falling in love with me.

Therapy helped me understand that I first had to fall back in love with myself.

I FLEW INTO LUKLA, the gateway to the Mount Everest region. It's considered one of the world's most dangerous airports due to the short airstrip, which ends at a cliff. The weather changes so quickly that flights are often canceled just as you have fastened your seat belt.

Once I arrived, I hired two porters, one to show me the way, and the other to help carry supplies. I was struck by the simplicity of their outfits: sweatpants, sneakers, and several layers of sweaters, threadbare and stretched from use. One carried a wheelbarrow-size bamboo basket on his back, which contained all our food for the six-day journey. So simple and rustic compared with me and other tourists in our high-tech nylon or spandex outfits and matching backpacks designed with specialized pockets for hiking gear and gadgets.

As we made our way up the mountain path, we passed through villages where I saw women in sun-faded floral blouses and oxidized nose rings and anklets, their saris tied up around their waists, their toes painted with a brilliant red vermillion powder, made from cinnabar. It's known as the promising color, and I wondered what promises lay ahead for them, and for me.

Hiking in that wilderness was almost a hallucinogenic experience: we walked past walls of wild rhododendron, bursting with glorious deep magenta blooms, the morning dew on their dark green leaves glistening, natural crystals catching the sun and reflecting it back. I took deep, intoxicating breaths of air so pure it tasted sweet on my tongue, intermingled with the scent of wildflowers and smoke from village cooking fires. It was a sensory symphony. Each day began and ended with a sky so Technicolor—from lavender to coral to sky blue—that I wondered, "Can something this beautiful be real?"

On the second or third day of the trek, I had just sat down for dinner when I heard soft voices in the distance. Children singing, I thought, and smiled.

The Nepali sky was a deep-sea blue with stars shining like diamonds, and the song that wafted toward me was "Twinkle, Twinkle, Little Star," in Nepali. My heart fluttered imagining the tiny faces singing. Was it a choir? A school? I did not know, nor did it matter. I was relishing the sweetness, which reminded me of my young self, so innocent, playing with those paper dolls, singing "Confidence" from *The Sound of Music*. Happy.

Then the children began to sing the Nepali version of "We Shall Overcome," and I was overcome by their magical chanting rendition and what it meant to me at that moment. I realized that I had been so focused on the business that I forgot my true love, the art of fashion. The numbers, not the nuanced poetry. And yet I was surrounded by inspiration in the purest form, from the salmon-hued sunset to the stars in the sky to the vermillion red and sun-faded florals and hyperreal rhododendron. I was eating rice and lentils with my right hand, as we do in Nepal, and said out loud, to no one, "My goodness, I know what my calling is!"

That trip reinvigorated my love, admiration, and appreciation for the Eastern world. I wanted to share that story, *my story*, in a more overt way. As I walked through those giant mountain vistas and rural villages, I saw clearly that beauty is not mutually exclusive from substance or grit. What spoke to me was the resilience and strength that I saw in the villagers. They lived hard lives, but still had radiant, infectious smiles. They still had optimism and joy. I wanted to infuse that into both my life and my work.

I decided that my next collection would be my way of inviting people into my world. A way of saying, "This is where I am from. This is who I am."

I SCHEDULED AN EXTRA week to see my family after the trek and went to a jazz festival in Kathmandu with my sister and some of her friends. It was a beautiful, crisp November night fragrant with the marigold and chrysanthemum flowers left over from the Tihar Diwali celebrations that had just happened. Those sweet scents intermingled with the freshly cooked momo and the jeri—sweet, deep-fried dough dipped in simple syrup. I was hungry for all of it and felt rejuvenated and inspired. Being at this festival with my sister, eating all my favorite Nepali delicacies, dancing to the beautiful jazz music intermixed with Nepali tunes was a continuation of the journey I began on this trip—to find myself.

Among the mostly Nepali crowd, there was a smattering of white folks—expats and tourists. But a tall, brown-eyed man with dirty blond shoulder-length hair stood out. He wore trekking pants and a worn-out plaid shirt and was holding a beer. While he was handsome, what struck me was how relaxed he seemed. I caught his eye, and he smiled, flashing the most gorgeous set of pearly whites. I felt a magnetic pull toward him.

"I'm going to sleep with him tonight," I told my sister.

I went over and introduced myself. His name was Sebastian, and I learned that he grew up in a rural town in upstate New York and went to Cornell University, which had an exchange program with Nepal. He was teaching English and said that he fell in love with the people and culture. There was an ease to him that I was immediately attracted to. I introduced him to my sister and, afterward, went back to his house. We started making out. There were dogs barking outside. The windows were open. It was a crazy, chaotic, magical night.

The next morning, I woke up before he did and saw that his apartment was a mess—there were clothes and books strewn all over the place, and dishes in the sink. I'm an utter neat freak, and this was the opposite of how I liked to live. But the joy I experienced with Sebastian quelled the critic in me. I was looking for possibilities. When he woke up, we went to get coffee, and, betting on hope, I asked if I could see him again that evening.

He smiled and said, "That sounds nice."

Back home, I told my mom about him.

"I only have three days left," I said. "Can he come stay here?"

"Of course!" she said.

My mother greeted him when he arrived later that evening for dinner. I left the two of them alone for a moment and was stunned when I returned to find them having an engaged conversation—in Nepali. Sebastian and I had been speaking English to each other, and I hadn't realized that he was fluent in our language.

Mami looked at me delighted and said, "He speaks Nepali so well!"

That was when I fell in love.

Back in New York, I kept in touch with Sebastian daily, via WhatsApp and text. We made a plan for him to come visit that spring. It was December 2013, and I had a collection to design. I had so many ideas, all inspired by my trek in the Himalayas. Mostly, I wanted to convey the optimism and joy I felt on that trip. I wanted to allow others to feel the thrill of wanderlust coupled with the compulsion of curiosity, without having to physically travel. This collection was about opening minds to possibilities beyond the borders of the Western world. It was about imagining where else one can find beauty and poetry. This time Nepal would not be merely hinted at, it would be placed on the runway for all the world to see.

I started with a mood board—images of monks, mountain people, sunrises, and sunsets. I wanted to transfer what I had experienced on that trip into knitwear and draping. I wanted to honor the fact that people in the villages wore fur and shearling in a powerful ode to the cyclical beauty of survival. Nothing was wasted: the meat was eaten; hides were tanned and turned into garments. Nourishment and protection. I wanted to marry that to my love for couture evening wear, which I translated into hand-embroidered beadwork and feathers and hand-draped chiffon dresses—worn with knitwear that was made by female artisans in Nepal. I knew this would create employment opportunities for these women, much like my mom did in Singapore all those years ago. I also had anklets made in Nepal out of oxidized silver, which were then attached to shoes made in Italy. East meets West. My clothes were never just clothes: each piece had a reason and a story. Luxury fabrics and materials made in Europe could exist alongside something handmade in Nepal. Belonging and unbelonging.

I was determined to use Nepali artisans' work in this collection, but also anxious about quality control and meeting deadlines. I sent samples back multiple times until it was right. It took time, training, and a lot of patience: I was trying to tell my own story, and the artisans' point of view was part of that.

The day of the show arrived, and I was more proud than nervous. I had poured my heart into this collection and was excited to share it with the world. I was fully embracing what Nepal meant to me. We started with the sound of the models walking with no musical accompaniment, in silence. Each wore anklets like the ones I saw the women wearing in the villages, which clinked together to make the most beautiful sound. A soft, clanging, *shh, shh, shh* rhythm followed by a soundtrack that included chanting and chiming, the sounds of my country. I wanted people to not just look at the clothes but to feel the emotions that went into making them. It was ethereal and everything I had hoped for.

But then I heard a commotion ripple through the crowd and saw a man jump onto the runway wearing a black silk robe, which he dropped to flash his ass to the audience. He was wearing a G-string and a fake plastic crown. It was vulgar and crude and broke the magical spell on the runway.

Amazingly, the models did not break their stride or gaze as he sprinted around them. Security quickly scrambled onto the stage and chased him away. I was so angry. I had no idea who he was or why he did it. I was about to go confront him, when a friend grabbed me and said, "Just let it go."

It was difficult, but I did. The show went on, and at the after-party, I decided to buy a bunch of fake crowns to hand out as party favors. I had since learned that this guy had also streaked the Oscars and the Grammys, so at least I was in good company. I wanted this collection to transport everyone to Nepal—and this brazen act reminded us where we were: New York City during fashion week. If I had learned anything by then, it was to not let anything deter me. I saw something special on that runway. The collection felt more me than ever before. An integration of East and West. Nepal in New York. I was on a path. I would stay my course. Bhai Halcha Ni.

CHAPTER THIRTEEN

Two days after the show, I had an appointment with Amber Mackenzie, the buyer for one of my biggest clients, a well-known online retailer for top brands. Usually our sales rep meets with buyers, but Amber was known to be tough, so I prepared to do the presentation myself. I was in my office when my assistant popped her head in and said, "Amber is here. She's in a mood."

This was her reputation. I had no reason not to like her, but she made me wary. I went out to meet with her. A handsome woman, she was dressed in a puffy jacket with fur trim, and cargo pants with heels. Ultimate cool-girl style.

Before I could even say hello, she said, "Let me get straight to the point—I hated the collection. I don't need cool from you. If I need to see a collection like this, I could buy a copy of *National Geographic*!"

"Okay," I said. For the sake of the business, I needed to stay composed.

"Stick to making pretty dresses."

She was being cruel and patronizing, but I continued to keep my thoughts to myself.

"I just don't know what to buy!" she continued, agitated.

"Well, let me walk you through the collection so I can explain things," I said, being very careful not to let my emotions show.

"I'm not sure I can carry this collection," she said.

I kept calm, explaining the love and attention I poured into each piece. By the end of our visit, she had plenty to buy and realized that she had overreacted. Her tone softened, but for me, the damage was done. I had put my heart and soul into this collection—and this woman, a powerful tastemaker, had shredded it. After she left, everyone on my team came to check on me.

"Are you okay?"

"I'm fine!" I said, but I was lying. I didn't want them to know how much her cruelty had rattled me.

THE GOOD NEWS WAS that Sebastian had arrived from Nepal to visit me on his way to see his family in upstate New York. We had been in constant contact since we met, and wanted to explore the chemistry we had both felt. I was brave when it came to launching my career, and a lot more cautious about matters of the heart. I've heard the phrase, "When you meet the person who is right for you, you feel it in your bones." I felt that with Sebastian, who also knew more about my home country than I did and spoke fluent Nepali. I didn't have to explain anything: he understood. It felt meant to be.

On the second day of his visit, he said, "I'm going to cook Nepali food for you."

By then, I had finally moved out of my East Village studio and into a loft off Washington Square Park, not far from Parsons. When I came home from work that evening, the table was filled with Nepali dishes. He made chicken curry, sautéed vegetables, saag, aloo bodi tama (a Nepali delicacy made of bamboo shoots and potatoes), and momo (my favorite). It felt like I was eating my mother's food, at my own table in New York. It was the comfort I needed at that moment.

A FEW DAYS LATER, I received an email from Amber Mackenzie.

"Hey, honey! I got an invitation to the Met Gala! I'd love to wear something by you!"

I thought, "Is she for real?"

And then I also realized that Amber Mackenzie wearing Prabal Gurung was a vote of confidence, as she represented such a major retailer.

"Of course," I responded.

We worked tirelessly on samples, and she chose a gorgeous outfit that we styled with jewelry and shoes. This was a huge investment: we dedicated days of labor and expensive material to make this dress. In the world of fashion, having someone as influential as Amber wear Prabal Gurung to the Met Gala was similar to having a celebrity photographed in one of your outfits—there was a ripple effect that could lead to more sales. It felt like a worthwhile investment. Two days before the gala, I got another email from her: "I just saw Riccardo Tisci and he fitted me with a dress from Givenchy—I must wear it."

Once again, I was stunned by her flippancy: Givenchy is part of LVMH, a huge conglomerate. I was an independent designer who had put time and resources into making this very special and expensive dress for her. I took a deep breath and responded, "You should wear whatever makes you feel best."

THAT YEAR, ANNA WINTOUR had invited me to attend the Met Gala—both cocktails *and* dinner. That evening, I saw Amber Mackenzie, and she looked totally forgettable. I had also asked Sebastian to come to the after-party to meet all my friends.

"Prabal, I promised my grandmother I would visit her in Old Forge," he said. "If these guys are your friends, then I'll meet them one day."

I'd never met anyone who was so unimpressed with the glam of the fashion world. It was surprising and refreshing.

And then, one month later, Amber dropped our line.

Amber's comment to "stick to making pretty dresses" really bothered me. I wanted to do so much more than that. I had found fame doing something I loved. People are always on the hunt for the next big thing—whether a trend, a designer, or both. I wasn't interested in that rat race—and yet I understood that a brand was supposed to have an identity—denim, American sports, sexy, etc. People want to know what your brand stands for. Mine was still style and substance, but I was constantly trying to figure out where I fit in. It was a question I had been asking since I was a child.

When I first launched Prabal Gurung, I began with nuanced references to Nepal—and began discovering my own voice as I grew my brand. My designs were my response to the world around me, and I wanted to continue to explore this idea: I come from the East, but my dream came to fruition in the West. I decided to continue on this route of blending these two worlds. I was beginning to see how fashion was not simply a way for me to make a living. It was a way to tell my story. I was also starting to see gender-fluid people, both Black and brown, wearing my clothes—at clubs, on the streets, in restaurants. I realized that the stories I was telling through fashion resonated with people far beyond rich Upper East Side women. I'd been mocked for wearing women's clothes my whole life, so to see there were so many others like me, who dressed this way, felt liberating. It proved my theory: beauty and glamour can come in a multitude of ways.

By now, Prabal Gurung was in more than twenty stores internationally, plus Bergdorf and Saks. Barneys had a change in leadership and finally had picked up the line, which was thrilling. We had started working with an international salesroom called Rainbowwave, which placed Prabal Gurung in high-end stores throughout Europe, the Middle East, and Asia. So once again, on paper, I looked like a success. But behind the scenes, there were still so many challenges.

Amber Mackenzie dropping us was a major blow to our business. We were still small, and so when orders came in from any store, we based our production on those precise numbers. That season, a store in Europe made a big order—which they canceled after we had made the product. The same happened with a smaller store in the United States, which meant that we were left with the inventory—and nowhere to sell it. Nor did we have the money to pay the factories that had made the clothes.

At this point, we owed $100,000, which was a lot of money for a small brand. It kept me up at night worrying. I didn't know how I'd pay these bills.

I knew these factories, and the people they employed, who were all, like me, hand to mouth. That's the reverse ripple effect in fashion, and there are lenders whose business is modeled on financially challenging moments like these. I wound up taking out a loan to pay off debts. The interest rates were high, so one missed payment meant another pile on of debt. This became a cyclical issue. Launching my line was easy. Maintaining and growing it remained the biggest challenge.

I am a creative person and a storyteller—but I also had to become an entrepreneur and a business leader, which I was teaching myself to do without an MBA. Always hustling, I happily did a collaboration with Target, which came with a big paycheck. That allowed me to pay some bills and also made my clothes accessible to more people. Kids on the street, and people at clubs and beyond would say to me, "We love your clothes but can't afford your line and are so happy that you're designing for Target!"

And I'll never forget one night at the Boom Boom Room, when I was out dancing with friends, someone said, "I love what you are doing. Bring your country home."

That really hit me: I knew that if I were to make Prabal Gurung a true success, it had to be bigger than just making clothes. It had to help break down the barriers of entry to the world of fashion and redefine who is chic. I was getting constant validation from beyond the white towers of fashion's elite—so why couldn't the Amber Mackenzie gatekeepers see the tremendous potential and possibility of embracing something outside of their own restrictive points of view? The industry tries to box you in: Are you preppy? Are you sexy? Amber wanted to put me in a box with that "keep making pretty dresses" comment, but all the beautiful misfits understood what I was doing. They saw me. I've never fit in any box, and frankly, I find that line of thinking incredibly boring—and dangerously suffocating.

For all these reasons, I was looking forward to a peaceful, calm summer without drama. I needed to breathe. My friends and I rented the same summerhouse share in the Pines, and this time, Sebastian joined us. We arrived on a Friday morning, and after spending the whole day at the beach soaking up the sun and catching up with my friends, I felt revived. That evening, we all went to Low Tea, a boozy, casual dance party by the water, which was always filled with music, laughter, and mingling. We headed over at 5:00 p.m., in order to catch that magic hour when the sky shifts from bright blue to lavender to pale pink as the sun sets. The warm, salty breeze caressing the half-naked bodies grooving around the dance floor was nothing short of magical.

This Friday was no different. The outdoor deck was teeming with men, in all stages of undress and already buzzed. Disco music blared. The joy and abandon were intoxicating.

I headed to the bar to order a drink, and as I was snaking through a crowd of mostly white though deeply tanned bodies, someone pushed me and huffed, "Fucking gaysians."

As always, that word triggered me. But this time around, I decided to let it go instead of reacting or fighting. I didn't want to ruin my weekend.

I ordered drinks and joined Sebastian and my friends by the tent poles where we liked to hang out. It was a beautiful day. I closed my eyes and took in the breeze and warmth of the setting sun: I wanted to forget what had just happened at the bar, what had happened with Amber Mackenzie, what had happened almost every time I entered a predominantly white space. I would not let it bog me down.

When I opened my eyes, I saw that the same guy who had made that comment was flirting with Sebastian. He looked like one of the cast members of *Jersey Shore* with his drugstore peroxide spiked hair and tanning bed–orange glow. I was annoyed but remained determined to not let him ruin my night.

Damien noticed my discomfort, and asked, "Are you okay?"

I nodded yes just as I heard a squeal.

"Who is the lucky, handsome devil?" Jersey Shore asked Sebastian in an overly dramatic and loud way as Sebastian pointed at me.

"Him? Oh, wow!" he looked shocked, and he made his way toward me. When he got to me, he said, "Gurl, congratulations! How did you get so lucky to catch this man?"

I took a deep breath and a large sip of my drink before saying, "First of all, don't fucking *girl* me. I'm not your girl, and second, *It is none of your business.* So just fuck off."

My friends around me were shocked—they didn't know what had transpired earlier. Instead of explaining anything, I went to the dance floor, where Sebastian joined me, clearly concerned—not about what I said, but about me. He knew how exhausted I was from all the racist bullshit. He smiled at me, and I was so relieved to have him to fall back on. He understood.

As the music played one disco number after another, my mood lifted. Dancing always does that for me. Plus, I was scheduled to go to a *Vanity Fair* shoot that Sunday to be photographed for a feature called "Cut to the Future" about designers on the rise. I knew and admired many of those who were also in the photo shoot and was excited to be included in the story. This stamp of approval meant a lot to me, especially after what I had been through with Amber.

I was already on my way to the city when I got a message from my publicist.

"You don't have to go to the VF shoot," her text read. "They said they don't need you anymore."

"Is the shoot completely canceled?" I typed back, confused. "Did they give you any reason why?"

Instead of texting, she called. "Hey, honey. I spoke with the editor and he's profusely apologetic. While he would not say specifically why you were dropped, it sounds like there was some behind-the-scenes foul play."

"What does that even mean?" I asked as a large knot formed in my chest.

"I wish I knew," she said, as exasperated as I was.

Not that it mattered: no amount of explanation could alleviate how devastated I was. I felt like I was the victim of the fashion industry's high school cafeteria–style antics: I was no longer invited to sit at the cool kids' lunch table.

The whole experience reminded me of Amber's cruel comments and behavior. I had to reach even deeper to not let that energy deter me. If anything, that narrow-minded pettiness was precisely what I wanted to help fashion break free from. I was sick of it. Rather than wallow in self-pity, I decided to focus on my next show. I understood then that the runway for me was not just about presenting my talent as a designer. I had twelve minutes of the fashion world's undivided attention. I was going to use it in a more meaningful way.

For my next collection, I leaned into my instincts, and combined all that I had learned about fashion in my career and infused it with the colors and patterns of Nepal. My team worked on a new fabric innovation that included a cloque jacquard inspired by those rugged mountain ranges, and made hyperreal prints of three-dimensional rhododendrons, like those I saw growing wild on my trek. The color palette was meant to emulate the vibrant Nepal sky from dusk to dawn: white, turquoise, lilac, amethyst, navy, and sunset coral.

Because this show was my love letter to Nepal, I decided to stage it at the post office in Herald Square. The show took place in September 2014. Shortly after that, Michelle Obama invited me to speak on a panel at the White House for her Reach Higher Fashion Education Workshop, with more than 150 high school students interested in a career in fashion. I was so excited to participate in something that I would have loved to go to as a teenager, and something I hoped my siblings and I could emulate with our foundation. At that point, we were still paying for girls to go to school and had plans to do more programming with art in education.

When I arrived at the White House for the panel, one of my fellow panelists asked, “Are you okay?”

Another asked, “How is it going?” clearly concerned.

I had no idea what they were talking about—until Caitlin mentioned that it must have been in reference to a recent *New York Times* review of my show. I’d stopped reading reviews several seasons prior, as the experience was so schizophrenic—some people understood what I was doing, others did not. I knew that if I pinned my self-worth on these critics’ columns, I would not survive. Still, when yet another person asked how I was holding up, I decided I had better read the review.

I found the review online and braced myself.

> **Lodged in the bowels, or more precisely the great heaving stomach, of the James A. Farley Post Office on Eighth Avenue on Saturday morning, I really felt for Prabal Gurung, who was showing there. The guy has gotten a little taste of the validation Michelle Obama has also given Jason Wu, and lots of celebrities like his stuff. But the “buzz,” as they used to call**

it—now it's probably more a frenzied tippety-tap—hasn't reached urgent levels, and convening hundreds of spectators in this municipal location seemed like a grim attempt by his handlers to amplify it.

My stomach dropped. First Amber Mackenzie, then *Vanity Fair*, now this.

While the reviewer mentioned one dress that she liked, she described the rest of the collection as, "if not exactly frightful, confusing. . . . Close-fitting, pieced-together pants purportedly inspired by, if not intended for, some kind of Himalayan trek were paired with mesh sweaters whose components had been jumbled, Mr. Potato Head–style."

Perhaps the most insulting moment came at the end: "In program notes, the designer tried to draw connections between the blistered new techno-fabric used to construct it and the topography of his homeland, Nepal. But, at the moment, he has lost his map."

All of the research and careful consideration that went into each piece I'd so lovingly designed was dismissed in four short paragraphs. It was hard not to take personally, especially given how much of myself and my culture I had poured into the collection. I was trying to give voice to a place where all the beauty in my life comes from, and in less than three hundred words, the reviewer ridiculed and silenced it. It also wasn't lost on me that of all the designers the reviewer could compare me with, she chose Jason Wu, a fellow Asian designer.

My mistake was reading this review right before joining a panel talking about my experience as a designer. I can't recall one question, as my mind was swirling around all the ways in which this particular review could damage my brand. By this time in my career, I'd developed a thick skin—but this felt personal.

After the panel ended, Michelle Obama said, "You did a great job." And then she looked at me, and said, "Keep at it."

It was as if she knew that I needed encouragement.

THAT REVIEW WAS A big blow: I was already facing business challenges. But I also knew that all the greatest designers—from Yves Saint Laurent to Marc Jacobs—had gotten bad reviews at some point. As a designer, I'm always willing to take a risk and fall flat. It would be one thing if it were a thoughtful critique of my work—but this was lazy journalism laced with subtle racism.

The challenges of growing a brand were hard enough. One bad review—in *The New York Times* especially—had real impact. The business was still in debt, which we were paying off at a high interest rate. And then we had a private client who placed an order for $80,000—which we fulfilled. And then she did not pay us. The ripple effect felt like it could lead to a crushing wave of more debt.

When I learned that the investor Silas Chou was looking at brands to invest in and was interested in my company, I was intrigued. He was a businessman from Hong Kong with a stellar track record who had propelled Tommy Hilfiger's and Michael Kors's businesses to be valued in the billions. Silas was well respected in the fashion industry as someone with a Midas touch.

He came to my office with his daughters. Veronica was my friend and an entrepreneur. She was also the president of Iconix China Group, which distributes brands like Badgley Mischka and Ed Hardy. Her younger sister Vivian, whom I was meeting for the first time, was going to lead his new venture, as Silas believed the future of fashion was a direct-to-consumer model called "see now, wear now."

Everyone in fashion was trying to figure out a model that did not end with slashed-down department store sales, so this model made sense to me. The whole industry was looking for new solutions that could help save margins and make their business profitable. I was tracking with him until he explained that I would have to lower my price point substantially, move my production to China—and move my design team and myself to Hong Kong.

Vivian explained all the new technology they were investing in for customer acquisitions, brand awareness, and marketing. It was impressive. As was Silas. I immediately liked him and how he doted on his daughters. I was utterly impressed with their vision for the future. It was radical and bold, something I'd typically be super excited about. However, a nagging voice in my head said, "No."

Perhaps it was the idea of moving to Hong Kong and leaving New York after finally feeling at home with my community and friends. Or perhaps it was the suggestion that I'd have to drastically change my designs to simple, wearable basics. Or perhaps it was when Silas mentioned that he had also been talking to Peter Som and Thakoon, other Asian designers who had been in business before me. I also did not like that he was clumping us together.

I felt so conflicted that I went to discuss the possibility with Anna, whose guidance had helped so much in my career so far. Over breakfast at her house, after listening to my story and trepidations, she said, "This is a great opportunity, Prabal. Silas is a smart businessman. You should take it. Opportunities like these don't come by often. This will help you grow." She paused, and then added, "But if your instincts are telling you something, then you should listen to them."

She helped me trust myself. In fashion, one is always told to strike while the iron's hot. But my goal was to build this brand steadily at an intentionally slower and more sustainable pace.

I also reached out to Tommy Hilfiger, who had been an avid supporter and adviser throughout my career.

"Why would you not want to do this?" he asked sincerely. He explained his amazing partnership and friendship with Silas and added that the decision to partner with Silas changed the course of his life, professionally and personally.

I was even more confused. Everyone around me was saying the same—and yet it just did not feel right. I contemplated the pros and cons. I knew this could change my trajectory, and perhaps help me realize my dreams of becoming a global brand. But then it hit me: throughout all these conversations, Silas never once asked, "What do you want?"

The pros—the potential to make an enormous amount of money and create global brand recognition—were enticing. But more important to me was the freedom to tell my story and the story of people whom the fashion industry has ignored thus far. Stories that made people feel seen, validated, and heard. In the end, I thanked Silas for his interest and said, "When Thakoon becomes a billionaire, I'll be waiting in line to meet with you again."

I WAS STILL ASLEEP on April 25, 2015, when my phone began buzzing. It was still dark outside, and Sebastian, who had moved in with me by this point, was still asleep next to me.

I grabbed my phone and saw a text from a Nepali friend:

"Have you heard the news?"

A 7.8 magnitude earthquake had struck just outside of Kathmandu, toppling buildings in the city and creating landslides and avalanches in the surrounding areas.

I started looking for news and gasped as the images began to fill my screen: that ancient city looked like a war zone. Buildings had crumbled into big piles of stone debris, cars were crushed, and people were covered in dirt and dust, looking dazed and confused. Panic gripped my throat and rippled through my body as I frantically tried to call my sister and mother, as both were in Kathmandu. Nothing went through—just the dull beep of a long-distance call that was interrupted by an automated voice: "Your call cannot be connected. Please try again later."

I pressed redial throughout the morning as I simultaneously searched for breaking news. The reports anticipated many deaths due to the epic destruction, and I began imagining the worst. When my mother finally answered her phone several hours later, I burst into tears.

"Mami! You're alive!" I shouted on the phone.

"Yes, kanchu, we're okay," she said calmly, though I could tell she was rattled.

She was in the airport with my niece as they were trying to get to Mumbai where Pravesh was now living.

"The damage is devastating," she said. "We felt the whole ground beneath us rumble. So many buildings demolished, so many lives lost."

My heart was in my throat.

Once I knew my family was safe, I reached out to my PR team. I had a platform and wanted to use it to raise awareness about what was going on. Nepal, so often overlooked, needed the world's attention.

I WENT ON NEWS programs and morning shows and did radio interviews. I'd never done this kind of press before and had no media training whatsoever. I felt anxious about how I was going to come across on these TV shows, but once I arrived on set, it was easy. This was not about me. I was also in constant contact with my mother, whose insistent resolve fueled my advocacy:

"Prabal, I hope the world does not forget us," she said. "Nepal needs aid."

I immediately reached out to a friend who was working at *The Huffington Post* named Danny Shea. He was able to connect me with someone at CrowdRise.

I called my siblings and said, "Let's start fundraising for on-the-ground response."

Thankfully, Kumudini had set up a 501(c)(3) for Shikshya, which was up and running in Nepal. That meant that all donations for the earthquake fund could go directly into any projects that needed funding. My siblings started focusing on the grassroots, on-the-ground operations, whereas I ramped up my speaking, reaching out to any news channel that would have me come on to talk about the immense devastation: the death toll rose to nine thousand people and more than twenty-two thousand were injured. There were aftershocks for seventeen days, and then another earthquake struck at a magnitude of 7.6, which took out more homes and buildings and killed more people. That was the primary impact; the secondary was the lack of infrastructure, access to clean water, and medical supplies.

Steven Kolb was among the first to donate $20,000 from the CFDA. Anne Hathaway, whom I had dressed once, gave a large amount, as did Kim Kardashian, whom I'd never met. I was so grateful for their generosity.

I WAS AT A fashion event when I experienced the first eye roll. "Here comes the savior," someone said cattily.

Another person chimed in, "That's one way to get press."

The gossip was that I was doing the fundraising to get attention for my brand. Of course, nothing could have been further from the truth. The panic I felt the morning I learned about the earthquake reminded me of how deeply connected I was to my home country. Places I'd grown up visiting were no more. I felt that part of my identity was at risk as well, and I wanted to do more than raise money for Nepal; I wanted to share its beauty, culture, and rich history with the world.

And so, fundraising aside, I decided to pour that energy into my work: my spring 2016 collection, presented in September 2015, went deeper into the Nepal that made me who I am. This time, instead of a soundtrack, I invited thirty monks to come to New York to start the show with a spiritual prayer as a way of saying thank you to everyone who had helped Nepal in the wake of the earthquake. I also shared my thoughts for the collection in the show notes, writing:

I wanted the world to experience a glimpse of what Nepal means to me. Stories that have been shared sitting on a hand-carved window seat overlooking the 15th Century Royal Palace Square. Monks chanting in the juniper incense-filled monastery in which I unfailingly visit to seek refuge every time I return home. Trails of self-discovery leading to the majestic mountains through which I have trekked. These are a few of the images that raced through my mind as I sat down to sketch my Spring Collection—a collage of my memories gathered.

Then visions in crimson, saffron, lemon, and blush hues floated down the runway. At the end of the show, I took the stage and spoke from my heart: "Today is about renewed faith in the goodness of humanity. Today is about the celebration of empathy exhibited. Today is about prayer and blessings for each of us here to follow our passion and make a difference."

All my life, I was looking for ways to integrate fashion and substance. I was constantly told, "It's just fashion. You're not saving lives." But the earthquake forced me into a new awakening: I learned that talking about issues that mattered to me came very naturally.

"Could I integrate advocacy and fashion?" I wondered. "Is that even a possibility?"

I saw the power I had to connect people with resources, whom I had met through the world of fashion, to Nepal at a time of need. And yet my own company was struggling more than ever. Our staff had grown, as had our retailers, so I hired an accountant to do our books. I was so focused on fundraising for Nepal that I didn't realize our funds were being mishandled until vendors started calling me looking for their payments. That's when I realized that our debt had bubbled up to over $1 million. As the majority owner, I was responsible for all of it.

This was a low moment for me.

I started doing appearances and collaborations to pay off the debt. I knew the road ahead was challenging; however, I had faith that I'd be able to pull it off.

Meanwhile, Thakoon was the absolute "It Boy" in all the press. His namesake store launched that same month. It happened to be on the exact corner where I had bumped into Ashish Singh all those years ago, when he predicted that I could never have my name, Prabal Gurung, on a Soho storefront.

One evening, as I was walking through that neighborhood, I stopped and looked at Thakoon's name written in large letters on his gorgeous new storefront, right next to Celine.

I remember standing in front of that glitzy, chic store and wondering, "Did I just make the biggest mistake of my life?"

CHAPTER FOURTEEN

It was my niece Vaidehi's coming-of-age ceremony, which is a big deal in Nepal. As I witnessed this young girl, my pride and joy, begin her journey toward womanhood, I felt more committed to creating stories where she and her brother could see themselves, two brilliant, beautiful Nepali kids, in expansive ways. To dream big knowing that they could be whatever they wanted to be.

Sebastian came with me on that trip. He loved being back in Nepal and hated living in New York City. He was working in media, had moved up the ranks, and was doing well professionally. We loved one another, but that magic magnetic attraction had waned. Our wants and desires were different. My work required that I be out in the world. It was demanding and hectic even for me—and impossible for him. He was a recluse who struggled with anxiety and depression. While our differences were obvious to us, our love for each other stopped us from talking about what was so clear: it was not working.

Of course, my mother noticed. The night before we were to head back to New York, she took Sebastian and me out for dinner.

"I'm concerned about your health," she said in her direct way. "I'm especially concerned by the amount you both drink. You both have put on massive amounts of weight. That is an indication of something deeper. What's going on?"

It was true—we'd both been drinking and eating, but not exercising. She saw something we didn't want to admit. I knew Sebastian was not happy in New York, to the point that he had started drinking every night. Rather than face the reality—that our relationship was not working—I joined him. We were in a rut. But I was not ready to face it, nor was Sebastian.

BACK IN NEW YORK, Donald Trump was dominating the news as he was running against Hillary Clinton for president of the United States. All the news channels were reporting on his *Access Hollywood* "grab them by the pussy" comment that had been caught on tape. No one in my orbit could fathom that Trump, the epitome of toxic patriarchal energy, had a chance at winning. For me, it was especially triggering, as the way he spoke about women reminded me of my father.

I was an early supporter of Hillary Clinton, who made history as the first woman in the US to be nominated to represent a major party in a presidential run. I relished the idea of America's first female president—as did my mother. I became very vocal in the media, participating in panels and making T-shirts to support her campaign. I'd been talking about feminism through my clothes and in the press and believed that Hillary Clinton as president was the embodiment of that. Plus, I understood the impact the first female American president would have on the world.

I was so inspired by this idea that I dedicated my spring 2017 collection, which debuted in September 2016, to all the radical feminists I adored, beginning with my mother. I evoked Gloria Steinem and Angela Davis on the runway, and channeled lines from Maya Angelou's poem "Still I Rise" into outfits and looks that confronted the antagonism between fashion and powerful women, disrupting the belief that women must sacrifice femininity to gain power, authority, and respect.

"Does my sassiness upset you?"

"Does my haughtiness offend you?"

I even stitched Emily Dickinson and Susan B. Anthony quotes onto the backs of blazers, on the fronts of dresses, and on the hemlines of pants. Intentional messages from strong historical women I admired, delivered in a subtle way.

"They threw things at me then but they were not roses" was embroidered in glitter-gray bugle beads on a black T-shirt, worn with black leather pants.

In my show notes, I wrote: "To my mother, who always wanted to change the idea of the higher you go, the fewer women there are."

THAT FALL, I WAS invited to the White House to see a screening of the documentary *We Will Rise: Michelle Obama's Mission to Educate Girls Around the World.* My mother happened to be visiting me with Vaidehi, so I was thrilled that I could bring them as my guests—and to use my American passport to get through White House security, as the Obamas represented everything I wanted to become an American for. There were not many designers in attendance, which made me even more emotional, as the film was about the importance of educating girls across the globe—precisely what our foundation Shikshya was doing in Nepal.

Afterward, at the reception, I introduced my mother and niece to the First Lady of the United States.

"To say we are so proud of Prabal is an understatement," Mrs. Obama said.

My mother's smile lit up the already dazzling afternoon.

On our way back to New York, I was floating. After we shared all the highlights from the afternoon, I asked Vaidehi, "Do you know why Trump is problematic?"

"Trump is very patriarchal," she said. "I understand why you're speaking out against it."

"This is something you will have to fight as you grow up," I said.

"I know!" she said dramatically. "You have made sure of it!"

We all laughed.

I asked my mom how she enjoyed the experience.

She nodded. "Lovely."

"Are you proud of me?"

She said, "I've always been proud of you. Not just today."

I sat back in my chair as the train rumbled north to New York, watching the landscape blur by, and realized that I was invited to that event because of her. She made me who I am. She must have read my mind, because she reached over and patted my hand. "Kanchu, you have not only found your joy," she said. "You have found your truth."

I'D ALSO DISCOVERED NEW ways to use my platform as a designer. I'd seen how I could use my influence to raise awareness and funds for Nepal following the earthquake. I wanted to use this influence to also do good in my new country, which I had sworn allegiance to when I accepted citizenship. The fear of a Trump presidency fueled many conversations about equality. "Diversity" became a buzzword even in fashion, where it had been dismissed throughout my career. As a queer Asian designer, I checked many boxes, so I was invited to be on many panels, specifically to talk about representation in the fashion industry. I've always been unflinching in my belief that beauty isn't limited to a Eurocentric definition. I began to see it as my responsibility not only to make beautiful and well-made clothes, but also to influence how the world views and defines beauty. As committed as I was to a more intersectional idea of beauty, I learned that I, too, was restrained by what that meant.

During one panel on the importance of diversity in fashion, a curvy woman raised her hand and said, "What about size?"

The moderator brushed off her question, and I saw the woman's face fall. She felt dismissed and overlooked. I knew how that felt.

I was in a cab on the way back to my office and could not stop thinking about that woman. I realized that I was also still very much in cahoots with an industry that set the standard of size 0. At that point in my career, I was still playing by those rules. I had started talking about feminism as a design philosophy and realized that I was being a hypocrite if I did not embrace body positivity. It was a diversity panel, which *should* include all marginalized experiences. And so it was my responsibility to address the body-shaming that I had both experienced and witnessed ever since I came to New York. I could connect the dots easily from fashion's then unhealthy fascination with thinness, to the insane body dysmorphia so many of my dear friends suffered from, to the anorexic model that was hired at Bill Blass. To be honest, I was also getting bored of seeing models who were all the same size.

I was having all these thoughts when my cab stopped at a light on Thirty-Fourth Street, and a bus pulled up with a banner ad for Lane Bryant, the plus-size fashion company. That was my epiphany. Back at my office, I started making phone calls, which led to a collection that I designed with Lane Bryant. That was a collection I was—and remain—incredibly proud of.

Yet again, though, there was resistance. A woman who worked in fashion PR approached me at a cocktail party a few days after the launch.

"Why are you designing for fat people?" she asked point-blank.

I felt the blood rise in my cheeks.

"Because of people like you," I said.

I knew, once again, that my instinct to always be inclusive and to radically reimagine beauty was the only way forward.

I'D BEEN CAMPAIGNING HARD for Hillary Clinton and was honored when the stylist Karla Welch asked me to design a look for the singer Katy Perry for an event the week before election night. I made a cobalt-blue pantsuit with a matching superheroine hooded cape that read "I'm with Madam President" emblazoned with rhinestones.

On November 8, 2016, I was at the Javits Center waiting for the results to come in, chanting along with Chuck Schumer, "I believe that she will win!"

My mother was in New York, and I wanted her to witness this historical moment: electing America's first female president.

When the results started to come in, the joy and jubilation began to dim. Over the next two hours, I'd never experienced such a rapid shift in energy in my lifetime: it suddenly felt like we were witnessing an unexpected death. When it became clear that Hillary had lost, there was silence underscored by a collective "this can't be happening" panic.

I remember climbing into a yellow cab that night with my mother and Sebastian and feeling crushed. What was it about feminine power that was so challenging to the status quo? How could so many people reject the idea of women in leadership? Matriarchal power is something I have always sought out—in my work, my life, my own self. Why were so many men—and, we soon learned, even women—afraid of it?

The next morning, when I went to get coffee, downtown Manhattan was eerily quiet. I had never felt or seen the city in such shock. People were either red-eyed from crying or still in tears. It was a collective loss, not just for us, but worldwide. The most deserving candidate did not get elected.

THAT DECEMBER, LESS THAN a month after the election, I was touched to receive an invitation to the Obamas' last White House soiree.

I'd been to a party at the White House once before, in January 2014, for Michelle's fiftieth birthday. I will never forget that birthday celebration. It was so colorful and alive. Vibrant and cool. I was dancing with Solange when Michelle tapped me on the shoulder and said, "I want you to meet Barack."

He said, "I've heard a lot about you!"

That night, I saw joy, optimism, and the promise of a nation that celebrates the beauty in diversity.

The mood was different this December. People seemed bewildered and already nostalgic. I felt scared. When I saw Michelle Obama, I got very emotional.

"Prabal, don't cry," she said. "You're going to make me cry."

I did my best to contain myself, but it was so hard. Everything I had believed about progress had come crashing down.

My mom had been with me for several months by then staying in the apartment in my building as she was now going back and forth, living in both New York and Nepal. She wanted to split her time between both. This meant instead of speaking every morning, I got to have breakfast with her. This was a dream for me, and she also got to see my day-to-day life—not just my work but my home life with Sebastian. Before she went back to Nepal that December, she sat me down.

"Sebastian is an amazing guy," she said. "I can only talk about you because you're my son. You're not the right person for him. You're insanely self-driven and ambitious—and using him for your emotional needs."

I understood what she was saying. Sebastian had terrible anxiety and had left his job in media. He was trying to figure out what he wanted to do next. I was up at five in the morning; he'd sleep until ten. There were so many days I'd come home, and he'd be drunk—so I just joined him. He'd been trying to tell me for quite some time that he was not happy and wanted a quieter life. I flashed back to a moment when he said, "Prabal, I'm never going to be good enough for you."

My mother said, "You've caged him."

In January 2017, I joined thousands of protesters at the Women's March in New York and was buoyed and inspired by the collective feminine energy I felt there—and throughout the country and world. I took a ton of photos of all the various placards, inspired by the messages: "We Are All Descended from Immigrants." "Respect My Existence or Expect Resistance." "Fight Like a Girl. Vote Like a Girl. And Grab Them by the Midterms." That was the collective energy we all needed to get through the next four years. I wanted to tap into it.

Before Trump was elected, Maria Grazia Chiuri, in her first collection for Dior, sent a model down the runway in a T-shirt that read, "We Should All Be Feminists," an ode to the Nigerian writer Chimamanda Ngozi Adichie's essay of the same title. Inspired, I decided to make my fall 2017 collection my own political protest—but this time in a more blunt, in your face way. I saw how powerful my platform was and wanted to wield it to make positive change. I knew that every time I did a runway show, I had the world's undivided attention for seventeen minutes: major newspapers, magazine editors, and celebrities would be writing about what they experienced. I wanted to make an impact.

And so, for the grand finale of my February 2017 show, I had all the models march down the runway, each wearing a T-shirt with a different slogan: "The Future Is Female." "Girls Just Want to Have Fundamental Rights." "Femininity with a Bite." "I Am an Immigrant." "Love Is Love." "Stay Woke." All the while John Lennon's "Imagine," interpreted by a female artist, blasted in the background. My more subdued attempts to incorporate feminism into my designs were not landing the way I wanted them to. I felt it was necessary to be this explicit.

This was my way to not give up hope. To fight back. And to use my platform, and fashion, to inspire and imagine a world where all the things we manifest become realized. It had worked for me in the past.

At the end of that show, I ran down the runway in a T-shirt that declared, "This Is What a Feminist Looks Like."

It resonated. People gave standing ovations, and bravos and hurrahs echoed throughout the space. We wound up selling a lot of T-shirts, with a portion of the proceeds going to Planned Parenthood, the ACLU, and Shikshya Foundation Nepal. That said, I was also made fun of by many in my industry: "Stay in your lane, Prabal. This is not a political rally. Keep it light and pretty."

Not a chance. The Trump presidency was even worse than we had imagined. And yet, it led to the galvanization of so many powerful movements, from Black Lives Matter to #MeToo. When *The Washington Post* exposé came out detailing the numerous sexual abuse allegations against Terry Richardson, a famous fashion photographer, I was enraged but also upset with myself. Why hadn't I said or done something sooner? Everyone in the industry knew that he was a predator.

I felt compelled to say something. On October 25, 2017, I made a post on Instagram that read:

> **We all have voices. We all matter. What will you say?**

In the caption, I continued:

> **It is important that we hold everyone accountable who worked with Terry Richardson. Not to shame them, but to understand the intention & motive behind their decision to turn a blind eye to his horrific actions. Clearly, they cannot say they didn't know, because we all knew. Every publication who hired him, every stylist who worked with him, every agency who sent models on his shoot, even the UPS delivery man knew.**
>
> **And I knew too. I have to admit that I heard the stories. I always knew them to be more than just rumours or industry gossip. While I never directly worked with him for one of my own shoots, I knew the truth. I shared it on my Facebook, retweeted some articles and followed the "slactivism" route (of which we all are guilty) but never truly engaged in the conversation. Never spoke up.**

So why, when so many of us know the same horrific truth, does it take us so long to get here? It might give us an insight into this world of fashion, that we love so much. It might teach us something about our hunger for power, money, chasing the cool, our lack of courage and above all human failings.

And while this ban can be masked as a semblance of progress, it does feel too little too late. Too late for the women who felt threatened, violated and scared.

To look forward, and advocate for real change, we need to ask each other and ourselves—How can we build better, stronger communities? How did we foster such a hostile environment, and why do we continue to follow a herd mentality even when we know better?

Once we truly dissect and understand this, only THEN we can possibly be free of repeating the same mistake.

That same day, a well-known celebrity stylist called me, upset.

"This is fucked up. Terry is a friend of mine," she said. "I cannot believe that you're speaking out against him."

"You've known me for a long time," I said. "I cannot stay quiet."

"You just want publicity," she said.

THROUGHOUT THAT YEAR, I used the runway as my political bullhorn. I launched a new line of T-shirts inspired by my runway show that spread messages of feminism, inclusion, and equality, and during another show, I staged a moment of silence and solidarity for all the women of the Me Too movement where models carried white roses on the runway. All of this advocacy led to Robin Givhan's writing an article in *The Washington Post* titled "Is Prabal Gurung the Most Woke Man in Fashion?" In the piece, she included the fact that I dressed Issa Rae and Kerry Washington for the Golden Globes and then donated the sales of those dresses to the Time's Up gender-equality initiative. She also mentioned that I had participated in an all-male panel on how men should be *listening* at this very moment.

There was a sense of change and revolution in the air that I'd never witnessed before. People were more willing to talk about important issues in public.

Cindi Leive, who was the editor in chief of *Glamour,* invited me to a dinner on November 13, 2018, called Conversations for Change, which she cohosted for Time's Up. Cindi had been a big advocate for women's rights and supported my career as a fashion designer. She was one of the few supporters of my advocacy work from the beginning, always encouraging me to continue on my path. I found her to be intelligent and kind. As I entered the room, I realized I was one of the very few men attending among a sea of incredibly inspiring women. It was my kind of party, and I felt immediately at ease. As each of these courageous women spoke, I was reminded of the women in my family and life who had powerful stories to share but rarely had the platform to share them. As I was taking it all in, I felt energized.

At some point during the dinner, Cindi came over to my table to thank me for coming. Then she looked at me and asked, "Prabal, how does it feel to be in this moment when the world, the culture, is finally catching up to you? You have been at this for such a long time without any acknowledgments from our industry or anyone else, for that matter, and speaking up at a huge risk to your career. Knowing you were on the right path must be really rewarding now, right?"

I didn't know how to answer her. I was surprised that anyone had noticed. I looked at her, trying to hide my tears welling up, and just said, "Thank you for saying that. Honestly, I was just being myself because my mom raised me and my siblings to speak truth to power. To question the status quo. It's the only way I know how to be. If anything, I'm grateful that this kind of conversation is happening now. It's long overdue."

As the night ended, I walked through Washington Square Park on my way home. There, I sat down on a favorite bench, one I've spent many hours on since my college days, and thought about what Cindi had said to me. I didn't fit within the narrative of what a fashion designer should look like or how one should behave. And over the years, I'd been called a troublemaker, disingenuous, or opportunistic. I'd also been on the receiving end of blatant racism and vitriol—both behind my back and to my face. Those people didn't know my life story or my struggle because I rarely spoke about it. That was before the "woke" era, and yet I was raised on conversations about politics, culture, and the world. We were encouraged to have different opinions and discourses because it often led to solutions. I realized that what I had been doing since the beginning of my career—speaking up—was also speaking up for that little boy in Nepal because no one, beyond my mother and siblings, had spoken up for him. I never thought these conversations about equity, representation, or visibility would happen in my lifetime. I knew it wasn't cool, but I didn't care. Being popular or universally loved was an unfamiliar feeling. I was just traversing through life as I knew it.

My shows, from that moment on, were a string of political statements. In 2018, my collections were called "Dreamers Awake," "We Are Stronger in Color," and "A Seat at the Table," which was my love letter to the women of the Eastern world.

I had begun using Asian models back in 2013. It was for the first show my mother was going to attend, and I wanted to open with Ji Hye Park, a Korean American model. Usually, the opening spot is saved for someone established, and back then, that meant a white model. Going with Ji Hye was a risk. But I knew what it felt like to grow up never seeing anyone who looks like you in these spaces. I wanted to add a new narrative—for my nephew and niece, who are both my reason for being. I constantly ask myself, "How can I make a better world for them?"

We opened with Ji Hye, and no one mentioned that as radical in the press or otherwise, which emboldened me to continue to push the envelope and further diversify my model lineup. All these years later, and with Trump in the White House, I decided that instead of just opening with one Asian model, I would cast all of the models to represent different Asian regions, from Singapore to India, Japan to Thailand, South Korea, and Nepal.

I WAS FEELING BOLDER in my creative choices but was also still inching out of the massive debts the company had accrued. Anna Wintour was the reason Tasaki reached out to me. It is the largest jewelry company in Japan and was looking for a new creative director. This was 2018, and the timing was impeccable. The company wanted a global presence to compete with Bulgari and Tiffany. I accepted the position gladly. That salary meant I could keep my business afloat and chip away at my company's debt. Plus, it was also a great alliance—stunning jewelry that complemented the couture clothes I was making.

When I went to Japan to meet the team, I was shocked to not see one person of color in any of the company's advertising or marketing campaigns. This was yet another industry to disrupt: fine jewelry only ever used white, fair-skinned models. I suggested that we used Liya Kebede—the model I'd tried to hire at Bill Blass—and was happily surprised that they were open to it. The next time I went to Japan, I saw Liya on the Tasaki billboard and was moved to tears.

Revolutions can happen.

I WAS INVITED TO dress an entire table for the Met Gala in May 2018 when Tasaki bought a table. The theme was "Heavenly Bodies: Fashion and the

Catholic Imagination." I wasn't just getting a seat at the table—I was getting the opportunity to create the table that I always wanted to sit at: colorful in every form. I invited and dressed supermodel Ashley Graham; Bollywood star Deepika Padukone; actors Diane Kruger, Gabrielle Union, and Eiza González; pop star Hailee Steinfeld; Japanese supermodel Hikari Mori; and Chinese supermodel Ming Xi. It was emotional and humbling to see my dream—that couture is stronger in color—come to life.

That was a night I will never forget. I thought back to taking Zoe to that Met Gala after-party years earlier, where we were two of only a handful of brown people at the entire party. And here I was, hosting my own table of dynamic, strong, smart, and diverse women.

THAT SAME SPRING, WARNER BROS. invited me to see *Crazy Rich Asians.* It was a luscious, beautifully designed and costumed American rom-com with an all-Asian cast. I was so moved seeing this kind of Asian representation on the big screen in America. It was also a love story, and to see two Asian main characters portrayed as desirable was powerful. It felt like a pivotal moment—important to celebrate and support.

I invited all my Asian friends in the fashion industry—editors, designers, stylists, and influencers—to host a screening. We were all so scattered throughout the industry, often pitted against one another. This was an opportunity for solidarity. I reached out to Phillip Lim, Laura Kim, and Dao-Yi Chow, as well as the likes of Radhika Jones, the editor in chief of *Vanity Fair*; Hanya Yanagihara, the editor in chief of *T: The New York Times Style Magazine*; and Eva Chen, who was then the Director of Fashion Partnerships at Instagram. I'd never seen this kind of Asian diaspora representation on the red carpet ever before. It was overwhelmingly emotional for many of us there. Looking at each other while taking the group photos was also being able to see ourselves, celebrated unapologetically, as our true selves, not cast as the model minority.

The experience made me realize how much I craved this type of community. Inspired, I reached out to Phillip Lim, who offered to host a dinner. I invited Laura Kim, Phillip invited the stylist Tina Leung, and she brought the restaurateur Ezra J. William. It was a night of getting to know one another and sharing stories. We laughed and joked and sang and danced. It was spontaneous and felt necessary. That same night, we all went to a party in Brooklyn called Bubble_T hosted by Asian queer youth. That was where the seeds of House of Slay, an inclusive space representing not only the AAPI heritage of its founders but all underrepresented walks of life, were planted.

Weeks before my tenth-anniversary collection debuted, in January 2019, I met with an investor who was interested in my company. I was introduced to him by a friend who assured me he would not micromanage me or my vision. He had also invested in major designers who were household names. Like Silas Chou, he was a billionaire who made designers millionaires. Besides, I never say no to a meeting. I was at a growth moment—and wanted to explore ways to do so organically. That takes capital. I went to his office in Midtown Manhattan feeling confident and optimistic.

His first question was a fair one: "What does your brand stand for?"

I explained, "For the longest period of time, Americana has been prescribed by the industry giants: Donna Karan, Calvin Klein, Michael Kors, Bill Blass. But that is just one point of view. America, to me, is not white-centric. It should be colorful, diverse, and celebrating each culture. That's what makes it so great. I want to define the new Americana."

He looked at me quizzically and said, "How are you going to define the new Americana when you don't look American yourself?"

There was a dead silence.

"You mean to say I don't look white."

He got flustered and said, "No, that's not what I mean."

I wanted to say, "You are a fucking racist."

But instead, I remained composed and said, "I've lived in America for twenty years. I am a citizen. I pay my taxes. More than 90 percent of my clothes are made in New York. I generate employment. I am socially and politically active in America's political system. I have challenged every conversation about what fashion looks like. And yet it's not enough. This is the reason I want to define a new Americana. A new chic. A new classic."

I didn't get the investment, but I did realize that everything I had been through prepared me for this moment.

I was already working on my tenth-anniversary collection when I pivoted: I asked Jose Antonio Vargas, the author of *Dear America: Notes of an Undocumented Citizen*, to consult on the collection, and deconstructed the idea of American classics. We were living in a moment when immigrants were being attacked—I am an immigrant, as are fashion factory workers, many undocumented. How was I to keep quiet? Once more, I spoke through my megaphone: the runway.

Originally, I was planning to stage the show in Hudson Yards, at the Vessel. But then I learned that the developer had done a fundraiser for Trump in the Hamptons and had raised $12 million. I was the first of many designers who wound up pulling out, which prompted the *New York Post* to write the story "Fashionistas Flee Hudson Yards over Trump Ties." In it, an unnamed source for Hudson Yards said they rejected me before I rejected them. When the reporter called me for a comment, I refused to dignify that with something I could prove was not true. The response was brutal. I heard from many people, including friends, "Prabal, you think you can save the fucking world?"

"Make America Great Again," Trump's divisive and dangerous motto, had activated all the racism, sexism, homophobia, and xenophobia that this country was tragically now known for. But I believed there were more of us than them. And my way of fighting back against these bullies had evolved. Instead of trading insults and throwing punches, I sent Black, brown, trans, and queer models down the runway with sashes that asked, "Who Gets to Be American?"

I explained my reason for dedicating this show, marking my twentieth year in New York, to immigration: "This is all deeply personal to me. Though my roots lay with my family in Nepal, this country is my home. America is where my heart is. I am an American."

CHAPTER FIFTEEN

I marked this milestone moment with a gorgeous coffee-table book, a visual diary of my career starting from my very first show. As soon as the copies came from the printer, I took a batch to Nepal. That book captured all that I had accomplished since I'd left.

When I got to Kathmandu, my siblings warned me that my father was upset because in my book, I had mentioned my mother but not him. Even though we had reconciled a few years earlier, our relationship remained challenging. I was still angry at the way he had treated my mother, and me. By now, Mami had moved on and was fully immersed in politics and other business ventures. She had also found her own inner peace through a silent meditation practice called Vipassana. She remained my North Star, my Wonder Woman. My mother rarely discussed how she felt about my father marrying her sister—but I knew it had to be painful.

On this trip, my siblings once again arranged lunch with our father.

As our car neared the restaurant, Pravesh said, "Here we go . . . brace yourselves."

As soon as we entered the restaurant, I saw my father's full head of thick silver hair, tanned skin, sharp darting eyes, and that big smile. He was wearing a pale blue shirt with a burgundy tie and a tailored suit. As always, his appearance and clothes had military precision. Always pressed. Always classic. It could have been his years in the police force or simply his narcissism. Regardless, he was disciplined, and I had to admire that about him.

His eyes welled up as we approached the table. I gave him a hug and noticed it was softer than I remembered, not the same robust bear grip I'd grown up with. Now that I could see him up close, I realized he looked weathered and slightly beaten down.

We sat and he started to regale us with stories of family, relatives, politics, and his latest favorite films. As always, he made us laugh. My sister was doing most of the talking, and then my brother, stoic yet thoughtful, was engaging with him in a very calm way. I was just taking it all in, nodding along, laughing.

And then, out of the blue, he looked at me and said, "Congratulations on your achievements."

I was startled by the sudden attention.

"Thank you," I said.

Then there was a slight change in his tone.

"You keep talking about your mother in all your interviews," he said. "What, I don't exist?"

I had anticipated this moment—but was not fully prepared to address it on this day. All these painful memories started racing through my head, flashbacks that I had learned to disassociate from to keep my sanity. I felt my breath quicken with my heartbeat as words formed like a script in my head:

"You were gone most of the years while I was growing up. We went many years without you in our lives. Did you even think or care what was going on with us? Or how the hell Mami was taking care of herself and three kids? On her own? Did you even bother to check in? Kathmandu was not a safe place for a single woman with three children. Those countless days of worry and financial struggles. The sleepless nights filled with tears—all because of your recklessness. You weren't there to save me when I was being beaten up and teased and taunted, not only by the boys in school but by our relatives, including your own sister. You just weren't there—but she was, each and every step of the way. Always there, always reliable. My constant. Not only is she my mother but she is my inspiration and a role model, so of course I speak only of her."

Instead, I said nothing. I loved my father, but he did not treat my mother well—at all. He might have mellowed in his old age, but I had witnessed moments when he was a monster. My mother raised me to be the person I am today. She deserved all the credit and more.

"You don't even know the whole story of your mother," he said, practically spitting out the words.

"What are you talking about?" I said.

He wrapped one arm around the back of his chair, bent the other in front of him, and started drumming the table with his fingers. There was a look of satisfaction on his face. I looked at Pravesh and Kumudini to see if they knew what was going on—they were awkwardly looking at their plates. I realized that I was the only one who did not know the story my father was harboring. Because I was the youngest, my siblings often kept upsetting news from me because they wanted to protect me. That had always frustrated me as a kid, and now, as a grown man, it made me angry. If I had been prepared for this confrontation, I could have defended my mother. Instead, I felt helpless.

"What the fuck is going on?" I demanded.

"Your mother was married before she met me!" my father said with a weird smile, as if he were proving some perverse point. I was stunned. I'd never heard this before. My mother had married my father at eighteen. She had already been so young. How could she have been married before? When I probed more, he gave half-baked answers and then made it out as if he had somehow rescued her—and that she was not as pure as I thought. That further upset me. I hated the fact that he had an upper hand—but I kept myself composed, out of respect for my mother. Still, I felt the pressure inside me building, like I might explode.

Just then, the waiter arrived.

"Desserts?" he asked.

"*No!*" I replied with such finality that no one questioned it.

My father paid the bill, we said terse goodbyes, and I stormed back to the car.

As soon as we were out of earshot, I turned on my siblings. "Did you guys know this? Did she tell you anything?"

"I've only heard rumblings a long time back when I went to Palpa with her," Kumudini said. "There was this older gentleman in the village who mentioned it to one of our uncles. I overheard it but somehow told myself I must have heard it all wrong. I didn't want to deal with it."

"She never speaks about it. Ever," Pravesh added. "And it's not my place to probe her about her past, which seems so traumatic that she wants to forget it."

I understood, but I still felt angry—and sorry that they had to carry this burden all these years. I wanted to give them a big hug, but they both looked so calm and serene that I realized that either they had come to terms with how strange life can be, *or* they were in full denial.

The car ride back to my mother's place was unusually quiet. We all were a bit deflated, shoulders shrunken, lost in our own thoughts. The air felt heavy and melancholic.

"Yup," Kumudini said. "Nothing has changed. Not even his gossip . . . just like our aunties."

That made us all laugh.

In Nepali society, gossip is usually associated with women—but our father was the most gossipy of them all, whereas our mother had neither time nor interest in petty conversation. Our laughter broke the sullen spell and added a lyrical layer to the hustle and bustle of Kathmandu and its mayhem of traffic, bumper-to-bumper cars, horns blaring, Nepali and Hindi music blasting. Giggling schoolgirls, the sarangi player on the street strumming his handmade guitar. The effects of the earthquake were everywhere—people zigzagged through the streets, stepping over the large cracks in the pavement or around the piles of rubble that buildings had collapsed into. And yet life continued. Resilience and grit. Beauty in chaos.

IT WAS MY IDEA to stop by the Buddhist monastery where we often went as children. It was dusk by the time we arrived. We all marveled that this sacred spot had not been touched by the earthquake. It remained the place of serenity I always knew it to be. The oil lamps cast an orange-yellow glow throughout the courtyard leading up to the temple, where the spicy-sweet smell of sandalwood incense intermingled with the monks' guttural humming and whirring prayer wheels. This was where I came as a teenager to calm my soul and get clarity. It was a safe space. My refuge. A place where I could breathe. But not that night. I was so disturbed by my father's revelation that I couldn't quiet the thoughts running through my mind: "How is it possible that my mother had a secretive past that I knew nothing about?" and "Could my father be that cruel, to make something like this up?"

My siblings both seemed to have heard something about it before, so there was truth to it. But not knowing the whole truth was more terrifying to me, as it let my mind wander to dark places. My mother had already suffered so much—her family being exiled as a child, giving up her dreams to go to London to study, experiencing domestic violence, and raising my siblings and me as a single mother while my father philandered. What else could she have endured?

I laid the straw mat on the temple's cool marble floor among the many other worshippers in prayer—and then sat down in lotus pose. I closed my eyes, let the chanting and humming surround my body, and felt something shift and dislodge within me. Tears were cascading down my face, dropping onto my thighs. I could feel the rivulets dripping from my chin. Beyond the horror of imagining what my mother may have experienced, I was undone by my father's cruelty. This was not his story to tell.

After what felt like an eternity, I got up, wiped away my tears, and went to find my siblings. Kumudini saw me first and, sensing my pain, also began crying. Pravesh kept his head bowed. Perhaps they, too, felt helpless. Or perhaps they were upset that they were unable to protect me from this news. They knew how sensitive I was—as a child, and even now.

"Let's go home," Kumudini finally said.

Before we entered my mom's place, Pravesh said, "Prabal, don't be in a rush to ask her about this. Think it through. Take your time. Wait until you are not emotional."

Pravesh, always pragmatic. Always the voice of reason.

I nodded.

That night my mother had prepared an incredible feast. She looked so happy to have all her children and grandchildren at her table, as Vaidehi and Arhant were there, too. Their innocent presence and my mother's joy eased the tension from what we had just encountered at lunch. I decided to wait to bring it up.

Back in Manhattan, I worked up the nerve to call her.

"Mami, is it true that you were married before our father?" I asked as gently as possible.

"How did you find out?" Her voice cracked, as if a stone had been dislodged in her chest. She sounded upset, which was rare for her. I wondered if it was because she had been holding this secret for so many years and had buried it so deep inside of her that it was painful to release. Even worse, it felt like my father was using this information to challenge my trust and love in her—even though he knew that was impossible. That evening, on the phone, she told me everything.

My mother and aunts loved to talk about their childhood adventures, so I knew that my mother was the first child born into the aristocratic family of the Pratap Ranas, and that they were exiled from Kathmandu by their first cousins, who remained in power. I knew that she grew up still enjoying the halo of prestige their titles granted them as the direct descendants of Jung Bahadur Rana, a name that still elicited awe. But, she explained, the financial ability to maintain that royal lifestyle was slowly and surely depleting. She was just fourteen years old—a year older than Vaidehi—and in boarding school when she got the news.

"A proposal came from a family of an older wealthy man, who was married with other wives," she began to tell me, in a slow-and-steady way, choosing her words carefully. "He had a great family lineage, and wealth. And he wanted a younger wife."

I felt ill.

I knew arranged marriages existed in Nepal, as did "child brides." But I never in a million years thought that term would apply to my mother. And yet, as she explained, marriage was a transaction between families, a business deal. My mother was the oldest of five sisters and had a few unmarried female cousins living with her family as well. The financial upkeep of the family and their lifestyle was challenging.

"I was the sacrificial lamb," she explained.

Her mother had already passed away, and her father was against it, but he could not dissuade her grandfather.

"He rationalized that this was a good matrimonial match because of the groom's status," she said calmly.

Mami said that she didn't remember much of the wedding except that it was a very low-key ceremony. At the time, she had no idea what was happening. Maybe she had blocked off that painful period of her life.

"Mind you, child marriages in Nepal were illegal at this time," she added.

This may have had something to do with all the haziness as well. Perhaps the family was doing it secretly? I decided to not ask too many questions and instead let her tell me whatever she was comfortable sharing. Afterward, she was sent to live with strangers, leaving behind her siblings and their countryside home for the bustling capital of Nepal. The only person she knew who lived in Kathmandu was Prem, her cousin, as he had moved there for work several years prior. She looked forward to seeing him, as they'd spent most of their early years growing up together. She considered him a big brother.

What she did not realize was that now, as a married woman, she no longer had the freedom to do as she pleased. Immediately after the wedding, her new husband had to travel, so she was left with his first wife and their children. That was when, while playing with children her age and even older, one of them called her "Little Mother."

She was taken aback, and asked, "Why do you call me that?

"Prabal, no one had explained anything to me," she said.

One day, Prem came to visit. He was deeply disturbed by the marriage, and after my mom told him how unhappy she was about being duped by her own family, Prem said, "I'm going to get you out of here. I'll come tonight at five p.m. Be ready."

That evening, my mother walked the long brick lane toward the gate with just the clothes on her back. As she approached the gate, the guards shouted, "Sano maharani?" ("Your Highness, where are you going?")

She ignored their questions and continued through the gate. Just outside, she spotted Prem, waiting for her half a block away on his motorbike.

"My heart was pounding as I quickened my steps," she said, her words coming faster now, too. "I climbed on the back of his bike, elated, and as he sped off, swerving in and around cars and buses in the busy city, I felt a freedom I'd never felt before."

As she told me this story, I had to hold back tears. She was only fourteen, still a child. And while she insisted that there had been no sexual relationship between her and her much older husband, I wonder if that's the story she chose to tell me knowing that I couldn't handle it otherwise.

My mother moved into Prem's tiny two-bedroom apartment and joined a nearby school. She made a core group of girlfriends who have remained her close circle to date. This was perhaps one of the best years of her life. She excelled in her studies and was popular, never afraid to question the authorities or challenge the status quo.

THAT NIGHT ON THE PHONE, we talked for hours, and she told me more stories that filled in the gaps of those I had heard as a child. I knew that she lived with my uncle Prem when she was younger, but I did not know the whole story. Back when he rescued her, he was a bachelor, and though their life was financially unstable, it was also full of promise. They often talked about their dreams: he was growing a fashion business, getting clothes made in India to sell in Nepal. She wanted to go to London to study and become either an entrepreneur, a feminist activist, or a politician. But fate had a different path for her.

She was fifteen years old and in the ninth grade when Prem met Manorama, who was a cabaret singer. Back then only people from a certain class were performers. The creative professions were looked down upon. If you were from a "good" family, you might hire them for your entertainment, but as a career or profession, it was forbidden. On top of that, she was married—to Prem's uncle! And had a child with him.

Manorama's husband was traveling for work when she met Prem. They had an affair and she became pregnant with Prem's child. This was scandalous and caused an uproar in Nepali high society. When Manorama left her husband to elope with Prem, everyone was outraged—except my mother. All that ever mattered to her was Prem's happiness.

Soon, Prem's businesses started to flourish—and a big gala was being planned for the opening of a factory in a place called Bhairahawa, outside

Kathmandu. Many Ranas, previously exiled, lived there, so it was exciting news for the extended family. Everyone was invited.

The night before the party, Manorama came to my mother's room.

"You don't have to come to the event," Manorama said. "Actually, it's better if you don't."

My mother, just fifteen, was confused. "Why?" she asked.

"Now that I'm pregnant with a girl, we no longer need you," she said. "Prem wanted me to let you know."

Hearing this enraged me.

My aunt Manorama had always been cruel—so this should have not been a surprise to me. Still, it was painful to imagine that my mother, once again, was kicked out of the only home she knew. Once again, her whole life was shattered. She wound up moving in with another uncle and said she'd never known a heartache like the one she had that night. She felt so utterly alone. Betrayed. Lost.

She did not have her parents. Her mother died when she was very young, and her father had ultimately allowed her to be married off as a child. I knew that this was the plight of women in so many places—and still could not believe that this had happened to my mother. Or that her grandfather, my great-grandfather, had played a role in the marriage. Worse, they did not want her back. Her running away had brought shame to the family.

Before Manorama kicked my mother out, she had introduced my mother to her cousin, my father, Baba Krishna Gurung, who was visiting from Singapore. My mother always said that she never considered marriage to my father—but then when he heard that Manorama had kicked her out of their home, he returned to Nepal and asked, "Do you want to get married and move to Singapore with me?"

My mom, caught completely by surprise, weighed her options. She had nowhere to go. Her dreams of going to London to study evaporated, and this option of marrying a new friend, her cousin's wife's brother, felt like a safe bet.

All these stories were like pieces of an elaborate puzzle, suddenly clicking into place. I understood why she never had shared her arranged marriage with me or my siblings. It was just too painful.

"Prem saved me from one arranged marriage," my mother said to me that same evening on the phone. "And Manorama placed me in another."

THIS NEWS SENT ME into a tailspin. I looked back over my entire life in a new light.

My mother was my Wonder Woman, my muse, my protector. She was the ten-armed goddess Durga who made sure I stayed on my destined path. She encouraged me to be myself. To dress up, apply makeup, sing, and wear stilettos. To find outlets for my art. To follow my dreams. Instead of being angry at her for keeping it a secret, I was even more in awe. All I had ever heard my mother say to my siblings and me was to pursue our dreams. To be happy. She was perseverance and grit personified. She never said why, and I never thought to ask. She was my inspiration and my saving grace. Everything I have comes from her.

CHAPTER SIXTEEN

It was a sunny, bright blue, cloudless sky. An uncharacteristically hopeful day in the summer of 2020, contrasting with the collective gloomy grays that had cast a pall over New York City for the prior few months.

I was riding a bike from my midtown office toward home, thinking about how much my life had changed in the last seven months. COVID-19 was our new reality—harsh, unsettling, uncertain, and exacerbated by all the hate and vitriol targeted at the Asian community. On top of that, my own company was in chaos and disarray.

In February 2020, Barneys New York, one of our biggest wholesale accounts, closed its doors and filed for bankruptcy due to compounding debts. That left many designers in a quandary, including me, burdened with debts and bills of our own. No one knew what the future looked like when the present was so discombobulated. "Sweatpants Forever" read the headlines in papers, sending jitters to brands like mine that did everything but that. We were at the mercy of government loans, our wholesale accounts (who were uncertain about their own businesses and the future of fashion), and our private clients' orders.

Trying to find ingenious ways to stay afloat and survive became my reality, which is why we pivoted to launch bridal. COVID had also caused a spike in marriages, which meant we were getting more brides, as well as bridal parties. They certainly couldn't say their vows at the altar in sweatpants. I was thrilled to be some part of their happily ever after.

MEANWHILE, AT HOME, MY own version of that had crumbled. Sebastian and I finally decided to part ways in January of 2020. I have a photo of the two of us hugging in the street that day. We loved each other so much that we knew we could not stay together. We wanted such different things in life, and for the other to be happy. I missed him terribly. I slept with his sweatshirt next to my bed for months, crying my eyes out.

The loss of my relationship and the uncertainty of business was devastating. COVID shut down not just New York City but the world. I was so grateful that I had already found a community with Phillip, Tina, Ezra, and Laura. They became my COVID pod, and we needed one another more than ever. Trump's vitriol was aimed at Asians, and his references to COVID as the "China virus" resulted in a direct rise in Asian hate crimes. So many of my friends had "escaped" from New York to go out to the country, away from the ambulance sirens and the protests that filled the streets daily. But for me, there was no place I would rather be. This was the New York I fell in love with.

I WAS LOST IN all these memories when a blast from a car horn shook me from my thoughts. I looked up and saw a bespectacled man, maybe from India, with curly, thinning, gray hair, holding the arm of a woman, perhaps his wife, dressed in a sari. They were essentially jaywalking—it was the car's right of way—and this petite woman had thrust out her arm, which was adorned with gold bangles, commanding the now honking car and its swearing driver to stop. Her fearlessness and fierce determination reminded me of so many women I knew back home in Nepal, mainly of my mother. That stunning mix of elegant and defiant, regal and resilient. This woman must have sensed my staring at her because in that moment, she looked at me, nodded, and smiled.

I continued biking, past the plywood-covered storefronts where colorful street art had started to proliferate up and down the avenues. "Black Lives Matter" was chalked on pavement and spray-painted on brick buildings and billboards, and George Floyd's and Breonna Taylor's faces were plastered on streetlamps and subway signs, lining my path downtown. All of this street art tapped into a collective desire—a demand of freedom for all. That everyone—Black, brown, trans—matters. It felt so raw and honest, as if the city had become an open canvas inviting all the unseen and invisible people to express their feelings. Art as storytelling. Art as therapy. It reminded me so much of the drawings I made as a teenager in Nepal, where I never fit in. I had found refuge in my sketchbooks. All these years later, those drawings transformed my life and informed my work as a designer. This protest artwork represented what was possible.

I was nearing Christopher Street when I heard RuPaul's "Supermodel (You Better Work)" wafting from Sheridan Square. The music got louder as I approached the park, just steps away from the Stonewall Inn, the legendary gay bar that gave birth to the gay rights movement, which was inspired and fueled by the civil rights movement. The rainbow flags were fluttering on the streets and in my heart. These movements were all interconnected: human beings have the right to live as we are, regardless of race, gender, or sexual orientation.

Christopher Street was quiet but for the music from the boom box. There was a small crowd that had gathered to watch a drag queen, probably in her sixties, perform. Her makeup was far from perfect—I could see the clumps on her eyelashes, the excessive gold eyeshadow glittering in the sun. I'd spent the last ten years sending models down runways in Paris, Milan, and New York, spending a fortune on hair and makeup, making sure every last detail—the drape of a dress, the arch of an eyebrow—was perfect. This was so far from that, and yet I was so moved by how beautiful this woman was.

"I Will Survive" started playing on the boom box, and her eyes lit up with those first lines. She began to dance, shimmying and spinning. Seeing the joy in her face, and how infectious that was to everyone who had stopped to watch her dance, was when I realized that these perfectly imperfect moments are precisely where the magic happens.

This was why I came to New York.

I CONTINUED ON TO Washington Square Park. As I parked my bike and wandered into the public square, I took comfort in the familiar. The regal, weathered chess players who have held court here for as long as I can remember. The fountain that on this particular summer day was shooting ribbons of water into the sky, frothy silver plumes.

Yes, the familiar was comforting. The future was uncertain. I knew it was going to be challenging, and my business could easily be collateral damage. Everything had shifted. Luxury and glamour were in the middle of a major transformation. But I also understood that I was witnessing an awakening of the universe—and that to me was exciting. I came to New York to be part of this revolution. I did not know where it would lead me, but I knew it was somewhere great.

I heard something, off in the distance. It started off faint, a murmur, and as I strained to see where it was coming from, it grew louder and more rhythmic: "Black Lives Matter! Black Lives Matter!"

The chanting became louder and louder to the point where I could not hear my own breath beneath my mask or feel anything beyond the wave of energy that quickly filled the square: protestors, representing every race and gender identity and ranging in age from toddler to octogenarian, most wearing masks and many carrying signs. "I Can't Breathe." "Say Their Names." "A Man Who Stands for Nothing Will Fall for Anything." "Silence Is Violence."

The crowd entered the park and quickly circled the fountain at its center, now chanting: "No justice, no peace!" the nation's summer anthem.

As I stood among the crowd, soaking it all in, I saw an older man who was introduced as an original member of the Black Panthers. He began to speak through a megaphone about how a revolution does not happen sitting at home. I scanned the park—there were thousands of people. That gave him hope, he said.

He then said something that rippled through my very being: "I never thought I would be around to see this," he shouted into his megaphone in a tone I can only describe as hopeful. "It is a long haul—we must stay the course. Change can happen."

In that moment, everything clicked for me. For as long as I can remember, my very existence has bothered people or made them uncomfortable. I was teased and taunted for being feminine. I was beaten and bullied for walking "like a girl." And while I'm certain it would have made my life so much easier if I had remained quiet, with my head down, I also would not be where I am today. I always fought back. I always agitated.

All I could think as I walked through the crowd was, "What an incredible moment we are living in! And how could I be anything but grateful?" And then I looked up and saw a rainbow, through the spray of the fountain, a Technicolor stripe against the leafy green canvas. It floated above the crowd, buoyed by their voices and the street music and our collective breath, a symphony of hope and resilience.

As I was thinking about all these things, my phone pinged.

I had read earlier that day that Joe Biden had picked Kamala Harris as his vice presidential running mate, and I was thrilled: the first Black and

South Asian female vice presidential candidate of the United States. Within hours of that announcement, someone from Kamala Harris's team reached out with a request: "Would you be able to come up with something suitable for her to wear to an upcoming event?"

They needed the suit in one week, and it had to contain all the hope that her candidacy signified. I wrote back immediately: "It would be my honor and privilege."

So much had happened since I first arrived in New York City to go to Parsons, just a few blocks away. I may not have been the first Nepali boy to ever have gone to that extraordinary place, but I was certainly the first—and perhaps only—one to have reached the highest rungs of the fashion world. And there I was, standing in Washington Square Park, where I had spent countless hours sitting on these very benches, sketching designs and dresses that went from color pencil fantasies in my notebook to silk chiffon or crisp taffeta or beaded velvet creations worn by Oprah, Demi Moore, Sarah Jessica Parker, and Michelle Obama. Getting to dress Kamala Harris felt like a trajectory continued, and a sign.

I would make a suit for Kamala Harris. I had no idea whether she would wear it, but that did not matter to me. All that mattered were the rainbow messages I was receiving that afternoon; it had led me to so much beauty in one day. I knew in my heart there was more to come.

As I began walking home, my phone buzzed again.

This time, it was my mother calling. Another sign.

After four years of what seemed like a dystopian reality under President Trump, the news of the Biden-Harris ticket was a ray of hope. I was all in to do my part. Anything and everything. Dressing Kamala Harris, our future vice president, was not just an honor—it was a privilege and my duty as an American citizen. I remembered what President Obama tasked me with on the day of the official citizenship ceremony: "I ask that you use your freedoms and your talents to contribute to the good of our nation and the world. Always remember in America that no dream is impossible."

Soon thereafter, Kamala Harris started to wear creations made by my team and me. I did not share those facts before the election because I wanted the world to focus on her leadership experience and capabilities. I wanted her to avoid the scrutiny that female public figures get over their appearances, the way it happened for Hillary Clinton and many others. When Madam Vice President wore a garnet double-faced wool crepe hand-tailored dress with a matching coat, both made in New York City, while attending the virtual Presidential Inaugural Prayer Service at the White House in Washington, DC, on Thursday, January 21, 2021, I was overcome with emotion.

It is nearly impossible to truly sum up the magnitude of this moment for me. To see Vice President Kamala Harris wearing our designs that morning, just one day after being sworn in as the first-ever female, Black, and South Asian American vice president of the United States of America, was my American dream coming true all over again.

My story is one that could only be possible in America: an immigrant who was born in Singapore and raised in Nepal and India, coming here—a land of endless possibilities—to pursue his wildest ambitions. I saw Vice President Harris in all her strength and grace, the child of an immigrant, like me, and I was reminded of the potential of this country. The power to make dreams come true, not just for the select few, but for everyone. I was reminded of my mother, sister, and niece, who could now look to the highest office in the country and see themselves represented. They could see their dreams are possible. I felt my hope renewed. That morning was a new day that held immense hope and promise as we united as a country behind President Biden and Vice President Harris and forged ahead toward a more just and equitable future.

THAT SAME SPRING, I received an email from Andrew Bolton, the chief curator of the Costume Institute at the Metropolitan Museum of Art, saying that he wanted to include the opening look from my tenth-anniversary show, "Who Gets to Be American?," for the Met Gala's 2021 exhibition *In America: A Lexicon of Fashion*.

It was a white cotton dress with asymmetrical sleeves, a side cutout with intricately placed handmade buttons, and a draped skirt under which a bouquet of flowers was lodged.

It was my nod at all things American: cotton and its deeply problematic past in America, a bouquet of flowers and sash that represented the pomp and pageantry of beauty competitions—a staple of American culture—married with a graceful sensuality of a sari and blouse from the East. Worn on the runway by Chinese model Lina Zhang, it was a collision of cultures, continents, beauty standards, and questions: Who gets to be American? To whom does America belong?

I was beyond moved by the recognition. And then *Vogue* published an article called "Made in the USA: A Glimpse Behind the Curtain at 'In America: A Lexicon of Fashion,'" in which the opening paragraph talks about my work. Andrew Bolton was quoted:

"The most ambitious exhibition to date from the Metropolitan Museum of Art's Costume Institute kick-starts with a question: *Who gets to be American?* A red, white, and blue silk sash from the grand finale of Prabal Gurung's 2020 10th-anniversary collection bears the phrase, and it greets visitors from the threshold of the Anna Wintour Costume Center. It's a query every immigrant must consider—but shrouded in golden light at the outset of a fashion retrospective, it takes on a new verve. 'It was important to open with that,' says Andrew Bolton, the Costume Institute's Wendy Yu Curator in Charge. 'It tackles this notion of acceptance and belonging, which recent events have brought to the fore. Of course, these are questions that have always been present—but there are moments in history when they're more resonant and resounding.'"

My dress would greet visitors from the entrance of the Anna Wintour Costume Center at the Metropolitan Museum of Art. It had a red, white, and blue silk sash featuring the phrase "Who Gets to Be American?" I was so moved that a piece from my tenth-anniversary collection—a deeply personal collection that had been deemed by some as too political or too "on the nose" (according to one critic)—had been responsible for inspiring the 2021 Met Gala exhibition.

I was grateful to Andrew, Anna, and everyone at the Met—for seeing me, and all the people I designed for. Unlike the investor who saw, in my non-whiteness, someone who could never be truly American, the Met curators saw us as an important part of the American past, present, and future. It felt as though we had powerful allies who saw and celebrated us for who we were.

WHEN I READ THE news about the Atlanta spa massacre in March 2021, I felt ill. It was not entirely surprising—my Asian friends and I had been tracking every assault and attack on our Asian friends since Donald Trump began referring to COVID as the China virus. But that attack, which left six women of Asian descent dead, ignited a spate of attacks on elderly Asian women.

As the attacks started to increase, I saw a video of a huge white man shoving a frail elderly Asian woman onto the ground, and then begin stomping on her with his boot-clad foot. It makes me feel sick to even write this sentence.

By then, my mother was living in the same building as me, near Washington Square Park. We found her the apartment in 2016, after the earthquake, because I thought it was safer for her. Now I was consumed with anxiety every time she left the building. I was so worried that I bought her a blond wig, sunglasses, and a hat.

That morning, I had a very difficult conversation with her.

"There have been some attacks," I began tentatively.

I saw her body stiffen.

"I know," she said. "I read the news."

"Please, don't walk around at night," I said. "And if you see someone coming toward you, be hyperaware."

I placed the wig, sunglasses, and hat on the table and added, "You might put this on when you go on your daily walks."

My mother stared at me without saying a word. I saw a flicker of disappointment in her eyes, but I was relieved that she took them with her when she left.

The next day, however, she came to my apartment for our daily breakfast together. Before she even said good morning, she placed the wig, sunglasses, and hat on the table.

"I want you to keep these things," she said. "I don't need them."

My heart sank.

She took my chin in her hand and made me look into her eyes. They had a spark in them. "Just get me a big strong walking stick," she said. "I will fight them off."

She continued, "I cannot pretend to be anyone other than who I am. In my mind, that is another way of giving in."

That made me smile. Of course she would not hide who she was. How could I ever have asked her to do so? This, after all, was the woman who taught me, again and again, to always be my true self.

CHAPTER SEVENTEEN

As 2021 was coming to an end, it felt like everyone kept hoping that things would go back to "normal." I knew in my heart that was simply not possible. COVID had exposed so many fault lines in the fashion industry—and beyond. As a result, many businesses were forced to downsize or shutter entirely. "Business as usual" meant the same hamster wheel of churning out one collection after another. There was no reflective pause, and certainly no road map for recovery. While the bigger labels had the deep-pocketed safety net of the conglomerates who owned them, the few independent brands still standing, like mine, had to start from scratch. I still believed in my own resilience and determination, but I was getting tired of being tested constantly.

On December 30, 2021, I sat down to take stock of the past year, and to look ahead.

The year 2022 promised to be busier than ever, and I knew that I needed to pace myself. As a creative person forced to take on the role of an entrepreneur, I felt my many cups were overflowing. I was already preparing for two runway shows, four collections, and trips to five different countries for work. I also had several public obligations and a seemingly endless list of things to do to keep it all afloat. For the first time in my life, I was unable to shake the feeling of impending burnout.

I decided to go for a walk, which I did whenever I felt overwhelmed: I started off in Washington Square Park and headed past Parsons School of Design, wandering through the West Village before ending on the Lower East Side. There, I saw young, creative people who reminded me of all those I had first encountered more than two decades earlier, when I first arrived in New York. These walks were my way of reconnecting with that wide-eyed Prabal, and a reminder of how far I had come. They helped keep me grounded in a city that urges you to soar higher and go faster.

On this evening, I decided to have dinner at Cafe Mogador, a restaurant I'd been going to since my Parsons days. There, I ordered a chilled martini with a twist, chicken tagine with lemon and olives, basmati rice, and, as always, baklava for dessert. I relished every bite. After I took the last one, I realized that I needed to find more of this kind of nourishing solitude. Quiet time to reflect—to feed my body and soul. And more than that, dedicated, uncompromised time to think about where I'd been and where I was headed.

I decided to make a public commitment to prioritize this type of self-care: it was more a promise than a resolution, and an odd one at that, as I usually use Instagram to post business news, coverage of collections, celebrities wearing my clothes, and other events related to the brand. This was a rare moment when I decided to share with the world what I *wanted* to do over the course of the year versus what I had accomplished.

I recorded the video at my kitchen counter and said, "I'm not big on making resolutions, but this year I decided to do one . . . taking time for myself, which is not my forte! Mindful solitude is what I want to do. I think being by yourself and mindful about your surroundings, what you see and feel and witness, will help me become even more acutely aware of where I am supposed to go."

The messages and DMs I received on that post were overwhelmingly positive: I still had no idea what that solitude would look like, or where I would find it. So I trusted that it would find me.

THAT WAS THE LAST deep breath I took before I jumped into the fashion industry's high-octane January. I was already knee-deep in preparation for my upcoming February show, designing, casting and styling models, securing the venue, selecting music, curating guest lists, and deciding who sits where. I loved the adrenaline of those sleepless nights in the weeks prior to sharing my collection with the world, the next chapter in the Prabal Gurung fashion book. On the day of the show, I kicked into a higher pitch of work mode: getting the models ready, sending them down the runway, taking my final bow. Then there were the media interviews, the after-parties, the press, sales, and more. It was another well-received show, for which I was thankful, and I was still being propelled by that energy when the AAFA reached out with the news that I'd been selected as the 2022 American Image Awards Designer of the Year.

This was a huge honor, and I was deeply humbled. It was not just recognizing me, but my entire team. It was proof that our work was resonating. It was making an impact, and for that I was grateful. I knew that these outward validations often translated into more press and sales, but they also made me wary. I felt like I had been walking a tightrope for my entire career—one wrong step, one distraction, and I could plummet. The feeling never went away, even after all these years. If anything, it intensified.

Perhaps I was suspicious because I'd never won anything until my late twenties. Or perhaps it was because for every high, I had experienced an intense low. Either way, all these awards started to feel more like career milestones than personal achievements. They did not change me: my heart still beat for the unseen. And I knew that every public acknowledgment meant that my visibility was a mirror for them as well as for me.

For the Met Gala that year I was dressing an entire table. The theme was "Gilded Glamour." I was so busy with designing dresses that I had no time to prepare a speech for the AAFA American Image Awards. When the day of the ceremony arrived, I rushed home after a busy day, quickly changed, and then jumped into an Uber. As I made my way to the Plaza Hotel, I realized that sitting by myself in the back of that SUV was the first time I had been alone, and quiet, for weeks. I was going to use that time to prepare a speech—but also for the first time in ages, I wasn't sure what to say. I was exhausted. The physical demands of the day, layered on top of two years of COVID-inspired chaos—including the uptick in Asian hate attacks—felt like more than I could handle. I'd been throwing myself into work as a way of buffering myself from the feeling that everything could fall apart at any moment.

I suddenly felt claustrophobic. I rolled down my window and let the spring air caress my face and fill my tight lungs—it was both painful and pleasurable at once. Yes, I was grateful for the recognition, but I also felt that teetering, tense sensation. Despite all the work being done around inclusion and validation in fashion, there was still so much more to be done. Instead of preparing remarks for the ceremony, I decided to simply tell the truth.

That evening, when my award was presented, I took the stage and spoke from my heart:

"This industry . . . has the power to change how we see each other. Yes, progress is being made, but it remains an industry that often rewards and celebrates only a particular idea of beauty—one dictated by the colonial lens and tastes; an industry that wakes up to the cultural movement hoping it will be a moment so they can go back to how things were."

People were nodding their heads in agreement.

"An industry where anyone who looks like me or [is likewise] from the marginalized and minority/BIPOC community is still a quota, a box to tick, a decorative display for the front of the house . . . while the boardroom and the decision-making tables remain blindingly white."

Many of the people I was critiquing were in that room—and I felt in my heart that they were ready to really hear me. I did not back down.

"We not only have to prove that we are equally good or better . . . but we also have to constantly fight for our Americanness, in both this industry, and this country. For the American Image Award [to be] handed to me—an immigrant, and a gay man of color—the irony of it all is not lost on me."

That got a few cheers, and chuckles.

I ended with "life without impossible dreams is not worth it. Realizing the impossible dream with passion and grit . . . well, what could be more American than that?"

As soon as I was done, many in that rapt audience leapt to their feet to give me a standing ovation. As I scanned the cheering crowd, I noticed the several designers in that room—both young and older, more established—shaking their heads in agreement, many in tears.

THE MET GALA WAS two weeks later, and my table was an example of everything I'd been fighting for all these years as my guests represented everything I believed in: dynamic, powerful, influential women who were unapologetically original and unabashedly graceful. I was grateful to Anna for inviting me to host and dress a table that reflected my ethos—and for her guidance in doing so. I was also aware of the privilege as one of the first-ever Asian fashion designers—not just from Nepal, but from the entire continent—to get the opportunity to do so. That fact was not lost on me. I reached out beyond the expected Hollywood celebrities and well-known socialites to curate a table of exceptional women who inspired me. I invited Deepika Padukone and Alia Bhatt for their first-ever Met Galas, as well as Michelle Yeoh, Mindy Kaling, Camila Cabello, Ashley Park, Denée Benton, KiKi Layne, Quannah Chasinghorse, and Grace Elizabeth. Together we checked many boxes: Asian, Black, Latinx, and Indigenous, each woman undeniably chic and powerful, a dazzling array of skin tones and experiences that proved my decades-in-the-making hypothesis: everything is better in color.

That same month, I flew to Los Angeles for Gold House's first inaugural Gold Gala, which was the inverse of many other galas I had attended for decades where often the deeply diverse table I had curated popped at the still overwhelmingly white events. At this event, we were the majority.

It was the first time the AAPI community came together to celebrate our existence and achievements, which was precisely the goal. As a board member and cofounder along with Bing Chen, Jeremy Tran, Kevin Lin, Maggie Hsu, Janet Yang, Jon M. Chu, and Michelle Lee, I was excited to turn this moment into a movement that would have a significant positive impact on the diaspora. The invitation laid out our intention: "The Gold Gala celebrates the most indelible Asian Pacific achievements to help project new, positive portrayals while also dismantling pernicious legacy stereotypes. Gold House is a cultural ecosystem—or family of companies—devoted to uniting, investing in, and championing the Asian Pacific diaspora to power tomorrow for all. It's not just about fighting hate but fighting for power that empowers all minority communities."

We had started Gold House as an antidote to the rampant rise in Asian hate we saw during the pandemic. The organization Stop AAPI Hate had published a report that found one in five Asian Americans had experienced a hate act in 2021 alone—deeply upsetting, but not surprising. We decided to combat this hate with solidarity: we rallied CEOs, celebrities, and beyond for our #StopAsianHate campaign to raise more than $10 million for victims of anti-Asian violence. But we also wanted to fight for what we love! Asian stories being told time and again in their glorious multitudes!

That year, the film *Everything Everywhere All at Once* was released, and racked up awards, more proof of our hypothesis. We hosted screenings and events to elevate the brilliance of those filmmakers and actors. We also launched a start-up fund and accelerator whose alumni have raised more than $1 billion in capital. We wanted to counter the stereotypes and prove that we are everywhere, making art and contributing to commerce. That we can no longer be overlooked or ignored. I want to note that since we began Gold House, AAPI has grown to include Native Hawaiian with the new acronym AANHPI, and that proves my theory that we truly are stronger together.

This gala was a celebration of all, and walking into this totally glamorous affair where the vast majority of guests were from the Asian diaspora, each person more beautiful than the next, was the party of my fantasies: a celebration of our existence. This was a pivotal moment. Everyone felt a renewed sense of purpose.

At Gold House, we wanted to create a road map for the next generations of designers, to give them guidance and the hope that their speaking their truth would not harm their businesses. I'd always wanted to have a seat at those established tables that historically didn't include people like me—with Gold House, we were able to create our own.

Back in New York, I dedicated my September show to the misfits who are too often forgotten, placing them front and center on the runway, to hopefully make the unseen feel seen—and loved.

And then, on November 10, Eva Chen presented the House of Slay with the CFDA Fashion Award for Positive Social Influence. Standing on the stage with Tina, Laura, Ezra, and Phillip, my newfound family, I felt that my fight for visibility was finally coming to fruition. All the work we'd done with House of Slay—a comic book, our social media posts, the parties, and panels representing the House of Slay—was reverberating.

To be recognized by the CFDA in an industry that relies so much on the Asian community—not just designers but all throughout—was again a collective celebration. Too often, we'd been sidelined or overlooked. Tina Leung and Phillip Lim accepted the award and spoke on our behalf. Standing together on that stage with Eva, we all had to hold back tears. This was so much bigger than the five of us. The first step toward resistance and change is showing up.

A WEEK LATER, I boarded a flight to Japan for my last trip for Tasaki as their creative director. My contract was up after six years, and my own company needed my full attention. It was an emotional trip for me, as Japan had finally opened after the COVID shutdown. The hunger and desire people had to connect and interact after being forced apart was palpable—in both New York and Tokyo. I felt that I had helped the company in profound ways, proving my hypothesis that change is possible and that diversity is beautiful.

Back in New York, I was asked to join the CFDA as a co–vice chairperson with my friend the designer Aurora James. That was announced in December, and this was the most meaningful milestone for me. I could plot all the ways the CFDA had helped me on my journey: from my early days at the incubator, to winning the CFDA/Vogue Fashion Award, to the countless mentorships and various awards and grants won over the course of my career. The CFDA was also the first organization to donate to the earthquake disaster relief effort I set up with my siblings in 2015. The organization had been an essential and integral part of my growth as a company, as a designer, and as a person: it is not an exaggeration to say that my impossible dreams became realized with its support and belief in me.

So to be able to sit on its board and do that for other designers like me was a powerful continuation of that work. I genuinely believe that the global fashion industry's soul and conscience both begin here in America.

We're at the forefront of meaningful conversations—about diversity, inclusivity, and sustainability as well as political and cultural accountability. We are a thriving community that roots for each other's successes. That camaraderie is intentional, and so it is a privilege to have the opportunity to help shape the future of American fashion. To have a seat at this table, in this position, with designers like Aurora James, Maria Cornejo, and Thom Browne meant that the changes that I've wanted to make in this industry for decades felt imminently more possible.

So MUCH HAPPENED IN 2022 that I barely had a moment to process any of it. Instead, I was surfing one wave of external validation to the next. I should have been fulfilled, satisfied, proud. Instead, I felt hollow. Something was missing—and I had no idea what. And that upset me, because it made no sense: I had reached the highest rungs of the fashion world. All those accolades and highlights, celebrating and being celebrated with fellow Asian artists and friends. I'd accomplished every single goal on that vision board that I hung in my East Village apartment many years before—and won more awards and appointments than I knew to even list.

So why did I still feel so empty?

Now that 2022, a banner year, was coming to an end, all I felt was utterly exhausted. My mother was in New York, and during one of our morning breakfast meetings, I shared my existential crisis with her.

"What else could I possibly want? When will it ever be enough?" I asked, feeling that same pain in my chest that made it hard to breathe.

"Maybe it's time for you to try Vipassana," she said in her calm, soothing way.

MY MOTHER HAD BEEN practicing Vipassana for more than twenty years by then. Known as "insight meditation," it's part of a Buddhist practice she began several years after her divorce. I have always marveled at my mother's dignity and strength in the face of such heartbreak and violence. What she's experienced over the course of her life would devastate most others, and yet my mother was grace personified. If you asked her how that was possible, she'd say, "Vipassana."

I FOUND A MEDITATION center in Massachusetts that offered a ten-day Vipassana retreat. There was a spot available that same month, so I signed up, and then immediately I began to panic.

The rules were stark: no phone, no talking, no writing, no journaling, no music. You weren't even supposed to look into the eyes of another person. For ten days. Instead, you would meditate from dawn to dusk.

Would I be able to sit still for that long? After so many years of running from one destination to the next, would I be physically able to stay quiet and still? To tolerate just me and my thoughts?

I'd heard of people quitting halfway through, or even after just a few days in. That was my biggest fear: while I knew that I was not a quitter, more than anything, I did not want to disappoint my mother. She was so thrilled that I was going.

It was a snowy morning in late December when a black SUV picked me up at my apartment to take me to the retreat. An Indian driver hopped out to help me with my bag, and I flashed back to the first taxi ride I ever took in the United States, from JFK to the East Village twenty years earlier. As we left Manhattan and made our way north, the five-lane highway gave way to long, winding roads, which were lined on either side by walls of pine and birch trees, moss carpets, and large fields dusted with snow.

To allay some of the anxiety I was feeling, and perhaps to delay my arrival to the Vipassana Meditation Center, I asked the driver to make a stop at Momo Tibetan Restaurant. I was feeling homesick and had typed "momo" into a Google search. The place was in nearby Amherst.

We pulled into the empty parking lot, and I wondered whether the restaurant was even open. Inside, I was the only person there besides the host, one server, and whoever was working in the kitchen. All the nervous anticipation I had felt in the car wafted away as the scents of my favorite Nepali foods surrounded me. Then I heard the staff speaking in Nepali and felt even more calm. I ordered momo, and after I finished one plate, I ordered another.

They tasted like serenity, like home. Content and full, I was finally ready to go.

When I went to pay, the host asked, "How was it?"

"Ghar ko yaad aayo," I responded, which translates to "It reminds me of my home."

She smiled and said, "We're so proud of you. Thank you for what you've done—we know you have a lot more to do."

Her words propelled me forward. As I got back in the car, the snow had intensified and was now covering the car and carpeting the trees like soft cashmere capes. I felt ready for the quiet solitude. Finally.

THE VIPASSANA MEDITATION CENTER had a large white clapboard house as its welcome center. There, a man with long hair and glasses showed me to my room, which was small, with a simple mattress, pillow, and blanket, and a window overlooking the garden. I unpacked and then texted my mom and siblings to say, "I've arrived. I will speak to you in ten days!" I then hit send and handed my phone to the man who had greeted me.

The calmness I felt in the car reverberated throughout my body. I was ready.

That evening, at orientation, I was assigned a seat at the dining hall and one in the meditation hall. The next morning, I was awoken by the clanging of bells.

The first meditation took place in the hall for one hour, followed by breakfast. Then we had an hour-long break before the next meditation started. That lasted two hours. Another break. Then we meditated in our rooms for an hour, before lunch. After that, we had an hour to walk around the premises. Then there was a two-hour meditation followed by tea. One more walk, before another meditation, then dinner, and then we meditated one last time in our rooms before going to sleep.

The first few days focused on breathing. Once I got the hang of that, I began to observe all these bodily sensations, from head to toe, then from toe to head. We're so used to outside stimulation that our mind stores all these memories. When it's allowed to quiet, it begins to rummage through all of these poignant personal experiences: Edon Richards. My father agreeing with my mother to buy me that paper doll back in Singapore. Kumudini scaring those teen boys away. Deep telling me to keep my head down as we walked to the dining hall at St. Xavier's Godavari. During one of these hallucinogenic mental slideshows, I even saw a neighbor whom I said hello to when I was seven years old.

The barrage of snapshots was a mental decluttering process. A sweeping out. A deep clean.

The first day was challenging. The second day even more so. On the third day, I was so uncomfortable that I decided to go for a walk in the woods. As my feet crunched on the snow and I saw my breath crystallize in the chilled air, I recalled my mother dropping me off at Godavari and unpacking the sweets by my new bunk bed. I also remembered watching her car drive through the school gates, leaving me behind. As these images flashed through my brain, I felt an intense, jagged sadness that was painful. I walked deeper into the woods, and the farther I went, the sadder I felt as all the painful memories from that time in my life began careening through my head at such lightning speed, they blurred together. It was almost more than I could bear. And then, out of nowhere, I felt compelled to sing a Hindi song that I first sang at Godavari. It is still my favorite song. It is about a girl who wakes up from a deep sleep and is stunned by the beauty of the world. She's surrounded by nature, as I was at that moment, and relishing how lucky she is to be alive.

I started to sing this song as I walked through the quiet, cold, serene woods. The sun was starting to set, shifting the sky from a pale blue gray to a pinkish purple. I felt like the girl in that song, lucky to be able to walk in such beauty—and to be alive in that moment. To have turned all the pain and bullying and heartache into art, stories, and song.

I began to sing even louder, breaking the rules of Vipassana, but also knowing that I always had to break the rules in order to find my place in the world. That epiphany further emboldened me: I began to skip, then sashay, and then dance in the woods by myself, among the trees now casting shadows onto the snow-covered trails that were dead quiet except for my voice.

SOMETHING SHIFTED IN ME that afternoon. Back at the center, I continued to meditate and thought of that Rudyard Kipling poem that became my mantra during middle school.

> *If you can meet with Triumph and Disaster*
> *And treat those two impostors just the same.*

Those lines translated to the Vipassana practice: you can experience joy and pain and learn to observe both in a similar manner.

This was what my mother had been trying to teach me my entire life.

"Don't get swept up by the highs, because the lows will be equally steep," she had said time and again. "Find the middle ground, kanchu."

ON THAT LAST DAY, I woke up and took a final walk. I stopped at a stream and noticed that the ice was slowly starting to melt. There was a warmth in the air. Besides the serene gurgling and the birds chirping, I could hear my breath. It was calm and steady.

It was early in the morning, and the sun was just turning the sky a crimson pink that signaled a new beginning. I was ready to go home.

I texted my mother and siblings from the car to say, "I did it!"

Kumudini wrote first: "Congratulations."

Then I called my mother. "Kanchu!"

When I heard her voice, I immediately began to weep.

"How are you feeling?" she asked.

I was unable to answer through my sobs.

"Why don't we talk when you get home?"

There, my mother was waiting for me.

Though she was always cool, calm, and collected, this was the first time I sensed her eagerness.

"How was it?" she asked, after a warm embrace. This time I was able to answer.

"I understand why you wanted me to do it," I said, smiling. "I finally feel free."

I saw tears well up in my mother's eyes as she reached for my hand across the breakfast table. Her delicate fingers wrapped around my wrist as she looked me in the eye and said, "You now understand that you have always had everything within you that you needed to be free."

I started to cry as she nodded her head at me, tears rolling down her cheeks.

"You've been trying to tell me this since I was a young boy," I said.

"And now, I don't have to tell you anymore," she responded with a warm laugh. "You have always been perfect just the way you are."

Afterword

The following November, I was getting ready for a Diwali party that my friends and I were hosting at the Pierre hotel. It is my favorite festival, one that celebrates love and light and hope. I decided to dress up: I designed a black velvet sherwani as an homage to my mother's family, as this was something her grandfathers would have worn.

The suit was made by twenty-five artisans in India and had more than one hundred thousand crystals and precious stones, including my mother's favorite green emeralds, hand embroidered onto a midnight velvet sherwani made in New York. The whole process took four hundred and fifty hours.

While this type of artistry and attention was something I'd done many times for my clients, I'd never designed something that elaborate for myself. But for this Diwali, I wanted to offer the world a glimpse of my mother's royal lineage. The glamour and beauty, combined with her resilience, are what has kept me grateful and grounded. This was my matrilineage.

Still, as I got dressed in my apartment, I wondered, "Is it too much?"

To start, the jacket weighed twenty pounds, as every inch of it was encrusted with jewels. As I slipped into it and felt its heavy embrace, I decided to go for it. I had spent my career uplifting others through my creativity: it was time to do that for myself.

I went to my mom's apartment to show her my outfit.

As I entered, I once again had reservations.

"All this embroidery?" I asked. "Is it too over the top?"

She looked at me, and with one raised eyebrow said, "Since when did you worry about being over the top?"

"I'm worried that it is too girlie," I said. "It is *very* sparkly."

She put up her hand to stop me from saying another word and then went to get something from her room.

When she reemerged, she was holding her great-grandmother's heirloom emerald earrings.

"Here," she said, placing them in my palm. "Wear these."

I put them on and had one last look in the mirror.

As always, she was right: I was beautiful. At that exact moment, I saw my five-year-old self, back in Nepal, sitting in front of Mami's vanity mirror, nervous and excited as she expertly fixed my smeared, messy red lips, my failed attempt to emulate her, using tiny brush motions as if holding a paintbrush.

Decades had passed. A lot had changed, but Mami's love and ability to see me were unwavering.

I turned to her; my eyes started to well up.

"Are you okay?" she said lovingly, holding my hands.

I nodded as I hugged her and headed out the door. I was more than okay. I had her. I always did.

I stepped out of my building downtown, got into my car, and headed uptown. I rolled down the window and was immediately embraced by the fall breeze of New York, a heady mix of exhaust and ambition. As we began to make our way uptown, I felt a wave of nostalgia as I realized I was retracing the very first taxi ride I'd taken all those years earlier. I had come to New York City with a crazy dream of becoming a designer and pulled it off—against all odds, despite the racism and elitism and homophobia I'd experienced. And yet, I was still that same hopeful dreamer. I was reminded of the opportunities that would have never been possible anywhere except here. My excitement at the possibilities of what lay ahead for me had not diminished, it had expanded. Because I finally understood. It was all within me, and it had always been.

The car approached the Pierre and slowed to a stop. As I stepped out in my full regalia, I was aware of people turning to stare at me. I had always been aware of those gazes all my life. But this time, I felt a profound shift. Instead of looking at me in ridicule, or as a threat, people were doing double takes, in awe.

The doorman smiled and nodded as he welcomed me.

As I walked into a sea of individuals of every possible shade of brown celebrating Diwali at the Pierre hotel, in the city where I had found myself, I felt like I was finally home.

Acknowledgments

The seed for this book was planted decades ago in Nepal, and the title came to me while I was growing up in India. It has taken me almost six years to bring these decades of stories to fruition—years of courage, self-belief, perhaps some delusions, manifestations, and many individual faiths. It's been arduous, emotional, cathartic, and, above all, profoundly humbling.

Gratitude—an immeasurable amount—is what I feel every time I reflect on my life, and especially my more-than-a-decade-long career. I believe I am the product of love, faith, and support from many people, mostly women and a few good men. For that and more, I want to thank the following people who've made this book and my dream possible.

The genesis of it all can be traced back to my dear mother, my mami. Her unwavering love and guidance have shaped every fiber of my being. Mami, you have been my rock, my guiding light, and the source of my strength. Your love has not only emboldened me to pursue my dreams but also instilled in me the resilience and determination to face life's challenges. You've shown me how to embrace hope and optimism for the future. Your wisdom and encouragement have grounded me and propelled me forward at the same time. The bond I share with my siblings, a treasure beyond measure, finds its roots in your teachings. You've always taught me to cherish and learn from them because they are the ones who will show me the way and shine a light on my path. I pray that in every lifetime, I am fortunate enough to be your child once again. Thank you for being the most amazing mother a child could ever ask for. You are my inspiration, my role model, and my greatest love.

Kumudini, if I have learned anything about the healing power of storytelling, it's because of you. From all the novels you've read, the movies you've seen, and the people you've met, the details shared made me feel like I was right there with you. You never left me behind, never made me feel alone. You let me play dress up with your clothes (the tiered pink dress was my favorite), and now I get to dress you up with mine. You taught me literature and science in school, and now you teach me about grace and discernment. You saved me when I was struggling and caught me when I fell. You fought battles for me and let me cry for hours without ever leaving my side. You encouraged me to pursue my dreams and kept your promise, showing up at every pivotal moment of my life. You have been there for me unconditionally, from indulging me in plates of momo, even though you dislike them, to encouraging me to make spontaneous but significant decisions that brought me joy. You are my sister, mother, best friend, and my biggest cheerleader, quietly and with dignity. You've taught me about creativity, art, curiosity, and checking my privileges, but above all, your quiet and diligent work has inspired me to do better and become better. You are an incredible daughter, sister, and friend, but most of all, I admire you as a mother. Looking at Arhant and Vaidehi, I know that the kind of people they are now is a testament to your relentless hard work as a mother, your unwavering support and love. It reminds me of Mami. The existence of this book is a testament to your influence. Your endorsement and approval were paramount, and your dedicated critique, hours of editing, in-depth analysis, and graceful enhancements greatly enriched this book. Thank you for setting the bar high without making it feel impossible. Words do not suffice for how much I love you. That may be my next book. We all know that you are the consummate storyteller in our family. I have initiated the process and started the engine until you are ready to jump on the bandwagon. I am happy to masquerade as a writer. I eagerly anticipate the day when the world receives the gift of your words on paper. You are the best sister anyone could ask for. I love you so much.

Pravesh, I have always been in awe of you. Witnessing your wisdom beyond your years, your kindness, your grace, and your unwavering generosity, regardless of status, has always inspired me. I understand that life is not a comparative game, but there is no doubt in my mind that you are a better person. I find solace in basking in your halo to elevate myself even slightly. Although I resented living under your shadow as I grew up, now, seeking refuge under the same shadow of wisdom and grace is what I look forward to the most. I appreciate your patience with me, especially dealing with the angsty kid who was always getting into trouble in school. From the moment I witnessed your captivating dance onstage to "Utha Utha Basumati" at St. Xavier's, which motivated me to stay up all night to ace the entrance exam, to your involvement in acting and directing numerous award-winning plays, you have always narrated your story quietly through words spoken by others, never boasting about your accomplishments. You implanted the idea of me coming to America with Kumudini, yet never sought recognition for it. Your intuitions are consistently accurate. Despite life not always dealing you the best cards, your ability to play the hand with equanimity, tenacity, and perseverance against all odds has been truly inspirational. Thank you for being my spiritual guide. Kumudini and you are my moral compass. Both of you set the bar high and laid out a road map, my following of which has made me a better person. You are my integrity barometers. I would not have come this far without both of you. You two are my lifeline and my best friends. Thank you for generously sharing your light.

As I was finishing the last chapter of this book, my father passed away on September 25, 2023. It was sudden. There were no prolonged goodbyes, nor a melodramatic ending. It was abrupt. He left this earth in a manner that felt familiar and exactly as I had expected, much like it had always been, even when he was alive. One minute he was here, and the next, he was gone. I despised that as I was growing up but found it endearing and a relief over time. This time around, I had no resentment because I had let go of my anger toward him and was finally on a path to making peace with my past. Then I realized that the relationship I never had when he was alive, I finally had upon his death. I was finally free from the last remaining constraints holding me back. I always felt free, but this was levitating. And finally, I am free to walk like a girl. Dad, I know you tried your best. Thank you for teaching me the importance of forgiveness. And thank you for the music, literature, and, above all, the levity—from crayons to perfume. Until we meet again, in peace.

Rajesh, thank you for unconditionally seeing, loving, accepting, and celebrating me without judgment. Your belief in me and my dreams has given me the courage to dream bigger, "impossible" dreams. It has helped me soar higher. Without you, it is possible there wouldn't be me.

Arhant, just like the meaning of your name—a perfected person who has gained insight into the true nature of existence and has achieved nirvana (spiritual enlightenment)—you've always been wiser beyond your years since birth. I left for New York the year you were born, but watching you grow up has been the most immense joy of my life. From the abandoned reverie to "Hips Don't Lie" to genuinely understanding the words of "Born This Way," from Hannah Montana to introducing K-pop to me decades before the world did, you've been uniquely on your singular path, unapologetic, unfettered. From your coming-of-age ceremony to your coming out, from an introspective loner to an assured empath, your growth has been an absolute joy to witness. Your creativity and art have been awe-inspiring, and I cannot wait for the world to discover more. But your clarity in living your life authentically and assuredly has inspired me to do the same. Your unapologetic existence has been a constant inspiration in my quest to be free. In you, I see myself and the life I should've had, but I am immensely grateful that you get to live it for both of us. You challenge me and keep me on my toes, and for that, I thank you. Thank you also for your edits and inputs for this book; they added more grace and empathy. Thank you for taking my picture for this book. We will always have that, besides all the memories. Thank you for being an incredible nephew, a kind and thoughtful grandson to Mami, and, most importantly, such a good friend to my sister. I love you with every fiber of my being and with all my heart. I hope you continue to live your life in truth, for it inspires us to do the same.

Vaidehi, you, my beloved niece, embody all my dreams, promises, and hopes. Each shared tear and every moment of joy we've experienced together has shown me the power of your unwavering love and unconditional acceptance, which have been my guiding light. Your presence has filled my world with hope and optimism, for which I am eternally grateful. Seeing you evolve into a compassionate and thoughtful individual has brought me immeasurable joy. To witness the strength that lies in you fueled by your unabashed and unapologetic femininity has inspired me to dive into mine. Your patience and willingness to share your world with me have been truly transformative. Every memory we've created—from our visit to the White House with Michelle Obama, to dancing and crying at the Laufey concert, to our cozy moments watching Harry Potter, to the horror movies we both love—they all hold a special place in my heart. Your nonjudgmental ear and our bond over our love for food, especially momo, are treasures I cherish dearly. I am also immensely grateful for your conscientious and valuable input in editing this book. Your diligence and careful attention have made this book even better, and it is a gift I sincerely appreciate. With all my heart, I want you to know how much I love and adore you. You are a remarkable soul, and I am truly blessed to have you in my life. You are my love, my life, my everything.

Liz Welch, my partner in crime, cheerleader, therapist, and kindred spirit, thank you from the bottom of my heart, my dear friend. This story would have remained a mere pipe dream, these words in my head just a thought, without your support and guidance. You are one of the few who have witnessed the depths of my soul that I've concealed for so long. Your endless empathy and unwavering encouragement have given me the strength to share my story. It is as much your triumph as it is mine. Thank you for walking me through the valley of words. I will forever hold these moments with you close to my heart. It's because of you that I have renewed faith in the goodness of humanity. I am eternally grateful. Bella is truly fortunate. At this perfect moment, I want to thank our dear friend, Elaine Welteroth, who brought us together. Thank you, Elaine. I hope we have made you proud.

Amy Sun, my incredible editor, I am deeply grateful for your unwavering support and the sense of safety you always provide. You are one of the kindest, most gracious, thoughtful, conscientious, soft-spoken, but assured editors/friends and encouragers I know. I cannot express in words how much I value your guidance, mentorship, and friendship. You have shown me the art of leadership with grace, precision, and kindness, and in you, I see the conductor of my orchestra, bringing the notes to the perfect pitch.

To everyone at Viking, led by the incredible editor-in-chief Andrea Schulz and publisher Brian Tart. Thank you for your belief in my story and for the role you each played in bringing this book into the world: Isabelle Alexander, Kate Stark, Emily Kimball, Tricia Conley, Diandra Alvarado, Brianna Lopez, Tess Espinoza, Madeline Rohlin, Angelina Krahn, Nicole Celli, Jessica DiDonato, Jason Ramirez, Nayon Cho, Cassie Mueller, Kristina Fazzalaro, Emily Fishman, Mary Stone, and Rebecca Marsh. Thank you for helping me realize this dream.

Georgia Bodnar, thank you for being the first to see the importance of this book in the world.

To everyone at CAA, especially Mollie Glick, who believed in my story the minute she heard the title, thank you for your continuous love and support. Christian Carino, Via Romani, Ali Ehrlich, and Kevin Lin, thank you for your belief, friendship, and love.

The pillars of our foundation, Shikshya Foundation Nepal: Rati Shah, Riva Thapa, Rupali Golchha, Kumudini Shrestha, and Pravesh Gurung, for relentless passion and empathy. I am so thankful for your love for the cause and the children. To all our partners, thank you for being on this journey with us.

Maya Rana Tufo, for fully embracing me unconditionally decades back. Dijju, you were and remain fabulous. You will always be my star.

Madame Vice President Kamala Harris, you are the epitome of the American dream. Seeing you run for the highest office of the nation and the world reassures my belief in matriarchal energy. This book is so much about that; this book is about you and your energy. Thank you for the support. Hillary Clinton, you remain an inspiration to me and my family. Thank you for your vision, resilience, dedication, and above all your warmth and love. You were one of the first who inspired us to dream big. I will forever cherish our Bollywood dance onstage in Mumbai.

Michelle Obama, thank you for making my American dream come true. Your love and support over the years have meant a lot to me, and your fiftieth birthday was the best dance party I've ever been to. Thank you for your belief.

Oprah Winfrey, thank you for inspiring me to live my dreams. Your truth made me realize my own and made me a better person. This journey started because of you.

Gloria Steinem, you have always been a hero and an inspiration to me. Thank you for making my runway show your first ever. It reassures me that I am on the right path. Thank you for your support.

Anna Wintour, thank you for allowing me to be my own person and for your support, advice, and honest opinions. I am eternally grateful. A large part of where I am and who I am is due to your guidance. Thank you from the bottom of my heart.

Caroline Brown, for your mentorship, friendship, and pragmatism, I am immensely grateful.

Lisa Joy, I am forever grateful to you for your unconditional love and friendship and for being there for me during one of the most difficult times of my life. I also appreciate your relentless quest to find me my love.

Karan Johar, you've become family to me. My go-to person to lay my heart out. You held me when I was crying, challenged me on the dance floor with our thumkas, and held the imaginary mic when I sang. Thank you for your love, wisdom, humor, and, above all, your friendship, which means the world to me.

Bing, with you in my life, I feel like I can take on the world. Thank you for always encouraging me to dream the biggest dreams, constantly reminding me that I deserve them, and helping me to make them happen. The work we do together with Jeremy and the Gold House team is one of my proudest achievements. Thank you for trusting me with your stories. I love you.

Paul, I am forever grateful for the memories.

My fellow Slaysians, Laura Kim, Tina Leung, Phillip Lim, and Ezra William, my life wouldn't be the same without the four of you in it. I am forever grateful that we had each other during one of the most challenging times of our lives. Love you with all my heart. And to everyone at the House of Slay, my love and gratitude.

Thank you, Radhika Jones, Ali Sethi, Sarita Choudhury, Hanya Yanagihara, and Salman Toor, for making me fall in love with New York yet again. You fuel my artistic soul.

The Avengers, who've been the rock during the most difficult times for our community, thank you for taking me in your folds: Ronny Chieng, Min Jin Lee, Jeannie Mai, Lisa Ling, Daniel Dae Kim, Daniel Wu, Jeremy Lin, Jose Antonio Vargas, Andy Kim, Joy Moh, Bao Nguyen, Benny Luo, Brad Jenkins, Melvin Mar, Tamlyn Tomita, and Viet Nguyen.

My mentors—Carolina Herrera, Cynthia Rowley, Domenico De Sole, Diane von Furstenberg, Ed Filipowski, Tommy Hilfiger, and John Demsey—thank you for your guidance and belief over the years.

I am forever grateful to everyone at the CFDA, especially Steven Kolb and Lisa Smilor, for their belief in my vision and support, especially during the earthquake in Nepal. It's an honor to serve as the vice chairperson at the CFDA; thank you.

Caitlin DiStefano, thank you very much for believing in my dreams and being willing to jump on this crazy ride for almost a decade. I will cherish what we built, and I wish you all my love.

Tiina Laakkonen, thank you for the magic you helped me create for the first few years, for your belief in me before the world had any faith, and for your love, support, and friendship.

Shan Reddy, thank you for carrying this dream forward with me now. It's been one helluva ride, but I am grateful it's been with you. You are my family.

Thomas Chen, thank you for being a friend and confidant. I am grateful for the sisterhood and laughter we share.

Amanda Fuhrman and Glenn Fuhrman, thank you for your belief, love, and support from the very beginning. FLAG Art and both of you have a very special place in my heart.

Thank you to my PG team, from each department, past and present, who have worked with me and not for me. It would take me pages to fully express my gratitude—I wouldn't have come this far without your beliefs and relentless hard work.

To my Tasaki family, thank you for these amazing few years. The pearls of wisdom are invaluable.

I just want to express my gratitude to all my friends who've now become my found family and have been instrumental in my personal growth. I am deeply thankful that so many of you are still a part of my life, and I cherish the journey that we are on together. Even for those with whom I may not interact frequently or whose paths have taken a different course, I am grateful for your role in my life's journey.

I am forever grateful to my friends from Nepal, old and new, who have let me be me, with their words or in silence. Deep Rana, you never ever asked me to dim my light. Thank you for your unconditional acceptance and friendship since we were kids. Samjhana Bhattarai, Ashish Maskey, Yogendra Shakya, Bikas Joshi, Satyendra Patrabansh, Sushma Joshi, Sarika Karki, Anil Keshary Shah, Shikha Prasai, Mridu Chand, Aman Adhikari, Sanjay Basnet, Deepak Thapa, Dhiraj Gurung, Abhaya Shrestha, Kendra Baruwa, Pragya Shah, Arun Karki, Abin Kunwar, Subid Wagley, Samjhana Pandey, Prerna Dewan, Dawa Sherpa, Sonam Ukyab, Kesang Sherpa, Triguna Basnet, Ashish Sherchan, Kashish Shrestha, Vijay Shrestha, Bijesh Shahi, Dhiraj K.C., Rishav Suwal, Rabi Karmacharya, Honi Tamu, Chewang Lama, Ajay Shah, Amit Karki, and Varsha Thapa.

Thank you to my friends from India, whose love and acceptance made me comfortable in my own skin and confident in my dreams: Bhupat Seemar, Pritika Kapur, Pranay Jain, Abhishekh Aggarwal, Ritika Chatrath, Anjali Gupta, Diya Mehra, Ruhi Dhand, Ruchika Mehra, Ashish Mehta, Anuj Bishnoi, Kimberly Coelho, Ashwini Salvi, Natasha Gonzales, Navraj Singh, Anu Mehra, Koel Purie, Aparna Bahl Bedi, Tanya LeFebvre, Anisha Bahl, Manish Arora, Vikas Malhotra, Shweta Bachchan, Kaajal Anand, Nitasha Nanda, Isha Ambani, and Natasha Poonawalla.

To my New York friends with whom I discovered the city for the first time, I am forever grateful for the memories: Rose Loveras Herrera, Matthew Plouffe, Abbie Lamb, Sarah Gunter, Rachael Fleming, James Gunter, and Greg Lawrence.

To my other New York friends, who make me fall in love with the city again and again.

Nell Diamond, Danny Shea, Barbara Bush, Isabel Wilkinson, and Kyle Hotchkiss Carone, thank you for the levity, love, support, and sometimes heated but never dull conversations, and for showing me the kinder side of America; you made me fall in love with her more.

Maggie Betts, all those inspiring conversations about life, creativity, and storytelling really helped me dream bigger; they fueled my soul. Thank you for your love and friendship. I love you.

Sam Spector, David Yassky, and Mike Andrus, thank you for your support, especially during the production of my first two collections from your apartments. I will always cherish those moments.

Adam Shapiro, Jeff Trosch, Shaun Lee Lewis, and Yuki James, I am forever grateful for your love and support and for the memories over the years, across the globe.

Damien Nunes, in the twenty-five years of our friendship, you have seen my dreams turn into reality, from the manifestation walls to the runways, and you have never once questioned them. Thank you for your quiet, unwavering support; I will always hold it dear to my heart. I love you.

To all the people of substance who I had the privilege of dressing, thank you for carrying forward my story: Beyoncé, Cate Blanchett, Julianne Moore, Sarah Jessica Parker, Zoe Saldana, Demi Moore, Margot Robbie, Kerry Washington, Greta Gerwig, Misty Copeland, Maria Sharapova, Gabrielle Union, Eiza González, Emily Ratajkowski, Gayle Rankin, Sarah Paulson, Jennifer Lawrence, Halsey, Alia Bhatt, Katy Perry, Deepika Padukone, Diane Kruger, Katrina Kaif, Nicki Minaj, Priyanka Chopra, Janhvi Kapoor, Sonam Kapoor, Laufey, Kiara Advani, Hailee Steinfeld, Demi Lovato, Venus Williams, Amanda Murphy, Padma Lakshmi, Michelle Yeoh, Reese Witherspoon, Ashley Graham, Gemma Chan, Bella Hadid, Awkwafina, Poorna Jagannathan, Candice Swanepoel, Caroline Trentini, Ellen Rosa, Gigi Hadid, Joan Smalls, Karlie Kloss, Liu Wen, Liya Kebede, Ming Xi, Rosie Huntington-Whiteley, Taylor Hill, Ugbad, and Pure.

To my friends and colleagues from the industry and beyond, thank you for impacting my journey over the past decade. I wish I had many pages to thank each of you, so I sincerely apologize if I missed someone: Elettra Wiedemann, Indré Rockefeller, Tina Craig, Jessie Betts, Calypso Lawrence, Mia Moretti, Monique Péan, Huma Abedin, Aurora James, Nicky Hilton, Fernando Garcia, Maggie James, Nancy Rogers, Bethann Hardison, Taylor Martin, Vanessa Barbosa, Ami Sehmi, Samantha Kain, Clara Wu Tsai, Nik Vallen, Alex Catarinella, Anjula Acharia, Furhan Ahmad, Hampton Carney, Anita Chatterjee, Hanuk, Dorothy Wang, Jonathan Zakarya, Ryan Verbic, Jordan Andino, Chris Habana, Dao-Yi Chow, Maxwell Osborne, Bibhu Mohapatra, Richard Chai, Eva Chen, Bryanboy, Jimmy Paul, Jin Soon Choi, John Pfeiffer, Joe Mangrum, Rachna Shah, Thierry Dreyfus, Andrew Serrano, Pascal Dangin, Paul Hanlon, Paul Wilmot, Alex Avalone, Sebastien Perrin, Shaun Beyen, Stevie Hyun, Susan Plagemann, Tala Yasseri, Gary Wassner, Bob D'Loren, David Bonnouvrier, Etienne Russo, Ivan Bart, James Scully, Megan Cohen, Lauren Cooper, Tyler Rose, Jin Kay, Michael Creegan, Opal Vadhan, Jonathan Morr, Cheri Bowen, and Tarana Burke.

To my extended fashion family who've kept me going with love, made me better with critiques, and always supported me by showing up, I thank you very, very much: Robin Givhan, Cathy Horyn, Nicole Phelps, Bridget Foley, Laird Borrelli-Persson, Leanne Italie, Vanessa Friedman, Eric Wilson, Booth Moore, Rosemary Feitelberg, Sally Singer, Hal Rubenstein, Laurie Brookins, Tim Blanks, and Sarah Mower.

For your love and support over the years through the lenses, the pages, and the muses, thank you: Caroline Issa, Edward Enninful, Cindi Leive, Joe Zee, Meredith Melling, Michelle Lee, Mickey Boardman, Miguel Enamorado, Anne Slowey, Sarah Harris, Sara Moonves, Virginia Smith, Glenda Bailey, Bandana Tewari, Kim Hasteriter, Long Nguyen, Lynn Yaeger, Lindsay Peoples Wagner, Mark Holgate, Samira Nasr, Nina Garcia, Versha Sharma, Mel Ottenberg, Alex Harrington, Alex White, Brad Goreski, Clare Richardson, Danielle Nachmani, Elin Svahn, Elizabeth Saltzman, Elizabeth Stewart, Erin Walsh, Jason Bolden, Jason Rembert,

Jeanann Williams, Jessica Paster, Mariel Haenn, Micaela Erlanger, Meredith Koop, Karen Kaiser, Karla Welch, Kate Young, Law Roach, Petra Flannery, Rachel Zoe, Wayman Bannerman, Micah McDonald, Shiona Turini, Ryan Hastings, Jamie Mizrahi, Mimi Cuttrell, Annabelle Harron, Rebecca Corbin-Murray, Ilaria Urbinati, Samantha McMillen, Thomas Carter Phillips, Thomas Christos Kikis, Tom Eerebout, Dan Jackson, Dan and Corina Lecca, Dan Martensen, Hans Neumann, Kevin Sturman, Kevin Tachman, Joanna Totolici, Michael Stewart, Lewis Mirrett, Bon Duke, Diane Kendal, Didier Malige, and many more.

For giving my vision, my story, a home, thank you: Elizabeth von der Goltz, Lauren Santo Domingo, Princess Deena Aljuhani Abdulaziz, Ikram Goldman, Ken Downing, Linda Fargo, Maria Lemos, Nicholas Mellamphy, Rickie De Sole, Roopal Patel, Brian Bolke, George Fountas, Yumi Shin, Tracy Margolies, Marc Metrick, Janice Elliott Morgan, and many more.

To all the women and men I don't know personally yet who have supported me in this journey, whether by wearing my clothes—buying, renting, or borrowing them—or through the countless words of encouragement you have shared via emails, tweets, and DMs, or perhaps a silent prayer you sent my way. I feel you, I feel the love, I feel the energy. For that, for seeing me: I thank you. From the bottom of my heart, from every ounce of my being.

And to you, the reader, who is now a part of this journey, I extend my heartfelt gratitude for your support and encouragement.

I hope you feel seen.

A little more free.

To be yourself.

To walk like a girl.

About the Author

Prabal Gurung is an award-winning fashion designer who has been at the forefront of American fashion since launching his eponymous label in 2009. He has been a relentless advocate for diversity, shattering beauty norms and championing inclusivity on the runway and beyond since the beginning of his career. His designs, a masterful blend of beauty, luxury, and edge, are as iconic as his commitment to social change. He is the co-vice chair of the Council of Fashion Designers of America; a cofounder of the Shikshya Foundation Nepal, a nonprofit organization creating a critical mass of leaders in Nepal; and a cofounder and board member of Gold House, a cultural ecosystem that empowers Asian Pacific leaders to power tomorrow for all. Prabal has written numerous op-eds and has been interviewed on major networks, leveraging his platform to address critical social issues, from racial injustice to gender equality, especially surrounding the Asian and Black diaspora. A true industry disrupter based in New York City for over two decades, he has become a prominent figure in the city's cultural and social landscape, and he is redefining the role of the fashion designer as a catalyst for positive change.